MARKET

<u>YOU ARE WHAT YOU THINK</u> by Neil C. Roth

1. Potential reading audiences:
   (a) College and adult ages in the Protestant tradition.
   (b) Supplemental reading for Christian college courses in Guidance and Counseling, Systems of Psychology, Pastoral Counseling, etc., Theories of Personality, Psychology of Effective Behavior.
   (c) General audiences of all backgrounds which exhibit non-sectarian philosophy and objective acceptance of other points of view.
   (d) Groups like AMWAY and Shaklee Products which stress the values of positive Christian-oriented philosophy in their sales approach.
   (e) Conferences conducted by the author throughout the United States - approximately 10 per year - potentially 300-500 book sales per year.
   (f) Travelers on rail, bus, or air who purchase books at newstands.

2. This book is unique and worthy of being published because:
   (a) Christian Rational Thought Psychology and Self-Therapy represent an old, and yet contemporary, approach to understanding human behavior and therapy.
      (1) It is Biblically-oriented and relies on the precepts and principles of the Word of God as constants.
      (2) It provides the reader and potential self-therapist with a practical and viable guide to effective self-diagnosis and understanding of one's thinking and emotional reactions.
      (3) It is premised on the fact that most people are not successfully coping with their lives and are, as a result, experiencing mild-to-profound emotional distress which is characterized by fear and despair. Consequently, these people have not learned how to think objectively and rationally and are generally confused about what to think.
      (4) It holds that people can change their negative, satanic, irrational thinking and emoting to positive, Christian, rational thinking and integrative emotional reactions. This can be accomplished if we learn to challenge and change our

irrational thoughts with the rational, love-oriented Christian thoughts of God's Word as typified by its precepts and principles.

(5) It holds that no psychological counsel or therapy can be completely effective without first dealing with the spiritual problems that man experiences. Always, at the bottom of man's emotional distress, we find irrationality, selfishness, and fear (with the exception of emotional distress that has physiological etiologies). These verities can only be effectively countered by a personal encounter with the Lord of Creation, Jesus Christ and His living Word.

(6) It holds that the motivation to change thinking and behavior comes not only from within man himself (a will to change), but more importantly, from God Himself in the Person of Jesus Christ.

(7) It accepts the learnings of other schools of psychology which are philosophically compatible with the precepts and principles of the Word.

(8) You Are What You Think will be followed by three kindred books within the next calendar year. These will be:

- The Ministry of Helping Others - a Primer for Christian Rational Thought Therapy.
- Learning to Relate - a guide to improving human relationships through Christian Rational Thought Psychology and Self-Therapy.
- Mid-Life Crisis - Causes and Cures - Thought and emotional stability through Christian Rational Thought Psychology and Self-Therapy.

(b) It challenges the egotistical, humanistic therapies that are prevalent in the western world today, and replaces them with a God-centered emphasis on the Word and the Lordship of Jesus Christ.

(c) It is a viable, novel, practical approach to achieving emotional control that has received wide acceptance in Christian Growth Conferences conducted by the author throughout the United States.

May our Lord bless you!!!
in christ,
Neil Roth

YOU ARE
WHAT YOU THINK

NEIL C. ROTH

authorHOUSE®

AuthorHouse™
1663 Liberty Drive
Bloomington, IN 47403
www.authorhouse.com
Phone: 1 (800) 839-8640

© 2019 Neil C. Roth. All rights reserved.

No part of this book may be reproduced, stored in a retrieval system, or transmitted by any means without the written permission of the author.

Scripture quotations marked KJV are from the Holy Bible, King James Version (Authorized Version). First published in 1611. Quoted from the KJV Classic Reference Bible, Copyright © 1983 by The Zondervan Corporation.

Scripture quotations marked NIV are taken from the Holy Bible, New International Version®. NIV®. Copyright © 1973, 1978, 1984 by International Bible Society. Used by permission of Zondervan. All rights reserved. [Biblica]

Published by AuthorHouse 01/28/2019

ISBN: 978-1-5462-7784-2 (sc)
ISBN: 978-1-5462-7783-5 (hc)
ISBN: 978-1-5462-7782-8 (e)

Library of Congress Control Number: 2019900929

Print information available on the last page.

Any people depicted in stock imagery provided by Getty Images are models, and such images are being used for illustrative purposes only. Certain stock imagery © Getty Images.

This book is printed on acid-free paper.

Because of the dynamic nature of the Internet, any web addresses or links contained in this book may have changed since publication and may no longer be valid. The views expressed in this work are solely those of the author and do not necessarily reflect the views of the publisher, and the publisher hereby disclaims any responsibility for them.

YOU
    ARE
        WHAT
            YOU
                THINK!

"For as he thinketh in his heart,
so is he" (Proverbs 23:7a).

by Neil C. Roth, Ed.D.

Thought and Emotional Control Through
Christian Rational Thought Psychology

Foreword by: David C. LeShana, Ph.D.

Dedicated to

Mary Joanne Roth,
my dearest wife,
and children,
Laurie and Edward.

I love you
and
thank you for
being you.

INTRODUCTION

The main purpose for this book is to present and examine the tenets of Christian Rational Thought Psychology. This is not a new or special brand of psychology. In reality, it has been around since the beginning of time when God first made man and communicated with him. It is clear that man has always been a slow learner when it comes to heeding God's ways, so His psychology is largely overlooked, and, in many cases, never discovered.

C.R.T. Psychology is premised on the idea that man, being made in God's image, must live according to God's laws, if he is going to survive, prosper, and be emotionally and spiritually fulfilled. The <u>C.R.T</u>. <u>Statement of Faith</u> will more fully explain its evangelical theological base.

For many years I have been working with people: as a sales representative for a major corporation; an ordained minister, having served eight congregations as pastor; a conference speaker and psychologist for over forty years; and, as a professor of psychology in eight different colleges and universities. These experiences have made me keenly aware of several things:

(1) That people generally are not coping successfully with their lives and are, as a result, experiencing mild-to-profound emotional distress which is characterized by fear and despair.

(2) That many people have not learned how to think objectively and rationally and are confused about what to think.

(3) That we can change our negative, irrational thinking, and the resulting distressing emotional reactions, to just the opposite-- positive, rational thinking and attendant integrative emotional responses. We really are what we think!

(4) That beneficial life-changing improvements in thinking and emoting will occur if we challenge our irrational, fear-oriented, satanic thoughts with the rational love-oriented Christian thoughts of God's Word as revealed in the Bible.

So many years ago, the ideas of C.R.T. Psychology began to fill my mind with all of their therapeutic possibilities. I saw C.R.T. Psychology as the viable answer to the cognitive and emotional needs of those who came for counseling. Generally, the concerns expressed were deeply existential ones, such as: "Why am I here on earth?" "What shall I do while here?" "What is my eternal fate?", etc. These questions beg for a constant, and, as a Christian, I knew of only one Constant--Jesus Christ and his Holy Word. So, C.R.T. Psychology and Psychotherapy have evolved out of the expressed needs of clients and parishioners to establish their spiritual roots on something permanent and life-changing.

I am convinced that no psychological counsel or therapy can be completely effective without first dealing with the spiritual problems that man experiences. For, when we leave God out of our helping, nothing is left to focus on except the patient's own self or the therapist. E. Stanley Jones once said, "Anything that leaves you centered in yourself or in something less than God, whether it is religion, psychiatry, or just plain secularism is leaving you off-center, for you are not God."*

C.R.T. Psychology focuses on God's desired will for man, namely, the loving of God with total devotion, and the loving of his neighbor as himself. The topics of this book include: thinking and emotions (chapters 1-3); the precepts, principles, and insights from the Word of God (chapters 4-7); and, guide to self-therapy (chapter 8). The final chapter, a brief epilogue, sums up the key tenets of C.R.T. Psychology.

I have chosen a popular, and yet sometimes technical style of writing (especially chapters 1-3), with a deeply-felt goal of sharing a practical, rather than theoretical, reading experience with you.

I am eternally grateful to the many people, who over the years of my development, shared of themselves in such helpful and loving Christian ways. These brothers and sisters said "we believe in you" and, thankfully,

---

* Jones, E. Stanley. How to be a Transformed Person. Nashville; Abingdon-Cokesbury Press, 1951, p. 36.

I finally received the message that I had worth, value, and potential. They all, without being aware of it, have greatly contributed to the making of this book.

One special person emerges out of the many, however! Without the loving assistance and encouragement of my wife, Joanne, this book might not have become a reality. She has encouraged me beyond measure and has spent endless hours in typing the many pages of theses, dissertations, and now the manuscript for this book.

Also, my special thanks to my son, Edward, and to my daughter, Laurie for their encouragement and Christian testimonies. A father and mother are most blessed and fortunate when their children have chosen the ways of Christ as their guide for living.

My special thanks to Dr. David L. LeShana, beloved President Emeritus of George Fox University and Seattle Pacific University. I am singularly honored by his willingness to write the Foreword for this project. He is a very special person who loves God and shows it!

My prayer for you is that this book will awaken and challenge your thinking, and cause you to firmly commit your thinking, emotions, and behaviors to the scrutiny of God's Word, and then to serve Him in righteousness and holiness all the days of your life! There are two kinds of people: those who stop to think and those who have stopped thinking. Please join with me as we pause to think!

FOREWORD

It is difficult to accurately describe the day in which we live. Some scholars have described it as the age of anxiety; others as the age of permissiveness, or the age of sensation. Political scientists and sociologists use terms such as "the technetronic era" and the "post-industrial society." A theologian has described our society as having no focus. Like a doughnut, there are good things around the edges, but there is no moral center.

Certainly, any apt description of our day must include the pervasiveness of pessimism. This is the "psychological plague" of the late 20th Century--and many Christians have discovered that even their faith has not provided immunity.

In the midst of this complex turmoil and confusion stands the Word of God. As it has for centuries, it provides both an analysis and a corrective for that which would confront us. Yet, when it comes to understanding and applying the Scriptures to our lethargic attitudes, far too many of us are more <u>shaky</u> about what we believe than are we <u>shaken</u> by what we believe!

The field of psychology today provides a case-in-point. On the one hand there are strong and growing schools of psychology, building upon the scholarly insights of others, yet breaking new ground of research and inquiry. Many of these scholars and practitioners, however, have no point of reference to the eternal truths of God's Word. On the other hand, there are some individuals who are grounded in the Scriptures but who either ignore or reject certain fundamental principles of human existence and behavior.

Between these extremes is a growing cadre of evangelical Christian scholars and psychologists who are attempting to integrate faith with learning and living, and who are striving to accurately relate the teachings of Scripture to the current mileau of human predicament. Dr. Neil Roth is part of this select group of men and women. As Professor of Psychology at George Fox University, he is conversant with the findings of modern research, and is knowledgeable about the traumas of our time. Together with his collegues, he knows the validity of the Word of God in meeting contemporary crises.

In this book, Dr. Neil Roth attempts to examine the psychological needs of an individual within the context of the Biblical premise, "As a man thinketh in his heart, so is he" (Proverbs 23:7). With candor, he deals with many of the psychological views that are in current vogue and offers an alternative perspective in his Christian Rational Thought psychology. It is a bold attempt to go beyond secular humanism and articulates an integration of faith with learning and living. As a practitioner, he offers some simple guidelines and suggestions, yet their context is not simplistic. He has attempted to glean the best from the world of current psychology and makes Biblically sound applications to daily living.

I am pleased to commend this study to you. It will require thoughtful reading, yet its principles are easily understood.

In the midst of this age of pessimism and confusion, I am glad for those voices that speak with clarity and hope. Things can be different! We can change! By God's grace, and with His help, we can become all that He has meant us to be.

David C. LeShana, Ph.D
George Fox University
Newberg, Oregon

I've read the book, YOU ARE WHAT YOU THINK, by Neil C. Roth and would like to offer the following comments:

Dr. Roth develops the concept of a biblically based rational psychology of life and its interpersonal relationships along with a self help step by step guide to assess the areas of emotional weakness and offers a sound scripturally based method for dealing with these areas of weakness. The use of the scriptures as a guide to judge our thought processes and behavior is clearly demonstrated. The concept of Christ as the prime example of counselor is beautifully developed. In this book Dr. Roth has aptly demonstrated the compatibility of Christian principles embodied in Christianity and psychotherapy.

The principles and precepts embodied in this book will be of benefit to a majority of patients seen in a general medical practice and I heartily recommend this work as a self help for persons whose lives are manipulated by fears, insecurities and loss of direction.

Stanley D. Kern, M.D.
Physician and Surgeon, General Medicine
Newberg, Oregon

I have reviewed the book, You Are What You Think!, by Neil C. Roth and would like to offer the following comments:

The author has an obvious awareness and expertise to develop a wholistic presentation taking into consideration the Biblical, anthropological and psychological interfacing in human personality. It is refreshing to observe the balance found in this book between psychological understanding and evangelical Christian commitment.

The professional practitioner, classroom instructor or lay reader will find some excellent practical guidance to the establishment of personal and emotional control. The concept of Christian Rational Thought is not only explained theoretically but practical steps are provided whereby the individual may chart a course toward a more balanced and controlled personality. The book, as a whole, offers much needed addition to Christian reading for those who take seriously some of the new areas of discovery in the development of an adequate personality and Christian lifestyle.

Leo M. Thornton
President
Western Evangelical Seminary

CONTENTS

1. Feeling Rough? You're Not Alone!.. 1
2. What is Learning and Thinking?.. 18
3. Thinking and Emotions: Friends or Foes?...................................... 37
4. The Foundation of C.R.T. Psychology--God's Word!.................... 70
5. The C.R.T. Person Precepts and Priority Principles....................... 92
6. The C.R.T. Seven Cardinal Insights For Living 123
7. Ten C.R.T. Progress Principles for Practical Christian Living....... 159
8. Achieving Emotional Control Through C.R.T. Self-Therapy 191
9. Epilogue.. 227

Appendix A 233
Appendix B 235

LIST OF ILLUSTRATIONS

1. Modified Christian Hierarchy of Needs 20
2. C.R.T. Model for Idea Development 32
3. The C.R.T. Mental Health Continuum 60
4. C.R.T. Priority Principles 106
5. C.R.T. Model Of The Mind 140
6. The Christian Rational Thought Model Of Man.......................... 164
7. C.R.T. Characteristics Of Man 166
8. The Desired Will Of God.. 197
9. The Eight C.R.T. Self-Therapeutic Steps For Straight Thinking 199
10. C.R.T. Thought Categories 200
11. C.R.T. Problem Appraisal Inventory (For Use In Self-Therapy) 203
12. Recap Of C.R.T. Person Precepts, Priority Principles,
    Insights, And Progress Principles... 206
13. C.R.T. Auxiliary Checklist... 208
14. C.R.T. Emotional Problem Guide 215
15. C.R.T. Personal Growth Covenant 222

Note: All Scripture references are taken from the Authorized King James Version of the Holy Bible, A.D. 1611, unless otherwise noted. (N.A.S. stands for New American Standard Bible).

CHAPTER ONE

FEELING ROUGH? YOU'RE NOT ALONE!

"Fear is unbelief parading in disguise."[1]

It takes little looking in life before spotting someone who is emotionally distressed. They are all about us! Husbands, wives, students, clerks, teachers, doctors, politicians, factory workers, farmers; you name it, most everyone has had or is experiencing emotional distress over something. "And, why not?" you might ask. "The world is a very unpredictable and alarming place in which to live."

Another person might be convinced that Murphy's Law is absolutely true; namely that, "If anything can go wrong, it will!" In fact, Paul Dickson, in his recent book, The Official Rules, has gathered together dozens of rather enigmatic and humorous rules that describe the pitfalls and potholes of life.[2]

Literally hundreds of fine books and articles have been written to attempt a description of why people are so emotionally upset. The next time you are in an airport book shop or shopping center bookstore, look up the "self-help" or "psychology" sections. I would be surprised if you are not amazed at how many books there are that deal with almost every facet of human behavior and emotional distress.

A crucial question is, however: "Is there really such a high level of emotional upset prevalent in the people of our nation as the helping professionals seem to proclaim?" Or, "Are these professionals trying to trump up business for themselves by decreeing a national mental health emergency?" You have perhaps heard of how the neurotic builds castles in the sky; the psychotic lives in them; and, the psychiatrist collects the rent!

The answer to the first question is yes, there really is a national mental health emergency in our country that is epidemic in its proportions! The answer to the second question is generally no! Helping professionals have more distressed persons to counsel with than they have time to handle and yet these professionals are not able to assist but a very small percentage (perhaps as low as 20%) of those who are in serious need of counseling or psychotherapy. It is true that many people still think that it would be personally embarrassing and degrading to see a psychological "shrink." They probably would not be so reluctant to recommend that other persons (outside the immediate family, of course) be attended to by the helping professional.

Many other factors hinder people from seeking professional psychological assistance. Among these factors are limited personal finances, fear of what really happens in counseling and psychotherapy, ignorance of available mental health resources, bad press from many possible sources, just to name a few.

EMOTIONAL SUFFERING IN THE PRESENT.

To highlight the seriousness of the emotional distress problem in the United States, look for a moment at the 1978 statistics of estimated incidences of major maladaptive behavior patterns.[3] Maladaptive behavior is considered by professionals to be behavior that is detrimental to the well-being of the individual and/or to society in general. Individuals included in the data were persons who were unable to successfully cope with some aspect of their lives. This inability to manage life is typically revealed in behaviors that are characteristically irrational in nature and highly charged with disintegrative emotional distress.

The report estimated that 55,500,000 persons suffered from minor to profound depression. Over 20,000,000 persons suffered from neurotic

You Are What You Think

disturbance.* Ten million reported alcohol-related problems with 1,000,000 individuals under treatment. In addition, over 200,000 persons attempted suicide, while 26,000 or more were "successful" in ending their lives. Over 1,000,000 students were reported to leave college each year because of emotional distress. Finally, there were over 200,000 reported cases of child abuse and over 10,000,000 persons arrested for serious crimes (190,000 persons are sent to prison and become part of the 500,000 persons who are in prison).

Obviously, these outdated grim statistics do not give the complete picture of emotional heartache that is being experienced in America today. Many more millions of our citizens suffer emotional distress and are "unreported" in the statistical data.

Families are still proud and attempt to keep their emotional upsets somewhat secret, if possible. It seems reasonable to predict that nearly one out of every two persons in our society is now, or will be, touched by mild-to-profound emotional distress that causes them to adopt self-defeating, non-productive behavior patterns. These behaviors will probably result in loss of self-esteem, general overall happiness, and physical health, not to mention life itself.

Ponder the unestimable personal losses that plague family and friends. The individual who unwisely perpetrates adultery, rape, or larceny soon experiences the hard consequences of breaking faith and may never again regain total trust and respect from family and associates. Responding to passionate voices, wooing one to enjoy forbidden fruits, and experiencing zest in life is often the siren call from Satan to "climb up fool's hill!"

How many persons lose or leave their jobs annually because of emotional problems? The Department of Labor estimates that the average American worker will change vocations at least six times during his working career. How many millions are changing because of emotional distress? Consider

---

* The neurotic individual "feels basically inadequate, evaluates everyday problems as threatening, and attempts to deal with the resulting anxiety by avoidance and defense-oriented reactions. The end result is a self-defeating lifestyle that blocks personal growth and self-fulfillment." Neuroses include: anxiety disorders (generalized anxiety disorders, obsessive-compulsive disorders, and phobic disorders); somatoform disorders (hypochondriasis, psychogenic pain disorders, and conversion disorders); and dissociative disorders (psychogenic amnesia and fugue, multiple personality, and depersonalization disorder) Coleman, Butcher, and Carson, 1980, pp. 205-242.

Neil C. Roth

the high number of middle-aged men that quit their positions after twenty to thirty years of service. Reason given--mid-life crisis--a catch-all term that includes a variety of personal-identity problems that men (and women, as well) experience during the middle years (40-55 years old) of their lives. These problems, notably existential in nature, probably have dogged their trails during the earlier stages of their lives, as well.

Consider too, the fantastic cost levied to our nation in the loss of productivity! Think of the work that is left undone, or not done on time, by those who call in "supposedly" or genuinely ill from emotional distress. Most physicians agree that a large percentage of their patients are suffering from psychosomatic illnesses. These are illnesses where psychological factors play a major part in causing physical disorders. Some of the classic psychosomatic disorders are heart attacks, peptic ulcers, migraine and tension headaches, hypertension, and anorexia nervosa, a condition where the individual refuses food or vomits after eating. (See chapter three for detailed discussion of psychosomatic complaints). Ultimately the person's body mass is greatly reduced and starvation is threatened.

As far back as 1955, researchers LeShan and Worthington suggested that perhaps the development and cause of malignant tumors might be influenced by psychosomatic factors.[4] This idea has gained in influence today with many skilled researchers focusing their energies on the problem. Notable work in this area is being done by the Cancer Counseling and Research Center of Fort Worth, Texas.

In addition to the usual forms of cancer therapy, numerous psychological techniques are employed such as: relaxation exercises, periods of imagery (here the patient visualized their white blood cells "doing in" their cancerous cells). Obviously, the placebo effect[*] is at work here with the patient's belief system, dramatically at times, altering the lethal course of the illness.[5]

It is interesting also to note that Hans Selye, who is widely known for his work on human stress, has shown that glucocorticoids (a stress-produced hormonal substance) have been shown to have paradoxical effects on the body. They seem to promote increased blood sugar for added energy and stimulate the distribution of blood, but inhibit body resistance to the control of infection and may allow other pathological influences to

---

[*] Placebo: a harmless medication or treatment which the patient believes to be a cure for his or her ailment. The "cure rate" is quite high with certain types of personalities.

You Are What You Think

develop.[6] It is noteworthy that many cancer researchers are more and more implicating the endocrine stress-response system as a key ingredient in the causation of many diseases from cancer to infertility. Let us hope that considerably more cancer research dollars will be allocated by Congress in the immediate future!

Added to the already overwhelming financial losses accruing to non-productivity is the factor of letting our friends in foreign countries take up the production slack, almost by default. This lack of productive resolve has been a key factor which has seriously undermined our industrial viability (witness the productive decline of the U. S. auto and electronics industries during the '70's and '80's).

All citizens are concerned about heavy local, state, and federal tax loads, but bear in mind that the lion's share of these collected revenues goes to care for those on the public assistance roles and for those under the care of governmental institutions or agencies.

Who are these persons that are being cared for? The physically and emotionally disabled (nursing homes and institutions for the mentally deficient and retarded); juvenile and adult offenders (group homes, detention centers, prisons); those persons on public assistance payrolls, and mental health programs sponsored by the local, state, and federal agencies concerned.

It all adds up to a tremendous drain of physical, emotional, and natural resources (represented by tens of billions of dollars annually) that are being expended to treat largely the symptoms of already entrenched maladaptive behavior patterns that unfortunately have a rather small probability of being changed by most human techniques in use.

Perhaps you have wondered, as I have often times, what would happen, if the many billions of dollars we spend yearly on assisting the emotionally distressed, and those that are lost to non-productivity, etc., (not to mention defense-spending) were diverted to needed projects like health research, increased energy exploration, food for the hungry, proper training, new jobs for the unemployed, and affordable homes for the homeless? This might be a very real possibility if only we could reorder our personal and national spiritual priorities to correspond to those set down by our Lord in the Holy Scriptures.

EMOTIONAL SUFFERING IN THE PAST.

Emotional problems are not something new to the human family of today. They have been around since the beginning of man's sojourn on earth. The chronicles of Herodotus, Thucydides, Xenaphon, Caesar, Josephus, and Gibbon, each reflect the intense emotional suffering that surrounded those persons they wrote about.

The Bible is replete with examples of great emotional distress. Listen to King David: "I am troubled; I am bowed down greatly; I go mourning all the day long" (Psalm 38:6). Or, hear King Solomon: "Therefore I hated life; because the work that is wrought under the sun is grievous unto me: for all is vanity and vexation of spirit" (Ecclesiastes 2:17).

Witness, as well, the emotionally distressed man of Gadara:

> Who had his dwelling among the tombs; and no man could bind him, no, not with chains: because that he had often been bound with fetters and chains, and the chains had been plucked asunder by him, and the fetters broken in pieces: neither could any man tame him. And always, night and day, he was in the mountains, and in the tombs, crying, and cutting himself with stones (Mark 5:3-5).

Each of these men were sorely troubled and were reacting very negatively to their life situations. Isaiah, the ancient prophet of Israel, perhaps described the plight of unregenerate man best when he quotes God as saying: "But the wicked are like the troubled sea, when it cannot rest, whose waters cast up mire and dirt. There is no peace, saith my God, to the wicked" (Isaiah 57:20, 21).

St. Augustine, reflecting on his sinful youth prayed, "Thou madest us for Thyself, and our hearts are restless until they rest in thee."[7]

Mary Carolyn Davis in her poem entitled "Feet," described the global existential vacuum that the non-Christian experiences, much like that of Augustine.

Hundreds of passages in the Bible describe the naturally sinful condition of man and reveal that there are very real and damaging consequences that will be incurred if God's physical and spiritual laws are

You Are What You Think

not heeded and obeyed. In a very real, and sometimes fatal sense, we inflict undue physical and emotional damage on ourselves because of a basic flaw in our character which the Bible calls sin. We will deal with the concept of sin and its consequences later in this chapter.

EMOTIONAL SUFFERING IN THE FUTURE.

Alvin Toffler, in his penetrating book, The Third Wave, lays a thorough foundation for understanding the decades of the eighties and nineties. He said,

> We, who happen to share the planet at this explosive moment, will therefore feel the full impact of the Third Wave in our own life times. Tearing our families apart, rocking our economy, paralyzing our political systems, shattering our values, the Third Wave affects everyone. It challenges all the old power relationships, the privileges and prerogatives of the endangered elites of today, and provides the backdrop against which the key power struggles of tomorrow will be fought.[8]

Toffler's new book, like Future Shock before, is unsettling at best. He describes a world that is to be battered by violent emotional and social upheavals. But, Toffler does not have the last word. Centuries ago, a lone Galilean forecasted a world that would be in chaotic crisis.

Let us now consider the words of Jesus Christ as He sets forth the conditions that will exist on the earth during the last days. (It is worth noting that most Bible scholars now feel that nothing prophetically can hinder Christ from keeping his promise to return to earth for his church at anytime!) Jesus' disciples had just asked Him what the signs of his coming and the end of the world would be. He said unto them:

> ...Take heed that no man deceive you. For many shall come in my name, saying, I am Christ (Savior); and shall deceive many (note the rise of pseudo Christs and their cults!). And ye shall hear of wars and rumours of wars (witness the proliferation of wars and the arm's races of our century!): see that ye be not troubled:

7

for all these things must come to pass, but the end is not yet. For nation shall rise against nation, and kingdom against kingdom; and there shall be famines, and pestilences, and earthquakes, in many places. All these are the beginning of sorrows...and because iniquity (lawlessness) shall abound, the love of many shall wax (grow) cold (Matthew 24:4-7, 12).

Men's hearts failing them for fear, and for looking after those things which are coming on the earth....(Luke 21:26)

But he that shall endure to the end, the same shall be saved. And this gospel of the kingdom (of God) shall be preached in all the world for a witness unto all nations; and then shall the end come (Matthew 24:13, 14).

Notice that our Lord does not forecast a very rosy picture for the end days. Deception and warfare will greatly amplify the emotional distress in the world, bringing about a critical atmosphere of sorrows and love-waxed-cold by lawlessness. Many are saying: "Let me off at the next world! I can't stand this one any longer!"

ANXIETY AND FEAR.

Furthermore, observe Christ's foretelling of how men's hearts would be failing them out of fear. Fear certainly would be felt because of the threats and calamities experienced through earthquakes and threats of, or actual war. But could it be that men's hearts are failing them because of a much much deeper fear that stems from the presence of the deep feeling, and perhaps inherent knowledge, that they will be ultimately judged for their earthly attitudes and actions? The writer to the Hebrews echoes this message when he quotes God in Deuteronomy 32:35, 36 and Christ in Luke 12:5. "...Vengeance belongeth unto me, I will recompense, saith the Lord. And again, the Lord shall judge his people. It is a fearful thing to fall into the hands of the living God" (Hebrews 10:30, 31).

The Apostle Paul reiterates the reality of a day of human reckoning with God to the Christians at Corinth. He said, "For we must all appear before the judgment seat of Christ; that everyone may receive the things done in his body (recompensed for his deeds), according to that he hath done, whether it be good or bad" (II Corinthians 5:10). The sure reality of a personal confrontation with almighty God at the end of our earthly lives, coupled with a certain pervasive fear and anxiety over the probable outcome, could point to the central reason for much of the emotional distress that people experience. It perhaps hinges on Kierkegaard's idea that anxiety is the "fear of nothingness," or that of becoming nothing if God's judgment removes us of our eternal identity.[9]

Robert Browning, in his tribute to the death of a dear friend, penned these lines in the poem, "In Memoriam" that describes man's deepest anxiety:

> So runs my dream; but what am I?
> An infant crying in the night;
> An infant crying for the light,
> And with no language but a cry.

The Apostle John described fear as having the ominous quality of emotional torment (I John 4:18). He supports the idea regarding the inate human fear of judgment when he describes the antidote for human existential fear and certainly the fear of the Divine Judiciary.

> Whosoever shall confess that Jesus is the Son of God, God dwelleth in him, and he in God. And we have known and believed the love that God hath (given) to us. God is love; and he that dwelleth in love (agape love--for God, others, and self) dwelleth in God, and God in him. Herein is our love made perfect, that we may have boldness in the day of judgment: because as He is, so are we in this world. There is no fear in love; but perfect love (that is, God's love shed abroad in your hearts by Christ Jesus) casteth out fear: because fear hath torment. He that feareth is not made perfect in love (I John 4:15-18).

The fear spoken of surely is related to more than fearing judgment, even though I believe this to be the central pervasive fear experienced by unregenerate man, and alluded to in this passage of Scripture.

Neil C. Roth

Man is also afraid of the future, afraid to commit himself to God because of what God might require of him, such as: having to change his life-style and behaviors; doing too much for the church; testifying on Christ's behalf; and, the fear of inevitable death.

Many of man's fears are also phobic in nature; that is, there seems to be no real external threat of danger that has brought about the fear. Emerson once said that "fear always springs from ignorance." Yet, while phobias are irrational in essence, many phobic persons, while consciously realizing their irrationality, are nevertheless unable to dispel them without therapeutic assistance.

That man is anxious, is probingly discussed by Rollo May, a clinical psychologist, who first trained for and served in the ministry. He has written some dozen books including the best sellers, The Meaning of Anxiety (1950) and Love and Will (1969). He states that:

> The evidence is overwhelming, however, that we live today in an age of anxiety. If one penetrates below the surface of political, economic, business, professional, or domestic crises to discover their psychological causes, or if one seeks to understand modern art or poetry or philosophy or religion, one runs athwart the problem of anxiety at almost every turn. The ordinary stresses and strains of life in a changing world of today are such that few if any escape the need to confront anxiety and to deal with it in some manner.[10]

It appears, then, that the general human family has been, and continues to be, beset by fears; some very real, but most very falsely founded. At the root is a basic sense of insecurity tied to perplexing existential quandries, namely: "Who am I?" "What am I here for?" "To whom or what am I responsible?" and finally, "Does someone, outside of my earthly associates, really care about me and my destiny?" In other words, "Where am I going during life and after life?" These questions have been carefully and adequately dealt with in the Holy Scriptures and will be discussed in a later chapter.

Obviously, it is proper and beneficial for us to fear those experiences, or their possibilities, that could bring us harm or even death. The red, hot

You Are What You Think

stove need be touched only once to reveal its mysteries. Need we jump off of the ten story building to discover what the outcome of our fall will be? Prudently, man does evidence some beneficial learning from past experiences where a healthy fear (often changed to respect) has inhibited capricious stumbling. The human fear of being spiritually exposed before the Living God at the final judgment is a legitimate and awesome fear that should cause any human to renounce his sin and join the ranks of the "born-anew" brethren.

E. Stanley Jones, one of the outstanding preachers and missionaries of our time, describes our world as possessing a "climate of anxiety." He notes that "unless the individual has inner resources which will make him immune to this invading climate, he will be afraid." Afraid of what? He feels, as do I, that there are more than the basic two fears that we are born with; namely, the fear of loud noises and the fear of falling. Dr. Jones continues by stating, "There is another basic (inherent) fear--the fear of the soul that is cut off from its central root God.... When we don't belong to God, then we belong to fear."[11]

Jones is careful to separate fears from anxieties. He qualifies that "Fear has a specific object, whereas anxiety is a vague and unspecified apprehension." He cites Otto Rank (and surely most Freudian psychological positions), and his view that there are two basic forms of fear experienced throughout our lives--life fear and death fear. Jones senses that the fear of living is really man's fear of being responsible. Life most assuredly brings responsibility to one's self, to others, and to God. He quotes Carl Jung in a very revealing observation about this evasion of responsibility. Jung says, "I no longer find the causes of neurosis in the past, (as Freud did) but in the present. I ask, 'What is the necessary task which the patient will not accomplish?'" So it is that so many human beings are backing out of being responsible to life because of fear.[12]

FEAR OF DEATH.

But what about the fear of death? Jones describes three key reasons for this fear and why individuals are attempting (ultimately they are unsuccessful in a physical sense) to avert death. He states that:

Neil C. Roth

(1) We are afraid of the unknown;

(2) We have not lived our lives the way they should have been lived, so we hesitate to go where 'we shall know as we are known;' and

(3) We are afraid that death is equivalent to extinction. The urge to live is strong with us.[13]

In his poem, "Prospice," Robert Browning wrote:

Fear death? --to feel the fog in my throat,
    The mist in my face,
When the snows begin, and the blasts denote
    I am nearing the place,
The power of the night, the press of the storm,
    The post of the foe;
Where he stands, the Arch Fear in a visible form,
    Yet the strong man must go:....

For sudden the worst turns the best to the brave,
    The black minute's at end,
And the elements' rage, the fiend-voices that rave,
    Shall dwindle, shall blind,
Shall change, shall become first a peace out of pain,
    Then a light, then thy breast,
O thou soul of my soul! I shall clasp thee again,
    And with God be the rest![14]

FEAR AND SIN.

Browning is echoing forth his faith in God that is reminiscent of Paul's words to the Corinthian Christians:

O death, where is thy sting? O grave, where is thy victory? The sting of death is sin; and the strength of sin is the law. But thanks be to God, which giveth us the victory through our Lord Jesus Christ (I Corinthians 15:55-57).

You Are What You Think

The fear of death has no dominion over he whose sin is covered and whose trust is in God!

Ironically, the personal existential anxiety underlying our identities and destinies cannot be shrugged off as completely learned behavior. Freud's great psychoanalytic contemporary, Carl Jung, felt that "anxiety is the individual's reaction to the invasion of his conscious mind by irrational forces and images from the collective unconscious."[15] Jung, the son of a protestant minister, probably wished to be accepted by his professional peers and so chose not to label these anxiety-producing irrational forces as the sinful or carnal human nature that the Bible so frequently describes.

The Apostle Paul, in his own inimitable judicial eloquence, relays this theme of an "invasion of irrational forces" by saying:

> Wherefore, as by one man (Adam--really Hebrew for man) sin entered into the world, and death by sin; and so death passed upon all men, for that all have sinned. For as by one man's disobedience many were made sinners, so by the obedience of one (Christ Jesus) shall many be made righteous. Moreover the law entered, that the offence might abound. But where sin abounded, grace did much more abound (Romans 5:12, 19, 20).

That sin has permeated the nature of man's personality should be of little doubt to most intelligent persons. Most of the psychologists today tend to overlook sin as the central symptom in client diagnosis and are almost totally inaccurate in their therapeutic approach which omits assuming that man has moral responsibility to our Creator, God! The surgeon who can open up his client, but has trouble "closing," is valueless to the patient. So it is, that the helping professional not only has the responsibility to assist the client in uncovering problem sources and achieving insight, but ethically, should be intellectually and spiritually able and ready to share God's counsel, and the message of reconciliation to God, as revealed through Jesus Christ.

A much needed and refreshing breeze has begun to blow about our great country in the areas of Christian psychology and counseling. Many Christian counselors, psychotherapists, and psychologists are beginning to exert their influence in the "helping market place" today.

Neil C. Roth

These professionals are products of numerous fine Christian and secular colleges, universities, and seminaries, and are evidencing genuine concern for helping distressed persons with their emotional and spiritual problems.

A leading authority in the area of psychiatry is the renowned Dr. Karl Menninger. He has written a cogent and provocative book entitled, <u>Whatever Became of Sin</u>? In it he states that:

> The wrongness of the sinful act lies not merely in its nonconformity, its departure from the accepted, appropriate way of behavior, but in an implicitly aggressive quality--a ruthlessness, a hurting, a breaking away from God and from the rest of humanity, a partial alienation, or act of rebellion.[16]

Surely, this describes the state of many relationships today that are blighted by the effects of sin. It is essential that we understand that individual sins are because the fundamental condition of sin is! Dr. Menninger's definition rings true and the qualities of sin described in his book are shockingly confirmed millions of times each day throughout the world.

This distress caused by sin, points to the fact that man desperately needs radical emotional and spiritual surgery by the only Surgeon capable of such a miraculous feat, our Lord Jesus Christ! In my opinion, the Christian helper is one who can "refer" these "humanly impossible" cases to One who is totally competent to heal! Paul said it so wonderfully well:

> There is therefore now no condemnation to them which are in Christ Jesus, who walk not after the flesh, but after the Spirit. For the law of the Spirit of life in Christ Jesus hath made me free from the law of sin and death.
>
> For they that are after the flesh do mind (attend to) the things of the flesh; but they that are after the Spirit the things of the Spirit. For to be carnally minded is death; but to be spiritually minded is life and peace.
>
> So then they that are in the flesh (carnal mind) cannot please God (Romans 8:1, 2; 5, 6, and 8).

You Are What You Think

THE MIRACLE THAT GOD SENT.

We needed a miracle and our Lord provided the means to become one with Him through his marvelous grace. Fortunately for us, Jesus views all sin as a curable condition. If this were not true, He would not have come to such a sinful world in the first place.

Please note, however, the numerous references to "mind" in the preceding verses. The spiritual transformation that God promises to us through his Son is a dynamic change of heart and mind. This change is accomplished by, and through faith in the veracity of what Christ has said.

Obviously, beyond acceptance of his Word must come the initial acceptance of his existence and Lordship in our lives. This faith, literally (in acrostic form) <u>F</u>orsaking <u>A</u>ll <u>I</u> <u>T</u>rust <u>H</u>im, is the base-line requisite necessary for admission to the Kingdom of God. The writer to the Hebrews (I hold this to be the Apostle Paul by virtue of writing style) said: "But without faith it is impossible to please Him: for he that cometh to God must believe that He is, and that He is a rewarder of them that diligently seek Him." He previously defines faith in this chapter as "...the substance (assurance) of things hoped for, the evidence (conviction) of things not seen" (Hebrews 11:6, 1).

To be sure, such words as carnal and spiritual mind, reason, and belief impinge critically upon our human destinies. For it is really how each of us manage or mismanage God's Truth that ultimately determines the quality, and oftentimes the length of our earthly sojourn, and more importantly, the possibility and realization of sharing a heavenly home with our Lord God and his people!

The title of this book was not selected by chance but by careful design. It expresses my firm conviction that <u>we are literally what we think</u>. Spinoza, in his <u>Treatise on the Correction of the Understanding</u> relayed his view of the importance of one's thoughts. "I saw that all the things I feared and which feared me had nothing good or bad in them save in so far as the mind was affected by them."[17] That our manner of thinking determines our practice is a well established empirical fact.

Furthermore, the Bible has stated this truth in numerous ways but perhaps most memorably in the words of King Solomon: "As he (a man) thinketh in his heart, so is he" (Proverbs 23:7). The New American Standard Bible states it: "For as he thinks within himself, so he is."

Neil C. Roth

But in what kinds of thinking are we then to engage? (Chapter two will thoroughly investigate the viable, and the not-so-viable, answers to this question.) The Bible does help us with an answer to this question. The Apostle Paul is stating an ideal here, but not an impossible one! Prayerfully he said:

> And the peace of God, which passeth all understanding, shall keep (guard) your <u>hearts</u> and <u>minds</u> through Christ Jesus. Finally, brethren, whatsoever things are true,...honest,...just,...pure,... lovely,...of good report; if there be any virtue, and if there be any praise, think on these things (Philippians 4:7, 8).

He then affirms the enablement to achieve the ideal: "I can do all things through Christ which strengtheneth me" (Philippians 4:13).

The verses just cited reflect the positive, developmental attitude that all Christians are to possess and experience. Again, you may be asking, "But how? Is it unrealistic or Polyanish to follow after such a positive admonition? Is this sticking one's head in the sand and ignoring the problems and evils that surround us in the world?" I think not! Our Lord is saying <u>be positive and redemptive, and by such attitudes, you can help others to grow and develop</u>.

Usually our negativism fails to solve problems. A nervous and tense woman once looked at a very expensive and beautiful rug and exclaimed, "I love the rug but moths will get into it!" There are many who see a "negative" in everything in life, and who fail to grasp the happiness and beauty. They are rather moth-minded!

We can either be a "negative" part of the problem or a "positive" part of the solution. Yes, the Christian should strive to see the problems of self and society clearly, but then endeavor, with insight, wisdom, and courage, to become a positive influence in the solving of such. How much better for us to expect the good in life and literally create it by our faith that it will happen! For real faith is when we believe in a thing enough to act upon it as if it were true. This principle applies particularly to our emotional well-being. We can learn to avoid emotional distress by changing our ways of thinking about God, self, and others.

Now, we shall continue on to chapter two and examine learning and thinking, and then proceed to chapter three and see how feelings and emotions interrelate with our mental processes.

FOOTNOTES

1. Brooks, Keith L. The Cream Book. Chicago: Moody Press, 1938, p. 88.
2. Dickson, Paul. The Official Rules. New York: Delacorte Press, 1978.
3. Coleman, James C., Butcher, James N., and Carson, Robert C. Abnormal Psychology and Modern Life, 6th Edition. Palo Alto, California: Scott, Foresman & Co., 1980, pp. 4, 205-242.
4. LeShan, L. L., & Worthington, R. E. Some Psychologic Correlates of Neoplastic Disease: Preliminary Report. Journal of Clinical and Experimental Psychopathology, 1955, pp. 16, 281-288.
5. Simonton, O. C., Matthews-Simonton, S., & Creighton, J. Getting Well Again. Los Angeles, California: J. P. Tarper (Distributed by St. Martin's Press, New York), 1978.
6. Selye, Hans. The Stress of Life, 2nd Edition. New York: McGraw-Hill, 1976.
7. Outline of Great Books. Edited by Sir J. A. Hammerton. New York: Wise and Co., 1932, p. 505.
8. Toffler, Alvin. The Third Wave. New York: Bantam Books, Inc., 1981, p. 10.
9. Kierkegaard, Soren. The Concept of Anxiety. Ed. and trans. by Howard V. Hong and Edna V. Hong. Northfield, Minn., 1976.
10. May, Rollo. The Meaning of Anxiety. New York: W. W. Norton & Co., 1977, p. ix.
11. Jones, E. Stanley. Growing Spiritually. Nashville, Tenn.: Abingdon-Cokesbury Press, 1953, pp. 33-35.
12. Jung, Carl G. Collected Papers on Analytical Psychology. Authorized translation by C. E. Long. London: Braillière, Tindall, and Cox.
13. Jones. op. cit.
14. Poems of Robert Browning. Edited by Donald Smalley. Boston: Houghlin Mifflin Co., 1956, pp. 296-297.
15. May. op. cit., p. 158.
16. Menninger, Karl, M.D. Whatever Became of Sin? New York: Bantam Books, 1973, p. 22.
17. Spinoza, Baruch. The Ethics of Spinoza and Treatise on the Correction of the Intellect. London: Everyman Edition, 1910.

CHAPTER TWO

WHAT IS LEARNING AND THINKING?

"Knowledge is folly unless grace guides it."[1]

LEARNING.

A classical definition for learning is: "a relatively permanent change in behavior that occurs as the result of practice."[2] The emphasis in this definition is on change: Change in response potentiality. The process of growth and maturation, in a physical sense, denotes change. So it is in the intellectual and emotional spheres of life. We say that the individual is acting and speaking as an adult if the formerly-held childhood attitudes and behaviors have been replaced by new, mature adult ones. Obviously, we know that learning has taken place if demonstrable changes are observable in overt behavior.

Learning tends to be relatively permanent and is closely tied to experiences in life. It applies to many different aspects of experiencing. Some of these are related to acquiring and mastering new skills, adding new information and knowledge, developing new interests, changing, redefining, or adding new attitudes.

Learning seems to be primarily accomplished as we respond to sensory stimuli in our environment. The effectiveness of human learning is contingent on the individual's sensory awareness of objects, conditions, or persons. Defects in an individual's sense organs can greatly alter the accuracy of sensory perception and can cause one's interpretation of events to range from slight understatement to gross exaggeration.

You Are What You Think

Furthermore, people learn in planned and unplanned ways. Formal learning is usually carried out in schools or supervised by a private specialist in a field. Some people feel that the only worthwhile learning has to take place in the schoolhouse. Nothing could be further from the truth! Actually, valuable unplanned learning takes place throughout our entire lives in unintentional ways. These ways reflect the myriad of positive and negative life experiences upon which all persons build their lives.

In reality, the learning we have accomplished throughout life becomes the real you-to-date! New learning, coupled with motivation and insight, will cause you to change into a slightly different person than you just were. This is born out in the theory of Abraham Maslow, and others, that man adapts certain behavioral responses hopefully to satisfy his basic needs. Maslow lists five: (1) physiological, (2) safety and security, (3) love and belongingness, (4) esteem, and (5) self-actualization.[3]

Maslow did not incorporate into his model the obvious spiritual needs that humans express throughout the world. Afterall, over three and one half billion of the world's population are estimated to have some kind of religious orientation. This surely suggests a spiritual craving for a better understanding of, and relationship with almighty God. Maslow did speak of metaneeds, metamotives, and B-values which were terms to describe self-actualized persons who had achieved special insight relative to the love of beauty, justice, love, etc., but he did not go far enough by discussing man's spiritual nature. Figure 1 is a modification of Maslow's Hierarchy of Needs.

Principles applying to need satisfaction:

1. Growth is gradual--shifts from one level to another.
2. Growth is progressive-- lower levels ordinarily need to be satisfied before higher needs will be strongly desired or striven for.
3. Lower needs do not disappear but assume lesser motivational importance.
4. The spiritual need can intervene at any hierarchical step and override through one's questing for and acquiring God!

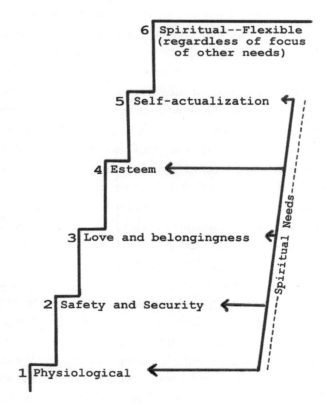

Figure 1. MODIFIED CHRISTIAN HIERARCHY OF NEEDS

It is important to note that the spiritual needs of man can, and do, override the pursuant meeting of all other hierarchical needs when the individual has experienced the "new birth" of life as found only in Jesus Christ (John 3:1-16)! Basic needs are no longer preeminent but become by-products of seeking God's will, and his kingdom, first and foremost (Matthew 6:33).

Accordingly, man, while learning certain behaviors and attitudes to use in his pursuit of need satisfaction, soon chooses which behaviors or attitudes that have proven to be most successful. These, of course, could be, and often are, very anti-social attitudes and/or behaviors, as well as those deemed socially redemptive. These attitudes and behaviors, after repeated rehearsal and appropriate (or not so appropriate) reinforcement (feedback from the environment), become rather enduring characteristics labeled by

You Are What You Think

psychologists as traits. The fact of the matter is that these traits (attitudes and behaviors) really are reflections of our learning. This learning (or life experience) becomes the "real you." Your heredity also plays a vital part in determining how you will respond to much that occurs in life.

In addition, the spiritual imprinting of God's image is a part of every human personality and cannot be dismissed by the difficulty of empirical validation. "So God created man in his own image, in the image of God created He him; male and female created He them" (Genesis 1:27) and later Moses amplifies God's crowning creative act (my homonoid egocentricity is showing!) by reporting how "the Lord God formed man of the dust of the ground, and breathed into his nostrils the breath of life; and man became a living soul" (Genesis 2:7). The fact that God made us to be living souls (personalities) and stamped our personalities with his spiritual image is indeed an awesome learning to ponder! Our human need for answers to the perplexing questions related to identity and purpose in life is better understood when we recognize that the image of God pervades our psychological and spiritual temperaments.

Meanwhile, let us resume our trek through some basic avenues of how learning occurs and develops. We discovered that behaviors and attitudes used to satisfy needs, tend to, after repeated practice, become unique personal traits. These are, in reality, the building blocks of your personality and character. Most psychologists agree that some individuals become persons that view themselves, others, and the physical world with responsibility and respect, while others adopt just the opposite perspective. Crucial to the actualization of this positive outcome is the early childhood presence of genuine human and divine love. Without generous doses of sincere love throughout life, the individual will be prone to view himself as an unloved and somewhat ugly person. Furthermore, this negative mind-set, unless checked early, will pervade the person's view of others, God, and life in general. This learning about love is so critical that we can tie virtually all of man's psychological and spiritual woes to his misunderstanding and misapplication to life of the Christian principles pertaining to love.

Chamfort once said that "There are more people who wish to be loved than there are willing to love." Tragically true, but in order for love to be effectively communicated, we must surely learn (as parents, spouses, and friends) that love cannot be expressed with a clenched fist or demanding

Neil C. Roth

voice! Love draws, leads, woos, respects. Later, we shall discuss this theme in greater length.

As living personalities (souls), made after God's image, we learn about life through personal experience and adapt characteristic ways of responding to life that are moderately predictable. Why? Because we are creatures of habit!

In the early part of the 20th century, the eminent psychologist Edward Thorndike advanced his theory of learning known as connectionism. He did extensive research with animals and children and formalized some previously thought, but vague, notions related to how we learn. Simply, he stated that (1) We learn best when we are ready to learn. That is, we all have our most optimal teachable moments. If we are forced to learn before we are really ready, Thorndike discovered that we would be annoyed. If we were ready to learn, satisfaction with the experience would occur (he called this the Law of Readiness).

He went on to state that (2) When we repeat or rehearse an action or behavior, we tend to strengthen the learning that accrues (this was his Law of Exercise). Really, he listed two aspects of this principle: the Law of Use and Disuse which simply stated that when we practice, we preserve and strengthen a behavior. When we do not consistently reinforce behaviors, they tend to become weakened by disuse.

Finally, he said that (3) If an activity or behavior tends to be satisfying, the strength of the behavioral connection is increased. The opposite is true when the activity or behavior is annoying, or less than satisfying. Thus, the strength of the behavioral connection is weakened and may be partially or totally extinguished.[4]

Much significant research on learning has been done during this century that merely supports the position taken by the Scriptures. The importance of human training and learning is frequently mentioned throughout God's Word. Consider: "Train up a child in the way he should go: and when he is old, he will not depart from it" (Proverbs 22:6). Surely, learning principles are implicit to the proper interpretation of this verse. "Train up"--stimulate the child with proper inputs about living as expressed by the Lord in the Word.

As a nation, we have witnessed the chaotic results of an era that disregarded the child-rearing counsel of God's Word and reaped the bitter

You Are What You Think

harvest of lawlessness and immorality. The spirit of the child must be preserved at all costs, through love and confirmation, but his will must be trained. This, hopefully, can be accomplished "gently," but, if need be, with stronger reinforcement, possibly by "warming up the child's seat covers!" But before that is resorted to, the parents should take care to establish the boundaries of their expectations for the child. Saying how far the child can go and quietly reinforcing those boundaries, without resorting to anger, will cause the child to respond early to their admonition and will.

More importantly, his will will be more amenable to God's will as he approaches the age of accountability and decision-making. Spare not the rod, and spoil the child (Proverbs 23:13) is wise advice to any parent. Many parents "give in" to their children's unbridled ways, thinking they will not be loved if they should discipline and occasionally punish the child. However, when there is no parental reinforcement, the child soon loses respect for his parents. Love often must say "no!" Confidently, remember that God's ways are always right and effective! After all, as man's designer and creator, He should know how we can best be taught, disciplined, and punished.

Furthermore, learn to trust Christ and commit your child into his care and then carefully follow his counsel by: (1) Being the right kind of parent: one who is totally committed to the Lord and his Word; (2) Valuing your child as a person who has been given to you as a sacred trust and opportunity; (3) Committing yourself to his development, using loving guidance (discipline) and loving punishment (without anger), if necessary. Do not, as a parent, fall victim to today's tragic dilemma where "everything in the house is controlled with a switch except the child!" and, (4) Affirming the child continually, conveying in word and deed that he is loved and respected for himself, over and above his behavior. Note, that it is extremely important to convey to the child that negative, selfish behavior can alienate him from harmonious parental, societal, and divine relationships if not corrected. Children must learn that natural consequences always follow the breaking of social and moral laws. If the above counsel is faithfully and prayerfully followed, then you can rely on God keeping his promise: "and when he is old (mature), he will not depart from it." In fact, research has confirmed that a majority of persons, upon reaching maturity (22--35 years of age) return to, and accept, a similar moral code that was held by their parents.

Neil C. Roth

Through this admonition and promise, we potentially see the inherent and explicit by-products of reinforcement of key learnings and their habituation. Froebel once wrote: "Think not that he is all too young to teach. His little heart will like a magnet reach and touch the truth for which you have no speech."

Continuing, review these scriptural admonitions tied to learning: "Thou shalt teach them diligently unto thy children" (Deuteronomy 6:7a), or; "Precept must be upon precept, precept upon precept; line upon line, line upon line; here a little, and there a little" (Isaiah 28:10). The instruction mentioned is directly related to the stimulus-response idea of learning held dear by most behavioral psychologists.

The final addition of the quality of free will is revealed by these words of Jesus Christ who invites all persons to become students (disciples) in his school.

> Come unto me, all ye that labour and are heavy laden, and I will give you rest. Take my yoke upon you, and <u>learn</u> of me; for I am meek and lowly in heart: and ye shall find rest unto your souls. For my yoke is easy, and my burden is light (Matthew 11:28-30).

These beautiful words of our Lord reveal truth that is liberating and redemptive in nature. By <u>learning</u> of Christ, our emotional and spiritual burdens may be lifted and rest for our troubled personalities is assured. The promise that such commitment to Christ and his school will not lead to confusion and anxiety, is affirmed by the promise of an easy journey with Christ as we occupy our yoke next to his.

Christ's spirit of meekness and lowliness is really the childlike spirit that He seeks to implant in his disciples. Lest we think that only those with boldness, education, and finesse are the only ones that can possibly fit into Christ's yoke, be reminded that we must become attitudinally as little children before entering into the Kingdom of God (Matthew 18:3). Nicodemus (John 3:1-16) was told he had to become "born-again." This is really God's call to the transformation and renewal of our minds (Romans 12:2). Of utmost importance is the early stimulation of children with quality spiritual sensory experiences. J. Edgar Hoover once said "Today's

You Are What You Think

unchurched child is tomorrow's criminal." We can go a step further: Today's adult is like the mirror's images presented to him in childhood.

An anonymous poet has beautifully described the potent influence we can have on the learning and character of the child. The poem, called "Heart of a Child,"

Along these lines, I strongly urge you to read Andrew Murray's great study called The School of Obedience in which he analyzes the purpose, character, and role of a true disciple in Christ's school for saints.

We could spend many pages citing scripture verses that describe learning and its effect when properly managed. Suffice it to say, contemporary learning theory, for the most part confirms anew the accuracy of the position taken by the Bible. Ronald L. Koteskey, in his book, Psychology From a Christian Perspective, confirms the thoughts just expressed by stating:

> Made in God's image, humans are cognitive beings who have the capacity for understanding and knowledge. God invites us to come and reason together with Him (see Isaiah 1:18). He can make such an invitation because humans are capable of reasoning. Since we are created in God's image, we can reason and increase our knowledge, but we must also realize that we are animal-like in that we are created beings, and thus finite. Our knowledge will always be partial and should be used carefully.[5]

Koteskey's reference to our human inability to know everything is highlighted by experience. The more we learn, the more we come to realize how little we really know. The old worn definition of education reduces the problem down to size: "Education (learning) is where you learn more and more, about less and less, until you know everything about nothing!" The point of concern raised from this backwoods wisdom, is that the focus and quality of learning is of paramount importance, lest we acquire large quantities of information (knowledge) but, in the end, find ourselves with little wisdom - knowing everything about nothing!

In continuing our discussion on learning, it is important to recognize that the totality of any situation is generally more than the parts we can identify. The Gestalt school of psychology emphasizes this postulate over and over: "The whole is greater than the sum of its parts." Simply put, this means that any person must be understood by analyzing more than his physical parts in order to accurately make up our interpretational information base. The person's intellectual, emotional, and spiritual frames of reference, plus the environmental and hereditary factors, must be evaluated in concert before we can begin to understand and more fully appreciate his uniqueness and motivation in life.

Insight (in Gestalt terms: an integration of the whole) assists us in better recognizing and understanding the meaning of the "Gestalt." The Gestalt position suggests that effective insight, surrounding this meaning of the "whole" is essential if viable learning in every area of life is to be totally relevant to the acquiring of wisdom, as well as knowledge.

THINKING.

Next, we shall consider thinking. Broadly defined, thinking is "the ability to imagine or represent objects or events in memory and to operate on these representations."[6] Webster cites many definitions for thinking but the most applicable meaning for our purposes is: "To use the mind for arriving at conclusions, making decisions, drawing inferences, etc.; reflect; reason: as, you must learn to think."[7]

Many psychologists have attempted to describe thinking but most admit that their theories are less than adequate. The problem is that our rather simply stated schemes cannot quite adequately explain the full range of characteristics that have been, or are being discovered about human cognition.

The stimulus-response position on thinking, developed by behaviorist Clark Hull, stated that neural bonds were formed in our brain cells between life events (stimuli) and our reactions to those events (responses). This thinking model has been recently likened as being analogous to the operation of a computer which is programmed (by the human) with information (stimulus) and upon demand returns the desired data (response). The problem with this conceptualization rests in its omission of many crucial human variables that contribute to thinking.

You Are What You Think

Beyond the computer, which, after all, is man's invention (and under his control), human thinking is more than a mere switching process within the brain between stimuli and responses. Thinking is an extremely active process that is bringing together one's perceptions, imagination, symbolism, words, conceptualizations, and even sub-vocal speech. It reflects the individual's awareness of the stimuli at hand plus his recall of past events and learnings. Indeed, what we bring to awareness is influenced by our mental set (mind-set refers to our readiness to respond to certain situations and not to others), wishes, needs, and intentions, to name just a few.

Obviously, this process of learning and thinking is carried on in the grandest of God's earthly creations, the human brain. Researchers are uncovering many previously hidden mysteries that will ultimately aid us in the better understanding of behavior. For example, we have known for sometime that the left hemisphere of the brain tends to manage the ability of expressing language. This function includes not only the management of speaking and writing skills but also those related to mathematics, science, and logic. The right hemisphere of the brain seems to specialize in the coordination of motor-spatial-perceptual activities and appears to house one's appreciation for the arts. Also, the capacity for fantasy is thought to be located here. Of course, the left hemisphere controls the right side of the body and the right hemisphere controls the left. This fact is made graphic when the blood clots in either cerebral hemisphere and often results in partial or complete paralysis (stroke) in the opposite side of the body.

Researchers have recently discovered that people differ in the ways that their brains function. For one thing, it is known that people possess hemispheric-dominancy. This finding points out that some persons are better able (by virtue of this dominancy) to better excell in left-hemispheric activities (verbal, language, logic) then those who are dominant in right-hemispheric functioning (excelling in the motor-spatial-artistic-kinesthetic functions). Hopefully, this discovery will have profound implications upon the choice of instructional methods and curricula in our educational institutions. In effect, not everyone learns best in quite the same way as do others. It is apparent that we must discover and implement more appropriate physiological and neurological learning strategies if we are to become effective in the actualization of our educational goals and outcomes.

Neil C. Roth

For sometime we have believed that students dropped out of our high schools and colleges because of boredom, changes in life goals, personal crises, etc. These reasons, and many dozens more, may represent only a tip of the "withdrawal-symptom" iceberg. Could it be that we have not presented learning material in a manner which could most easily be analyzed and understood by the student who had to function with either left or right cerebral-dominancy. In other words, some persons seem to learn best when they can have a "hands on" experience with the object or concept in question. If only teachers (particularly in the upper grades and in college) could begin to acknowledge this fact and implement appropriate didactic methods, perhaps a greater number of students would begin to view their education as exciting, relevant, and useful. Perhaps our national school drop-out rate would begin to significantly subside!

I would refer you to the intriguing work of Dr. Marcel Kinsbourne (focusing on the area of cerebral-hemisphere specialization in normal persons), for further reading on the subject.[8] Gozzaniga, in his research, has dispelled the notion that mental unity exists in the functions of the brain's hemispheres.[9] This is born out when in a near miraculous way, after severe injury or surgery is experienced in one hemisphere of the brain, the other hemisphere takes over and slowly begins to function on behalf of the lost capacity.

There does seem to be a unitary constant present in the human brain that is witnessed in the act of problem-solving. Regardless of the nature or the difficulty of the problem, Lester and Alice Crow suggest that thinking seems to involve six key processes. They are: (1) direction; (2) interpretation; (3) selection; (4) insight; (5) creation; and (6) criticism. It is interesting to observe how thinking occurs on different levels such as in the acquistion of information, reflective and creative thinking, reverie or daydreaming, and aesthetic appreciation.[10]

Let us now look at the six key thinking processes and their implications in better understanding thinking. The <u>first</u> mental process is <u>direction.</u> Here, we are attending to certain goals because of inherent or stimulated interest. All of us have a certain mental set that causes us to respond to certain stimuli and not to others. Our response to a particular situation can be and usually is quite predictable. An example of how different persons (with the unique mental set) respond to the same stimuli is somewhat

You Are What You Think

revealing. Consider, that a beautiful mountain property, with cabin, is being viewed by many different professionals. Would they view it in the same way? Probably not. The banker may be concerned about its monetary value; the musician may see a place to play inspiring compositions; the minister may be concerned about the people living there, etc. Truly, mental set and beauty do seem to be in the eye of the beholder.

Mental process number <u>two</u> has to do with <u>interpretation</u>. Broadly defined, interpretations are the various meanings that we have in our minds to explain what has been personally experienced in life. These meanings are influenced greatly by what we have thought about our past life encounters; our present experiences, and last, but not least, future anticipations or expectancies. There are numerous kinds of possible interpretations that we make to ourselves, such as: reasons, evaluations, assumptions, ideas, impressions, beliefs, opinions, conclusions, stereotypes, and expectations.

It is not surprising to see then that everyone has a slightly different interpretation of life than other persons. Of critical importance is the understanding that our interpretations of events are so integrally linked to what "we perceive" in the world, not by what may "really" be! Here, we must begin to look at the factors that distinguish the degree and quality of the person's perceptions. Crow and Crow suggest eight factors that are important variables for perceptual understanding:

1. The sensitivity of his sense organs (poor hearing or sight).
2. The degree of stimulation that he receives from the elements of the situation (loud-soft; hot-cold; etc.).
3. His previous training and experience.
4. The details to which he attends at the moment (focus of attention, etc.).
5. The extent of the integrative process (how well can you put together the facts of the situation and interpret them accurately).
6. The energy expended in concentration.
7. The feeling tones of pleasantness and unpleasantness that accompany an experience.
8. Training in sense perception.[11]

Neil C. Roth

Obviously, few persons are consciously aware of all or some of these perceptual factors while in the process of interpreting a life experience. We should, however, be alert to the overriding influence of our attitudes, motivations, expectations, and feelings while we are perceiving events. Our sensations are indeed representatives to us of the "raw" data of life experiences that are tied to our thought processes which then create for us personal meanings.

What is it that we must learn about our interpretations of life that can greatly benefit us in our adjustment and personal relationships? First, it seems that we must acknowledge that for any situation there may be more than one possible interpretation possible from the same sensory data. We get ourselves into the right/wrong or either/or box if we miss seeing other points of view. Secondly, many times we have received too little information or incomplete data upon which to form an accurate opinion. Thirdly, the data we receive may be contrary to previous experiences and future expectations. Perhaps delaying your interpretation will allow you time to integrate the new information and perhaps see the event in a novel and helpful way. In a way, you would have gained insight and experienced a "good Gestalt!"

The central lesson to be learned, then, is to practice being somewhat tentative in your interpretations! A key task for the individual is to consider "beyond" the information that is supplied and learn to draw accurate inferences about the world and its multitudinous personal events. Jesus' words caution us in this regard: "Judge not, that ye be not judged" (Matthew 7:1). We cannot really ever know enough about another person to adequately and accurately evaluate "where he's coming from or going to." Besides, when we attempt to throw mud at another, we always end up with dirty hands!

Crow and Crow's third mental process is that of selection. Here, the individual can believe everything that he hears and sees, or he can enlist some of the strategies of reason and logic to test possible assumptions and interpretations about life. An understanding of syllogistic reasoning can be most helpful for preparation for learning how to think more objectively. I would strongly recommend a good book in logic (or a college course, if possible) for valuable personal enrichment in this area.

In selection, we must be aware that most of us tend to be more subjective than objective, more critical than commendatory, more generalized than specific, and possessing oftentimes such a desire to believe something that

You Are What You Think

we fail to do our investigative homework. This homework (refer back to section on interpretation) should include: reviewing relevant pertinent facts; evaluating accuracy and adequacy of data, and checking to see if our extreme views (usually generalized) are justified by the information available. More about selection will be discussed in later chapters.

The <u>fourth</u> mental process has to do with <u>insight</u>. A broad definition of insight might be: the discovery of viable relationships or significant personal meanings from one or several experiences in life. Webster states that insight is: "The ability to see and understand clearly the inner nature of things."[12] Sigmund Freud, of psychoanalytic fame, saw insight as an emotional and intellectual understanding of the causes and dynamics of one's behavior. We have all experienced insight during our lives. Statements like: "Eureka, why didn't I think of that before?" or "I've got it now!" express insights that most of us experience from time to time.

Mental process number <u>five</u> in our discussion has to do with <u>creation</u>. In this activity, new and creative thoughts emerge as we set our minds on solving a problem (or problems) that lie between us and our creative goal. Initially, the person prepares by analyzing the facts; his mental set with all of its conceptions; and, then moves toward realization through illumination, sometimes inspiration, and particularly, hard work! Someone once said that, "Inspiration in presentation is perspiration in preparation."[13] Sometimes the best creative acts are born out of our failures. Inspiration is crucial, but hard, consistent effort has been responsible for more creative acts than one might assume.

Finally, our <u>sixth</u> process has to do with <u>criticism</u>. Here the individual tries to objectively evaluate the effectiveness and viability of solutions being tested in real life. As in the scientific method (see Figure 2),

----

<u>Step 3</u> Synthesis
(The bringing together of all pertinent facts)

<u>Step 1</u> Thesis
(New idea--untested)

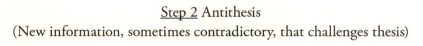

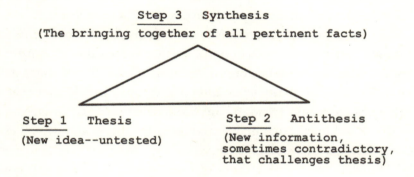

Figure 2. C.R.T. MODEL FOR IDEA DEVELOPMENT

the individual places himself (a composite of his will and volition, sensing, thinking, feeling, and doing) into an intellectual stance of stating a new idea (thesis); then, he tests it and links it to previously held notions that were once partially or totally effective. As a result, old unproven notions, or newly discovered facets of the discovery, may be modified or discarded. In any event, a new creation emerges from our thinking (antithesis). Then, as objective feedback confirms the validity and reliability of our tested thesis (or plan, creation, etc.), the "final" product or behavior emerges (synthesis). The synthesis step ultimately becomes the thesis step in a new quest for more advanced ideas. The process is really describing the steps often used in our development of ideas. Furthermore, this means of thinking is always open to change and creative improvement and should continue to assist us in critical thinking throughout life.

Harold H. Titus, a philosopher, has captured perhaps the best essence of what we have been attempting to describe about learning and thinking. He said:

> Life is not something that can be put under a microscope, enlarged, and directly observed. When we attempt to dissect and to analyze life, it seems to disappear. Life is a principle of unity or organization. We can say that man is alive; yet we seem to

You Are What You Think

know life only as we apprehend it within ourselves. Mind is of a similar nature. Thinking, feeling, appreciation, and a sense of values are central in individuality, or personality. They are the very things that give sense and meaning to the human venture and the universe itself; yet they are not things that can be counted, measured, touched, and seen. The very existence of science and philosophy depends upon the assumption that the mind can distinguish between true and false judgments. The existence of art and religion depends upon the ability of persons to appreciate values and to distinguish between them.[14]

Obviously, learning and thinking go together and form much of who we are as persons. As we learn to use our minds (by thinking), we gain skill in assimilating and synthesizing our experiences and form sound (oftentimes, not so sound) interpretations of reality as we see it. We are not omniscient creatures (as is God), and accordingly, not all things can be objectively reasoned. In fact, many things we believe deeply in (like God, veracity of documents and traditions, the world of our fellows, etc.) have to be taken largely by faith.

One writer, Arthur F. Holmes states that:

Formal logic has limited power; it can neither establish the truth of the premises a deduction uses, nor wholly avoid the subjectivity of the philosopher, nor prove the logical necessity of free actions and unique events. Its primary value is as a negative criterion in exposing inconsistencies and fallacies, and positively in helping us see things as an ordered whole.[15]

To be sure, there is a higher wisdom than man possesses. The Apostle Paul, in writing to the church at Corinth, stated that: "Your faith should not stand in the wisdom of men, but in the power of God" (I Corinthians 2:5). As Paul continues to develop this theme of God's power and wisdom and points to the fact that we are to experience the same, we are reminded that:

Now we have received (as Christians), not the spirit of the world, but the spirit which is of God (see Romans 8:1-10); that

33

we might know the things that are freely given to us of God. Which things also we speak, not in the words which man's wisdom teacheth, but which the Holy Ghost teacheth; comparing spiritual things with spiritual (I Corinthians 2:12-13).

What a blessing and assurance it is to know that, as his redeemed children, God, through his Holy Spirit, teaches us how and what to think! God's Son, Jesus Christ, was acknowledged by his contemporaries as: "...one having authority..." (Matthew 7:29); as one who was true (John 14:6) who taught the way of God in truth (Matthew 22:16); and, as one that was a "...teacher come from God..." (John 3:2). He is one to whom all authority has been given in heaven and on earth. Who else can we go to with such credentials?

Jesus said, as He prayed to his Heavenly Father:

And now come I to thee; and these things I speak in the world, that they might have my joy fulfilled in themselves. I have given them thy Word; and the world hath hated them, because they are not of the world, even as I am not of the world. I pray not that thou shouldest take them out of the world, but that thou shouldest keep them from the evil. They are not of the world, even as I am not of the world. Sanctify them through thy truth: thy Word is truth" (John 17:13-17).

Our Lord has laid out for all his followers the plan of salvation (from ignorance, irrationality, selfishness, waste, and judgment) which in effect is a plan that entails the regeneration of our attitudes and affections and the reformation of our thinking and learning processes, so that we, through our faith, trust, and obedience to the Word might be conformed to his image and experience the joy of which Christ spoke (John 17:13). With great enthusiasm, the Christian can confidently affirm that the Christian life is much, much more than just a reasoned exercise of measuring or evaluating the rightness or wrongness of one's acts!

It is that "joy unspeakable and full of glory" that the songwriter wrote about. It can be, with God's Holy Spirit enthroned within, what Paul wanted us, as well as the Ephesians, to grasp hold of. He commands us (Christ

You Are What You Think

through Paul) to be filled with the Spirit and to speak "...to yourselves in psalms and hymns and spiritual songs, singing and making melody in your heart to the Lord" (Ephesians 5:19). This attitude of praise would not, or could not be unless something miraculous, by transformation, had happened to our personalities and to our very outlook on life and death.

Paul earlier describes how we must learn of Christ by being "renewed in the spirit of your mind; and that ye put on the new man (and woman), which after God is created in righteousness and true holiness (holiness of truth)" (Ephesians 4:23-24). Fortunately for us, God's paramount desire for man is that he be redeemed from sin, shame, and judgment. This can occur only through personal faith in his Person and atonement. As we walk in and with God's Spirit, our lives will experience the cleansing of spirit, motive, and deed by obedience to the Living Word, Jesus Christ, and his words. Someone once said: "Nature forms; sin deforms us; school informs us; but only Christ transforms us."

William E. Gladstone once wrote the following lines that are even more relevant to the crying spiritual needs and concerns of our day. He said: "There is but one question of the hour: how to bring the truths of God's Word into vital contact with the minds and hearts of all classes of people."[16] This, after all, should be our most sought after goal in life.

Solomon affirms this admonition from a wise heart gained from bitter experience. He said: "Let us hear the conclusion of the whole matter: Fear God, and keep his commandments: for this is the whole duty of man" (Ecclesiastes 12:13). Such simple words, but profound counsel!

FOOTNOTES

1. Brooks, Keith L. <u>The Cream Book</u>. Chicago: Moody Press, 1938, p. 42.
2. Hilgard, Ernest R., Atkinson, Rita L., and Atkinson, Richard C. <u>Introduction to Psychology</u>, 7th Edition. New York: Harcourt, Brace, Jovanovich, Inc., 1979, p. 598.
3. Maslow, Abraham H. <u>Toward a Psychology of Being</u>, 22nd Edition. New York: Letton Educational Publishing, Inc., 1968.
4. Marx, Melvin H., and Hillix, William A. <u>Systems and Theories in Psychology</u>, 3rd Edition. New York: McGraw-Hill Book, Co., 1979, pp. 53-56.
5. Kotesky, Ronald L. <u>Psychology from a Christian Perspective</u>. Nashville, Tenn.: Abingdon, 1980, p. 90.
6. Hilgard, Atkinson, and Atkinson. <u>op</u>. <u>cit</u>., p. 608.
7. <u>Webster's New World Dictionary</u>, College Edition. New York: The World Publishing Co., 1968, p. 1515.
8. Kinsbourne, Marcel, and Smith, W. W. Lynn, eds. <u>Hemispheric Disconnection and Cerebral Function</u>. Springfield, Ill.: Charles C. Thomas, 1974.
9. Gozzaniga, M. S. <u>The Bisected Brain</u>. New York: Appleton-Century-Crofts, 1970.
10. Crow, Lester D., and Crow, Alice. <u>An Outline of General Psychology</u>. Totowa, N. J.: Littlefield, Adams & Co., 1966, pp. 212, 213.
11. <u>Ibid</u>, p. 94.
12. Webster's Dictionary. <u>op</u>. <u>cit</u>., p. 756.
13. Doan. <u>op</u>. <u>cit</u>., p. 134.
14. Titus, Harold G. <u>Living Issues in Philosophy</u>, 3rd Edition. New York: American Book Co., 1959, p. 166.
15. Holmes, Arthur F. <u>Faith Seeks Understanding</u>. Grand Rapids, Mich.: Eerdmans, 1971, pp. 51-52.
16. Doan. <u>op</u>. <u>cit</u>., p. 36.

CHAPTER THREE

THINKING AND EMOTIONS: FRIENDS OR FOES?

"For feelings come, and feelings go,
And feelings are deceiving,
My warrant is the Word of God
Naught else is worth believing."[1]

FEELINGS AND EMOTIONS--WHAT ARE THEY REALLY?

Many different ideas have been offered to try and explain what it is to experience feelings and emotions. We all have had our share of feeling dejected, pleased, apathetic, anxious, loving, hateful, elated, depressed, and so on. Sometime, for fun, make a list of the feelings you have experienced during the day. You will probably be very surprised at how many different and varied feelings have been identified.

WHAT ARE FEELINGS?

Some psychologists use the term to describe the emotional coloring of one's everyday experiences. Really, everything we do probably is colored by some shade of feeling tone. In a particular sense, feelings are sensing part of that deeper quality known as emotions. Obviously, feelings are physiological and experienced in the sensations of contact, pressure, temperature, and pain that are transmitted through the skin (for example: sense of touch). Webster states that:

> Feeling, when unqualified in the context, refers to any of the subjective reactions, pleasurable or unpleasurable, that one may have to a situation and usually connotes an absence of reasoning ('I can't trust my own feelings'); Emotion implies an intense feeling with physical as well as mental manifestations (her breast heaved with emotion).[2]

Edward Titchener, an early English psychologist (1867-1927) suggested that feeling had only a dimension of pleasantness--unpleasantness associated with it. This was a rejection of an earlier view by Wilhelm Wundt (1832-1920), a German psychologist who stated that feelings have also the dimension of "strained--relaxed" and "excited--calm."[3] Tichener's notion that feelings are primarily keyed to pleasantness--unpleasantness qualities is reflected in the hedonistic theory that purports that life's key aim is the pursuit of pleasure.

WHAT ARE EMOTIONS?

Other psychologists, Coleman, Butcher, and Carson, define emotion as "a strong feeling accompanied by physiological changes."[4] Furthermore, William James, a Harvard psychologist of the late 19th century (brother of Henry James, the author), and Carl Lange, a Danish physiologist, developed a theory of emotion about the same time. This theory, known as the James-Lange Theory described the steps to emotional arousal as occurring when the individual perceives an "emotion-producing stimulus" which in turn activates "visceral and skeletal responses" which then elicits "feedback to the brain from bodily responses" which then "produces the experience of emotion."[5]

A differing view was advanced by Walter Cannon, a physiologist at the University of Chicago (1927) who stated that the thalamus of the brain played the key role in emotion. The theory, amplified by Bard in 1934 (now known as the Cannon-Bard Theory) explained emotion as coming about when the individual perceived the "emotion-producing stimulus"

You Are What You Think

which then is "processed by the thalamus, which simultaneously sends messages to the cortex (of the brain) and to other parts of the body." The result of the messages: (1) to the cortex--emotional experiences are produced; (2) from the thalamus--the visceral and skeletal responses are activated.[6]

Later researchers have discovered that the hypothalamus, as well as parts of the limbic system, and not the thalamus, are the centers of the brain most associated with emotional responses. Stanford University psychologists Hilgard, Atkinson, and Atkinson have concluded that:

> In view of the complex interaction of neural and hormonal signals, it is difficult to determine whether the physiological responses precede or accompany the emotion. Emotion is not a momentary event, but an experience that takes place over a period of time. An emotional experience may initially be activated by external inputs to the sensory system; we see or hear the emotion-arousing stimuli. But the autonomic nervous system is activated almost immediately, so that feedback from bodily changes adds to the emotional experience.[7]

The physiological mechanics leading to the production of emotional response are complex and perhaps will never be fully understood. We do, however, know that our emotional experiences have certain identifiable qualities that help us to distinguish how we feel. The first is degree of feeling. This is experienced as in a sudden (hardly detectable) qualm of emotion to the most magnificent of passions.

The second degree is that of hedonic tone. Here, unpleasant to pleasant tones are experienced (note: the term hedonism is the early Greek doctrine (after Epicurus) that states that the pursuit of pleasure and happiness is the greatest value and goal of life).

A third degree deals with the unifying or disunifying emotional outcomes that tend to enhance or inhibit adjustive behavior. Unifying emotional experiences (like loving, hoping, pleasing) can help the individual to experience an affective richness that will encourage and stimulate a positive, creative world outlook. On the other hand, disunifying emotional experiences (like angering, depressing, fearing) can depleat one's emotional

Neil C. Roth

and physical strength and ultimately, if prolonged, begin to destroy the person, body and spirit.

A <u>fourth</u> member degree of emotional experience is related to <u>intricacy</u>. This involves the mix of emotions that we experience from time to time such as love and anger, as evidenced in great passion or in romance. Jealousy may possess both contempt and awe as emotional intricacies. Emotions are never totally pure. They are much like the different hues of color that comprise the rainbow. Hence, we often have ambivalent (variable or mixed) feelings about an experience in life. On the one hand, we might love to attend a certain social function because of its location. But, down deep, we might fear the prospect of meeting a detestable former associate, while still harboring bitterness to the program committee for not asking us to be the keynote speaker.

The <u>fifth</u> and final degree in our discussion of emotional experience is that of <u>motivational</u> <u>strength</u>. Emotions, depending on their powerfulness or weakness, cause one to react by behaving in rather predictable ways. The angry person may lash out with hostile behavior or he might withdraw and pout. The loving person will typically move toward other persons in helping ways. In a real sense, the motivational emotional strength determines the degrees and kinds of emotional responses that the individual will choose to express himself to others.

Carl Jung, the great Swiss psychiatrist and author, once described four functions that explain how an individual apprehends external and internal stimuli. "<u>Sensation</u> tells you that something exists; <u>thinking</u> tells you what it is; <u>feeling</u> tells you whether it is agreeable or not; and <u>intuition</u> tells you whence it comes and where it is going."[8]

It is not difficult to see that emotional reactions, regardless of how the aforementioned qualifying degrees interrelate, cause certain physiological changes to occur in the body. A situation that arouses anger will surely produce certain physical symptoms such as increased heartbeat, tenseness, headache, etc. But what about emotions that are not (as commonly explained by many) activated by life events? Are there physical causes that contribute to emotional delight and distress? The answer is unequivocally, yes!

I am not, within this context, alluding to the opium-like substances called endorphins that are produced in the brain and pituitary gland as a result of stimulation. I am referring specifically to those emotional

You Are What You Think

reactions that stem from organic (arising from a physiological or anatomical deficiency or defect) dysfunction. Causally, this can include any breakdown in bodily function due to mutagenic or congenital effects, glandular upset and metabolic imbalance, neural-organic-muscular-deterioration (associated with aging), disease, injury, brain infections, and tumors, to name a few.

EMOTIONAL DISTRESS DUE TO ORGANIC DYSFUNCTION MUTAGENIC (HEREDITARY) DISORDERS.

For example, it has been discovered that the rate of affective disorders is noticeably higher among relatives of persons with affective psychosis than with the population at large. Slater discovered that approximately 15 percent of the offspring and siblings of "manic depressive" patients under treatment had experienced the same emotional symptoms. Only 0.5 percent of the general population experience this disorder.[9] Other studies back up this finding with regard to frequency and concordance rates (Abrams & Taylor, 1974;[10] Rosenthal, 1968,[11] etc).

I would encourage you to review any recent text on abnormal psychology in order to get a more intensive view of the emotional problems that are by-products of a host of mutagenic effects (hereditary deviation or variation that is transmissible as a dominant or recessive trait). These maladies effect the entire range of systems associated with the body.

GLANDULAR DISTURBANCE.

Our glandular system, namely comprising the exocrine (duct) and the endocrine (ductless) glands exert significant influence over our bodily development and behavior. The exocrine glands assist in digestion (the salivory and gastric glands, as well as the pancreas and liver all play a part), as well as when we experience emotion, with the sweat and tear glands perhaps being brought into action by the endocrine secretions. The endocrine glands, in their secretion of hormones, greatly influence our behavior. Also, these endocrine secretions (1) regulate the maturational rates of bodily processes, (2) control the chemical changes constantly

Neil C. Roth

taking place in living tissue (metabolism), and (3) assist the body to maintain chemical equilibrium (homeostasis)."[12]

Since the endocrine system is, for the most part, under the control of the central nervous system, serious endocrine disorders can bring about "significant changes in personality, memory, and mental functions, as well as medical and neurological problems."[13]

Frequent disorders are associated with the thyroid and adrenal glands. Thyroid disorders result in mood, behavior, and cognition changes due to an overproduction of the hormone thyroxin. This condition is known commonly as hyperthyroidism (Grave's disease).

Also, iodine deficiency can contribute to this malady. Symptoms may include excessive sweating, tremors, abnormal weight loss, anxiety and apprehensiveness, and marked agitation. The undersecretion (production) of thyroxin causes what is called hypothyroidism (or myxedema). Psychologically, a person suffering with this malady appears to be afflicted with a severe depressive disorder. Weight tends to increase, with a resultant sluggishness, concentration and memory problems, and lethargy.[14]

Secretions from the adrenal glands (namely the cortex) control stress reactions and secondary sex characteristic development. The hormonal secretions of the medulla manage strong emotional experience. When the adrenal cortex under-produces its hormones, Addison's disease may be the result. Symptoms may include "depression, anxiety, irritability, lack of motivation, fatigue, and decreased sociability."[15] Cushing's syndrome may occur if the adrenal cortex is too productive. "Obesity, atrophied muscles, lability of mood, and fatigue" are common symptoms.[16]

METABOLIC UPSET.

Much space could be devoted to just listing the numerous metabolic (metabolism involves the chemical and physical processes that continuously are occurring in living organisms and cells) disturbances that bring about emotional disturbance and sometimes severe physical handicap and mental retardation. Some of these conditions are Alzheimer's disease, Cushing's syndrome, Gaucher's disease, glycogenosis, Hunter syndrome, Niemann-Pick's disease, phenylketonuria, and Tay-Sach's disease.

You Are What You Think

AGING AND SENILITY.

Some diseases are primarily associated with aging and often bring with them profound losses of friends, emotional and physical health, wealth, and self-esteem. There are several degenerative disorders that are considered presenile such as Alzheimer's and Parkinson's disease, as well as Huntington's Chorea. Parkinson's disease afflicts 500,000 people in the United States and is caused by some type of brain fever, or encephalitis. Impairment of fine body movements, plus tremors and facial rigidity characterize the disease.[17]

We are all somewhat familiar with the presence of senility in the elderly. Senile dementia causes mental deterioration that is associated with atrophy and cerebral degeneration. Patients typically display any or all of these behavior symptoms: "disoriented, agitated, paranoid, severely depressed, delusional, delirious, or hallucinatory."[18] These persons are often found in nursing homes and may appear to be untreatable. Certainly, a genuine senility is essentially incurable. But, accurate diagnosis is essential to guarantee that the older citizen is not stuck away in a nursing home or state hospital for senility when it may not be the culprit. The individual may be suffering from nutritional or metabolic problems that produce senile-like symptoms. Furthermore, he may have a treatable depression that is a rather normal reaction for some to have toward certain situations, like being neglected by loved ones, or being placed in a rest home. Oftentimes, the loss of a spouse, and/or friends, causes many to just "give up" on life. Their symptoms may appear very much like those of senility.

EPILEPSY.

To continue, epilepsy must be mentioned because of its high incidence of prevalency in our nation's population. Epilepsy is a group of disorders that effect the brain and produce momentary lapses of consciousness and generalized convulsions. In actuality, there exists abnormal electrical discharges within the brain cells that produce a condition known as dysrhythmia.

The most severe epileptic seizure is the Grand Mal which is characterized by loss of consciousness, jerking (convulsive-like) movements, and after regaining consciousness, a sense of overall confusion.

Neil C. Roth

The Petit Mal and Psychomotor types are typically shorter in duration but, as in Grand Mal, stimulate some serious emotional reactions. Epileptics suffer often from social adjustment and discrimination problems and may develop low self-esteem.

The use of certain drugs like phenobarbital or phenylethylbarbituric acid, have helped the epileptic raise his convulsive threshold. Other drugs like Mesantoin, Trimethadione, and Primidone have also been rather effective in treating both Grand and Petit Mal seizures.[19] Some of the causes of epilepsy include high fever, brain tumors, trauma, infections and inflamations, deprivation of oxygen (anoxia) and genetic predisposition.[20]

It must be noted that Multiple Sclerosis, that crippler of the central nervous system, produces symptoms of depression in many of its sufferers. This dreaded disease, for which there is no known cure, afflicts hundreds of thousands of our citizens, particularly those between twenty and forty years of age.[21]

BRAIN TUMORS AND FEVERS.

Our discussion about the so-called organically-caused dysfunctions concludes with the mention of brain tumors and infections. Abnormal tumorus growths in the brain can cause marked personality changes leading to such psychotic behavior symptoms as hallucinations and atypical sensory experiences. Often, the tumor expands so rapidly that the person responds catastrophically to life stresses. This occurs because of a more and more constricted ability to function mentally.

Encephalitis is a general term for one type of brain infection that is caused by bacterial or chemical viruses. In addition, "sleeping sickness" is one common form which is characterized by "extreme lethargy and almost excessive sleeping, followed by a period of hyperactivity and hyper-irritability. Even delirium and convulsions can occur."[22]

Another type of brain infection is the result of the advanced stage of syphilis. This venereal disease, caused by the bacterium Treponema pallidum, is nearly always conveyed during sexual coitus. Occasionally, the unborn child will receive syphilis from the mother. Symptoms include generally a rash, small sores on the lips and genital area. The bacteria may

You Are What You Think

remain latent for years and then invade the body and destroy tissue and cause what is known as general paresis. Between 2 to 5 percent of those afflicted by syphilis will develop paresis. "Mental symptoms can include lethargy, poor emotional control, intellectual deterioration, irritability, and occasional delusions of grandeur."[23] Paralysis usually sets in with the victim getting progressively more incapacitated.

It is no secret that there are millions of persons who are at this moment experiencing from mild to severe emotional distress because of physical illness. Sometimes the psychological damage that is suffered is far greater than is the organic result of the lesion. The suffering person not only has to adapt to his physical malady, but also to the idea (and to the possible debilitating or handicapping effect) of his disability. Many serious disorders cause their human bearers to experience subtle but pervasive emotional mood swings that may adversely effect behavior unless professional psychological help is readily available. This is especially true when one loses a limb, an eye, one's hearing, or has facial damage. The loss of a familiar physical landmark brings on a panic and amplifies one's sense of insecurity. Long ingrained manic-depressive traits might tend to unleash more serious neurotic and psychotic tendencies as a result of the physical trauma.

PSYCHOSOMATIC COMPLAINTS

But dozens of the illnesses that plague us are really caused by our psychological reactions to life and its stress. Some of these so-called psychosomatic illnesses can be fatal for some and surely crippling for many others. Let us look at a few of the more common psychosomatic complaints.

HYPERTENSION.

Curiously, when emotional problems cause physical distress, that distress causes new and sometimes more harmful stress! Cardiovascular problems (heart) are promoted by anxiety, which leads to prolonged tension which, in turn, increases the blood pressure, heart rate, and cardiac output. Hence, the emotions of dejection and despair are often experienced.

Neil C. Roth

Stress is generally linked to coronary artery disease, angina pectoris, and myocardial infarction. Life stresses often stimulate the individual to feel hostile and convert this emotion to vascular hypertension which would encompass such ailments as gastrointestinal problems, fatigue, and head discomfort.

MIGRAINE HEADACHES.

Nearly 12 percent of our population are afflicted with hypertension, which is, in effect, high blood pressure. Sixty thousand deaths a year are attributed to it and it is a key factor to a million or more deaths a year from cardiovascular disease and stroke.[24]

In addition, migraine headaches, are thought to be caused by disturbance in mood of those who tend to be perfectionistic personality types. It is estimated that about nine out of ten of these headaches may be tied to emotional tension. Women seem to suffer more with migraines than men. It is estimated that 50 million Americans suffer from recurrent tension and migraine headaches.[25]

ANOREXIA NERVOSA.

Some individuals, who exhibit such behavior characteristics as introversion, dependency, perfectionism, self-fishness and stubbornness, and extreme conscientiousness with regard to "duty" or "duties," may be affected with anorexia nervosa. This ailment, which is more common with females than males (20 to 1), claims the lives of at least 3 to 4 percent of its sufferers. It is a disorder where the individual refuses to eat, or vomits after eating, resulting in loss of body mass and possible death by starvation.[26]

PEPTIC ULCERS.

Peptic ulcers also are the resulting by-product of one's inappropriate reaction to life stress. They are the most frequently observed symptoms that trouble the alimentary system of the body. The list of stressors that

You Are What You Think

effect this system are almost endless but they all seem to have as a common denominator: anxiety and fear. Of course, many other complex emotions emanate from these two central ones. Mucous colitis and Ulcerative Colitis are often diagnosed as stress-induced dysfunctions.

BEING OVERWEIGHT.

Obesity, needless to say, remains probably one of the nation's top health problems. Most doctors in the medical profession accept the standard that obesity exists if one's weight is 20 percent above the standard for a particular age, height, and sex. The overweight person often overeats to compensate for his psychological inadequacies, and after gaining more and more weight, reinforces his already low self-esteem with a negative physical self-image.

It has been estimated that one out of every four Americans is obese. It has long been known that obesity effects longevity, energy levels, and self-esteem. Such programs as "Weight Watchers" and "TOPS" have greatly aided thousands who have needed weight-reduction assistance. Emotionally, overweight persons may feel somewhat depressed, inferior socially, insecure, and rejected. The image of the "jolly" obese person often is a compensatory action adopted to give an appearance of emotional well-being.

DRUGS.

In our day of heavy dependency upon drugs for every crisis, it is wise to become well informed with some of the more commonly used types which fall in the stimulant and depressant classifications. So many of the non-prescription drugs sold over the counter are sometimes potentially capable of altering our emotions if taken in great doses, or too often. This is particularly true of cold and allergy remedies which tend to be highly suppressant. This is also true of barbituates, which are used in the suppressing of some forms of pain.

Some other familiar depressants are: chlorpromazine, Vitamin B 12, Phenobarbital, Sulfonamides, Corticosteroids, and Rauwolfia alkaloids. Commonly prescribed stimulants or antidepressants (these are opposite of the so-called sedative or hypnotic drugs) are: Dismethylimipramine (Pertofrane or Norpramine), Nortriptylene (Aventyl), Amytriptylene (Elavil), and Imipramine (Tofranil). More familiar are the stimulants like coffee and tea and the suppressant qualities of alcohol. Also, there are the "uppers" and "downers" associated with street drugs.

For sometime, we have known of the sometimes tragic effects of using L.S.D. and Heroin. Not only are physical and genetic damage possible, but psychologically, almost irreversible effects are repeatedly witnessed and validated. Emotionally, the sought-after high, particularly with Heroin usage, requires increasingly heavier dosage, until the body literally "short-circuits" and what we know as an "overdose" occurs, sometimes tragically ending in death.

It is fascinating to note that the body itself produces opium-like substances, called endorphins, in the brain and pituitary gland. These substances provide us with that "natural high" feeling when adequately produced, but when underproduced, it is thought to perhaps contribute to the addict's craving for drugs.

Some have espoused the virtues of marijuana and have moved for total legalization of its use. Certainly, much can be said for its use with glaucoma and cancer patients, but apart from controlled medical purposes, the drug affects human beings in a generally harmful way. Apart from recent research, centering on possible genetic effects, I am referring to the marked loss of one's ambition and enthusiasm, and the almost total inability of many "hooked" on the drug to assume and maintain responsibility in their lives. This loss of drive and motivation to be a worth-while citizen is reflected in the symptoms of lethargy, depression, wishing for a new artificial high, and antisocial behaviors that typically tend to disregard the law and the rights of others. For more information about drug abuse, contact the National Institute of Mental Health in Washington, D.C., or the Director of Mental Health in the state in which you reside.

Continuing, brief mention of some additional physiological causes of emotional upset should be made. Some of these physical causes are linked to improper diet, allergies, pre-menstrual distress, chemotherapy, and conditions such as hypoglycemia. With hypoglycemia, severe depression can be experienced when the blood contains little glucose (blood sugar). In addition, the person may be restless, dizzy, and irritable, as well as

You Are What You Think

depressed. Physicians can conduct what is known as the glucose tolerance test for the individual and, if hypoglycemia is diagnosed, a special diet may be advised or a prescription of insulin. Sometimes persons prone to diabetes, or diabetics themselves, may experience a hypoglycemic attack that will emit quite severe symptoms such as confusion, delirium, syncope disorientation, fugue states, stupor, or coma.[27]

To sum up this section, it is important for us to recognize that perhaps ten percent (or more) of the persons in our world are responding in sometimes emotionally stressful and life-altering ways, to the physical dysfunctions they experience. These dysfunctions can be brought about by mutagenic effects (eg: organ not functioning or malformed; limbs missing, brain deficiency, etc.); injuries sustained before or after birth; diseases encountered before or after birth (prenatal--congenital types) such as cancer, paresis, multiple sclerosis, cardiovascular complaints, etc.; psychosomatic illnesses such as migraine and hypertensive headaches, peptic ulcers, backache, hypertension (high blood pressure) and stress-related cardiovascular problems; malfunctioning systems, such as the endocrine glands, under or over secretions; or, the central nervous system, afflicted by a brain tumor or infectious fever; and substances ingested, such as improper nutrients; excessive or insufficient vitamins, chemicals, and roughage; various drugs, beneficial and deleterious, etc.

My prime reason for presenting the foregoing discussion is really very simple: so that you might be made perhaps more aware that approximately one out of every five persons (this may be too conservative a figure) is hurting physically and emotionally and may be having some considerable difficulty coping with the stress of living! These persons are often reinforcing their physical dysfunctions by their use of disunifying emotional strategies like fear, hostility, hate, bitterness, etc. And so, oftentimes, a vicious circle is established where preliminary ailments (physical or psychological) induce new ailments that in turn breed their own new symptoms. Sometimes, it is quite a task for the physician, psychiatrist, or psychologist to discover which came first, "the chicken or the egg?"

For the Christian, a discussion such as this should reinforce the dictum of our Lord when He commanded us to not judge one another (Matthew 7:1-5). Not only should we keep our interpretations tentative (which too often become judgments), but how could we possibly ever know enough to fairly and accurately judge another fellow human being? Surely this knowledge, regarding physical dysfunctions and other causations of physical and emotional distress, should cause us all to be more loving and patient with others, perhaps allowing that they just might be the "one out of the five" who are physically and emotionally afflicted.

THINKING AND EMOTIONS.

Let us now look at our feelings and emotions and analyze their close relationship with the quality of our thoughts. Perhaps greater than 90 percent of our emotional experiences are really a by-product of what we are thinking about a situation at any given time. This statement is easy to demonstrate and confirm. As an example, imagine that you are thinking (at this very moment) that "it would be wonderful, and I would be most happy, if my tax refund check comes in the mail today." In effect, you are anxiously expecting some money in the mail and, if it truly comes, happiness, relief, excitement, etc., will be your emotional experience. Now, the mailman comes and you eagerly gather the mail, and wow! The check from the government is there. Your feelings? They were just as you had thought. You expected to be happy, relieved, excited, and you were.

Let us say the check did not arrive, but in its place was a nice form letter from the Internal Revenue Service that politely informed you that your previous year's income tax return was to receive special attention by being audited! Would you feel happy and relieved? Probably not, unless you are prone to masochism! No, you probably will be excited, but also experience some strong feelings of apprehension, fear, anxiety, and perhaps anger, particularly if you were audited just the year before.

The point is, that our feeling and emotional responses are merely reflections, or physical reactions, of what we are thinking. They are like a barometer of what our personal expectations are. When your check came, you were excited and happy. You were hopefully expecting it to come. When it did, your expectations were met and the resultant emotional response was as you planned. If the check had not come, your expectations would not have been met and the resulting emotional reaction would be very predictable. Why? Because you probably said to yourself "I will be less

You Are What You Think

than happy (dejected) if that check doesn't show up today." So, you were unhappy! In other words, if things had worked out, a positive emotional response would have been experienced. If things had not worked out, negative responses all the way! Why is this?

First of all, most persons really believe that their happiness or sadness in life is the direct result of the events that touch them. In actuality, most of us are taught to believe that when something wicked or damaging occurs, our emotional response should be akin to anger, despair, or sadness. Even when less traumatic situations occur (like not getting enough praise for something or having our favorite T.V. program switched), we sometimes tend to catastrophize them and experience exaggerated negative emotional responses. In effect, we have learned to respond rather predictably to so-called negative events in negative ways. In reality, these negative situations are those that did not happen as we had hoped or expected them to.

Throughout the history of man, descriptions of his general attitude toward life have been recorded. There have always been examples of loving and hateful people (the Bible is a treasure-chest of such cases) who have exhibited their philosophies of life through behavior. Christ reaffirmed this when He said: "Out of the heart proceed evil thoughts..." (Matthew 15:19). Again, Solomon speaks: As a man "thinketh in his heart, so is he" (Proverbs 23:7a). The word heart (Greek: Kardia) in Scripture refers to many aspects of man's personality and spiritual nature. Merrill Unger has described the heart as "the inner-most center of the natural condition of man." He goes on to state that the heart is:

(1) The center of the bodily life, the reservoir of the entire life--power (Psalm 40:8, 10, 12);

(2) The center of the rational--spiritual nature of man; thus when a man determines upon anything, it is called to 'presume in his heart to do so' (Esther 7:5); the heart is the seat of love (I Timothy 1:5) and of hatred (Leviticus 19:17) and the center of thought and conception. It knows (Deuteronomy 29:4, Proverbs 14:10), it understands (Proverbs 8:5; Isaiah 44:18; Acts 16:14). It is also the center of feelings and affections: of joy (Isaiah 65:14); of pain (Proverbs 25:20; John 16:6); all degrees of ill will (Proverbs 23:17; Acts 7:54; James 3:14); and

(3) The center of the moral life; so that all moral conditions, from the highest love of God (Psalm 73:26), even down to self-deifying pride (Ezekial 28:2, 5), darkening (Romans 1:21) and hardening (Isaiah 6:10; 63:17), are concentrated in the heart as the innermost life circle of humanity (I Peter 3:4). The heart is the laboratory and place of issue of all that is good and evil in thoughts, words, and deeds (Mark 7:21; Matthew 12:34).[28]

Scriptural evidence abounds with the idea that the heart of man represents the totality of his very being. Obviously, the term heart, in a global sense, encompasses more than the physical organ, but involves the soul, strength, and mind too (Matthew 12:30). These things have been said to point out that the strength of one's belief system motivates him to respond to life in certain characteristic emotional ways. So it is, that the very core of the emotional life is seen in the human will. Most of the "<u>can nots</u>" in our response to duties or opportunities in life are essentially "<u>will nots</u>!" Why is it that most persons do not live up to their level of education and insight? Frankly, they "will" not to.

When crimes are being tried, the defendant's motive for committing the offense is keenly evaluated with sentence-severity hinging directly upon that motivation. Earlier, Christ was quoted as saying, "Out of the heart proceed evil thoughts." Solomon said it a slightly different way: "Keep thy heart with all diligence; for out of it are the issues of life" (Proverbs 4:23). What is meant by these statements of concern?

I sincerely believe that man learns early in life to perceive the world in positive or negative ways. In essence, his world includes the numerous physical components such as nature, man-made goods, and his own body. In addition, and more importantly, he learns to relate to God, himself, and others in the same ways, either positively or negatively. If the individual has been fortunate enough to have been exposed to a positive, loving, supportive home, and affirming outside relationships in most cases, his character will reflect self-confidence and a generally high degree of optimism toward people and life, in the main. In all of life, the law of sowing and reaping is present and binding upon all of us! The breaking of certain laws, whether they be physical, social, intellectual, psychological,

You Are What You Think

or spiritual, always result in the experiencing (though sometimes deferred) of natural consequences.

So it is, that many who grow up viewing life negatively have been the "beneficiaries" of the same negative attitudes and behaviors which have been practiced by their parents. These children, with their unruly behavior and negative attitudes, are most often the net result (or consequence) of their parent's violation of many different laws of living. It is not difficult to see how the practice of sinning has been passed down from generation to generation. We have surely inherited the "skills" of sinning that are essentially by-products of a moral deficiency and spiritual bankruptcy. Sins are because sin is! The Apostle Paul defined sin broadly as falling short of the commandments and the glory of God (Romans 3:20; 6:23).

The world view of presumptuous and habitual sinning, and an almost universal devotion to be rebellious to God underlies, in large part, man's dilemma! How can he remove his psychological and spiritual chains and become truly free? To be sure, man cannot become free from sin without some competent help. Who is capable of providing such help when it seems that no earthly human has it completely all together? Jesus Christ promised an abundant (John 10:10) and free (John 8:32) life for all that will truly believe on and trust in Him. What a claim He has made! But obviously, there is something very, very wrong in the world, for there seem to be few who are able to claim they are truly free and living such an abundant life as Jesus promises.

In reality, many adolescents and grown people are choosing the ways by which they wish to view life. The child, however, is at the mercy of others for some time and will not be always capable of evaluating the reasonableness or the morality associated with the numerous issues of life. When the time is developmentally right for rational thinking, most persons are so greatly handicapped by irrational and self-destructive notions, that they are essentially emotionally, intellectually, and spiritually crippled.

Sigmund Freud described the mind-set of patients that he treated as that of being motivated to live (Eros) or to die (Thanatos). What was Freud really observing in his client's display of a death wish? I believe it was their fear, anxiety, and despair to live. This fear to be is essentially a fear to trust God with our development and destiny.

Neil C. Roth

Other psychologists have discussed this tendency of man to be negative and fearful. Carl Jung saw man as essentially introverted or extroverted. This, he felt, was largely due to the innate collective unconscious mind that is full of primordial images inherited from past generations that are created by fear-produced neurotic tendencies of his ancestors. Jung believed that "anxiety is the individual's reaction to the invasion of his conscious mind by irrational forces and images from the collective unconscious"[29] Could Jung have been alluding to man's original bent toward sin and sinning? Both he and Freud recognized the evil bent in the natures of their patients.

Karen Horney saw people as being bound by varying degrees of neuroses (fear to be and fear to live) that produced behaviors characterized by moving toward, moving away from, or moving against other people. The "moving" toward another person could be a healthy sign of emotional stability on the one hand, but on the other, a sign of neurotic dependency and anxiety.

Alfred Adler saw the newly-born human as essentially inferior and reinforced as such by others for a long period of time. Because of this experience, the child developed a sense of dependency and subordination to the parents. Consequently, Adler felt that most persons spend their lives striving for security and superiority. Of course, this is a deluded belief that one could be above or better than others, so, there arises a deep-seated inferiority complex, often masked by a rather repulsive superiority complex. Adler once humorously described this by saying: "It is as if a man feared that he was too small, and walked on tiptoe to make himself seem larger."[30] Adler felt that all of man's emotional conflicts were tied to his inability to relate well in social relationships. We could take the point one step further and say that man's broken interpersonal relationship with God is the primary source of his sense of inferiority and insecurity.

It is interesting to follow the development of ideas regarding the self over the past century. When boiled down, these notions partially reflect the mind-set or self-concept of the individual. As the individual learns to satisfy his psychological needs (discussion on needs in Chapter 2), traits are formed and the ego, or self-concept begin to emerge. It has become clear from research that human needs do not change with age. In addition, people, regardless of their so-called normalcy or abnormalcy, race, sex, color, or religion continue to experience an unaltered urge to fulfill their

You Are What You Think

needs. The ego then emerges as a by-product of our need-fulfillment behavior patterns and becomes a mediator between the individual and the world.

Psychologists would much rather replace the term "abnormal" with defective and the word "normal" with effective with regard to the ego's success in its job as a mediator. In effect, the ego's main task is to fulfill the individual's needs and keep him alive and well. The ego is concerned with establishing a sense of identity within a person's consciousness that impresses awareness that "I am I!" Someone once said, "A man needs self-acceptance or he can't live with himself; he needs self-criticism or others can't live with him."

This latter phrase of the just used statement points us to consider another function of the ego--that being reality testing and judgment. A rather humorous story is told of a missionary who went to serve the Aborigines in Australia. After months of somewhat fruitless service, the missionary was approached by the chief who exclaimed: "We have no god which we can obey like you do in following the god strapped on your wrist." The point is, that the vital true self, or ego, should, if functioning effectively, be accurately and objectively monitoring what is really going on within our life-space. To continue, the ego is responsible for how aggressively we interact with our social and physical environments.

There are several interesting ways that psychologists look at the self. First, the self is viewed as it relates, by virtue of self-acceptance to self-rejection, to the (1) personal self, (2) physical self, (3) moral-ethical self, (4) family self, and (5) the social self. In addition, the self is described as containing real, imagined, measured, and ideal components. The <u>real self</u> is who we really are (as God can only know us); the <u>imagined self</u> represents who we think we are; the <u>measured self</u> is how standardized psychological tests describe us to be; and our <u>ideal self</u> is who we wish to be.

Hopefully, most persons are attempting, often abortively, to shed their imagined selves and find their real selves. This can happen when the individual is willing to face himself honestly and courageously, and accept the counsel of experience, others, and God's Word. He then can pursue the ideal self from an accurately-assessed real-self foundation. It is clear that no man can begin to grow as a person until he admits to who and where he is as a person. This is essentially the same process that Maslow was describing

Neil C. Roth

(using different terms) in the person's striving for self-actualization; that is, the need to be on the "track" in life that seems to fit one's self best.

Then, there is the vast world of learning to like and love yourself with all of its various hues of past, present, and future fantasies, realities, and aspirations. The following anonymous poem, entitled "Myself," describes beautifully our human dilemma in understanding who we truly are.

I have to live with myself, and so,
I want to be fit for myself to know;
I want to be able as days go by
Always to look myself in the eye.

I don't want to stand with the setting sun
And hate myself for the things I've done.
I want to go out with my head erect;
I want to deserve all men's respect.

But here, in the struggle for fame and wealth
I want to be able to like myself.
I don't want to look at myself and know
That I'm a bluster, and bluff, and empty show.

I can never hide myself from me
I see what others may never see;
I know what others may never know:
I can never fool myself and so
Whatever happens, I want to be
Self-respecting, and conscience free.[31]

The self is a many-splendored thing--like a diamond reflecting its multi-intensive lights. Whether we call it--id, ego, superego--child, adult, parent--anima or animus--ego or self--an adequate description of who we are still defies us. For further discussion on man's self, refer to Chapter 7 and Figure 6 (the C.R.T. Model of Man), and to Chapter 6, Figure 5 (the C.R.T. Model of the Mind).

You Are What You Think

During our time, Thomas Harris, a psychiatrist and founder of the Institute for Transactional Analysis in Sacramento, wrote a best-selling book entitled, I'm OK--You're OK.[32] In it he described four basic psychological life positions (or attitudes toward people, events, and things) that characterize the lives of human beings. These positions are really euphemisms for the earlier pronouncements of Freud, Jung, Horney, Adler, Sullivan, and many other prominent psychological spokesmen.

Harris felt that a basic state of self-respect and other-respect must exist if one was to experience positive growth on every level and effective relationships. This is known as the optimum adult-level life position, number one, called I'm OK--you're OK. The individual who chooses this position decides to be positive and hopeful about life, and others, and capitalizes on the good. He gets on well with others and tends to be affirming them with commendatory language. He feels joy, laughter, and warmth in his life.

Ideally, he is that person that the Apostle Paul speaks of in I Corinthians, chapter 13, and in Philippians, chapter 4, verses 8-9. He is that person the poet described when he said: "Two men were behind bars: one looked out and saw mud, the other saw stars." He is the one who believes that the "as if" principle of William James really works. James once said, "If you want a quality, act as if you already had it!" Optimally, the "I'm OK--you're OK" person truly believes in himself, his God, and in others. He repeatedly reminds himself, "others live here, too!"

But, Harris described three other life positions that were not quite so indicative of emotional and social health. The second position, I'm OK--you're not OK, describes the individual who is afflicted with a dominant superiority complex. This individual projects his own sense of insecurity and inferiority upon other persons. Typically, his words like "I object" or "How dare you?" reveal feelings of arrogance, defiance, and perhaps outrage. He is prone to be paranoid and wishing to rid himself of others. This person is perhaps unable (without able assistance) or unwilling, or both, to look at himself honestly and realistically. Thankfully, the Holy Spirit is constantly endeavoring to work his work of conviction and education in our lives so that we might come to see ourselves as God sees us. It goes without saying that other people are surely suffering with our

Neil C. Roth

egotism. (See Romans, chapter 8.) Someone once said, "The clock that strikes the loudest doesn't always keep the best time!"

The <u>third</u> life position depicts the person who feels "not OK" about himself but "OK" about others (<u>I'm</u> <u>not</u> <u>OK</u>--<u>you</u> <u>are</u> <u>OK</u>). Comments like "I never can," "you know," or "I don't know" are masking feelings of embarrassment, melancholy, and depression. The depressive urge to "get away" from others describes this person's social relations. This introjective stance of inferiority is brought about generally by lacking parental and societal emotional support and affirmation. This deficit generally leads to an "I'm dumb," "I'm worthless" self-concept. Parental statements like, "Why can't you be like your brother or sister?" or "Everyone else made the team, what happened to you?" can reinforce the false idea in his mind that he is inferior to other persons. In this regard, and of major consequence, is the fact that often the inferiority feelings are erroneously linked to a sense of worthlessness as a person, instead of being understood as a less than successful behavior that is independent of one's human value. Accepting the criticism and disdain of others may be one of the most difficult lessons to learn in life. We start this process by recognizing that we are not, and cannot be totally adequate, knowledgeable, or skilled in all things.

Accordingly, Dr. Harold Lindsell has said, "We have to make peace with our limitations."[33] Recognizing our true capabilities and accepting them honestly as our own is a true mark of courage! Axel Munthe was right when he said that "A man can stand a lot as long as he can stand himself."[34] It seems clear, that a low self-esteem, coupled with repeated rejection, sets the emotional stage for failure and possible suicide.

The <u>fourth</u> position is <u>I'm</u> <u>not</u> <u>OK</u>--<u>you're</u> <u>not either</u>. This is a position ladened heavy with negatives and potential suicide and/or homicide. The afflicted person sees no good in life, in himself, or in others and reflects a caustic attitude of pessimism. He is a person who suffers emotional seasickness throughout the whole journey of life. He is repeatedly stating to himself: "It's no use;" "It's just no good;" or "Nobody understands." His feelings are characterized by humiliation, depression, hostility, exasperation with himself and others. He has essentially given up with social relationships and has become somewhat schizophrenic (loss of contact with reality).

You Are What You Think

In summary, these life positions reflect one's upbringing and current mind-set. In essence, they reflect the respect that we hold for ourselves, others, and, most importantly, God. Optimally, the "I'm OK--you're OK" person is respectful, loving, and optimistic about self, others, God, and life and is striving, with God's help, to become his best self. He is a winner in spirit.

The "not OK" person adopts attitudes and behaviors that are depreciating of self and others and generally views himself, and sometimes others, as possessing little or no worth. He is typically lacking in self-confidence and chooses self-defeating behaviors that seem to guarantee and perpetuate his being a continual loser.

The "I'm OK--you're OK" person says, "If I don't try, I can't win;" whereas the "I'm not OK" individual says, "If I don't try, I can't fail." We learn to view life with optimism and faith or assume a lesser, less noble perspective that causes us to cheat ourselves, and others, of the best that God wishes for us. Tragically, these wrong attitudes toward people produce wrong effects in the body. We do experience physical reactions when we think of some people and their behavior. Statements like: "He drives me nuts," "She's a tonic," or "I feel like a million," reveal how the emotional passes over to the physical. William James once said, "The greatest revolution of my generation was the discovery that human beings, by changing their inner attitudes of mind, can alter the outer aspects of their lives." For an excellent commentary on Transactional Analysis, see <u>Born</u> <u>to</u> <u>Win</u> by Virginia James and Dorothy Jongeward.

In actuality, the individual who is afraid "to be" (see Paul Tillich's book, <u>The Courage to Be</u>)[35] is afraid to face himself, others, and life honestly and courageously. Thinking he is achieving safety, he instead launches himself onto a sea of retreat-from-reality. In essence, these persons are those suffering largely from self-induced neuroses and psychoses! The "I'm OK--I'm not OK" labels can be easily interjected into the C.R.T. Mental Health Continuum (see Figure no. 3).

Neurotic* and psychotic individuals are choosing maladaptive attitudes

---

* Most all persons have used neurotic tactics throughout their lives, but fortunately, many learn from feedback (received from others, reading, the Holy Spirit, etc.), which can lead to insight and to beneficial changes in attitudes and behavior.

Neil C. Roth

	"Optimal" Mental Health	"Partial" Mental Health	"Minimal" Mental Health	
	REAL WORLD (Healthy Position)	QUASI WORLD (Neurotic Position)	FANTASY WORLD (Psychotic Position)	
L O V E o f C h r i s t	----------COURAGE TO BE----------			F E A R o f l i f e
	Positive self-concept	Negative self-concept	Negative self-concept	
	.Faith in Jesus Christ.	.Employs ego-defensive attitudes or behaviors to shield oneself from seeing things as they really are.	.Emotional withdrawal complete.	
	.Transformed thinking "Mind of Christ."		.In most cases cannot return to real world (at will) without therapeutic assistance.	
	.Love for God, Self, and Others.			
	.Reality-orientation.	.Can emotionally withdraw from, and return to the world at will.	.Set, irrational thinking.	
		.Confused, irrational thinking that is still pliable.		

Figure 3. THE C.R.T. MENTAL HEALTH CONTINUUM

With
Love-Fear Polarities

and behaviors in an attempt to escape from unpleasant or unmanageable aspects of their world reality. But to where do they escape but to a far worse hell; to the false safety of withdrawal, hopelessness, depression, and irrationality. Note, that the mental health continuum can only be traveled when the individual is ready to show courage to move away from fear and move toward love. He may move slightly beyond the neurotic zone, from time to time, but can never be completely set free from it until he faces up to the reality of Perfect Love in the Person of Jesus Christ. Only those who personally know the Master of Creation can fully forget the guilt, failure, and shame of the past, face today with optimism, and view the future with

You Are What You Think

supreme confidence. Why? Because they are forgiven, redeemed, and soon to be glorified!

Some of the neuroses and psychoses, however, are not caused by life stresses but by organic and sometimes hereditary causes. For example, some types of schizophrenias are thought to be genetically caused. The neurotic and the psychotic have made a choice not to face life honestly and rationally! This ultimately (unless help is received) will bring about undue physical and emotional suffering in themselves and other persons.

But what about the so-called normal person, who is relatively free of neurosis and who manages his own affairs in a generally responsible manner and takes into account the value of other persons in his world? Earlier in this chapter, the point was made that our emotional responses are a by-product (or a reaction) of our interpretations (thoughts, perceptions, etc.) of the events of our past, present, or future anticipations or expectations! So it follows then, that we must be able to <u>choose</u> <u>to</u> <u>react</u> to life according to the information we have received and selected from others and every life experience. These personal reactions are typically ladened with emotions and stem largely from what we think. So it is, that the so-called normal person (like you and me) can choose to think and act rationally and realistically.

A vital question begs to be answered: "Does our thinking really make any demonstrable qualitative difference to our lives in particular?" "Does our thinking specifically impact our physical, intellectual, emotional, and spiritual well-being? Absolutely, yes! Hopefully, your continued reading will confirm this optimism on my behalf.

Let me take a moment here to thank you for reading this far. The background you have been exposed to is essential in order to fully appreciate what the balance of the book will attempt to convey.

Let us now look at the central thesis of this endeavor: Since we realize (1) that perhaps more than 90 percent of the emotional reactions that we experience are by-products of our thinking; (2) that a large proportion of our distressful or unpleasant feelings and emotions are caused by irrational thoughts and ways of thinking; it has been overwhelmingly demonstrated in present times, as well as in the past; (3) that the individual can change these distressful and destructive feelings and emotional reactions to unifying, productive and satisfying ones; and (4) by learning to challenge

Neil C. Roth

the irrational thoughts, and replace them with constructive and redemptive rational thoughts.

But, you might ask: "What are constructive and redemptive thoughts? The remaining chapters of the book will fully explore the answers to this vital question. Akin to answering the previous question, is the need to look at what constitutes reason and logic as they apply to human behavior.

Let us sample the thoughts of several spokesmen who are considered experts on this subject. Probably, the foremost leader in the field of rational-emotive psychology and therapy, and the one to whom I am indebted for the stimulation to develop C.R.T. Psychology and Therapy, has been Albert Ellis. In his classic book, <u>Reason and Emotion in Psychotherapy</u>, (1962) Ellis has developed an extremely common sense approach that assists the individual in evaluating whether or not his thinking is based upon rational, integrative thoughts or irrational, disintegrative ones. Ellis proposes a list of twelve basic thoughts that he feels are irrational for people to maintain. His therapeutic approach, called Rational-Emotive Therapy quite assertively zeros in on these irrational ideas with the client in an attempt to produce insight and productive cognitive and behavioral change (For further discussion, see pages 197-301).

But Ellis, although probably the first to fully develop a rational-emotive therapeutic school, is not alone in his view that irrational thinking is a chief cause of emotional distress and maladjustment to life. Throughout the centuries, B.C. and A.D., men of courage, insight, and faith have been calling the world to reason. Men of ancient and more recent days like Epictetus, Plato, Marcus, Aristotle, Socrates, Aurelius, Francis Bacon, John Locke, Immanuel Kant, Thomas Paine, have each, in their own way, espoused the virtues of objective, reasonable thinking. Contemporaries with Ellis have also picked up on the therapeutic value of rational-emotive themes. To mention just a few--Adler, Alexander and French, Berne, Dollard and Miller, Dubois, Eysenck, Kelly, Phillips, Rotter, Thorne, Wolberg, and Wolpe.

Ellis has laid for us a clear statement of rational-emotive philosophy that is foundational for our continuing discussion. He states that:

You Are What You Think

Man is a uniquely rational, as well as a uniquely irrational, animal; that his emotional or psychological disturbances are largely a result of his thinking illogically or irrationally; and that he can rid himself of most of his emotional or mental unhappiness, ineffectuality and disturbance if he learns to maximize his rational and minimize his irrational thinking.[36]

Maxwell Maltz, the author of the best-seller, Psycho-Cybernetics, holds that ideas (thoughts) are changed by other ideas, not just be will. He says, "Remember that both behavior and feeling spring from belief" but, he cautions, "rational thought, to be effective in changing belief and behavior, must be accompanied by deep feeling and desire.... It is the job of rational conscious thought to examine and analyze incoming messages, to accept those which are true and reject those which are untrue."[37]

Lest you think that I am advocating "pure" rationalism as the cure for all human ills, please rest assured that human reason, without divine guidance, is at best, limited. Furthermore, according to God's Word, we are told that our "faith should not stand in the wisdom of men, but in the power of God" (I Corinthians 2:5). One of the wisest mortals, King Solomon, said that "The fear (reverential respect) of the Lord is the beginning of knowledge: but fools despise wisdom and instruction" (Proverbs 1:7). He went on to state that "Wisdom is the principal thing: therefore get wisdom: and with all thy getting get understanding" (Proverbs 4:7).

From 1781 to 1790, Immanuel Kant (professor of logic and metaphysics at Königsberg University, Germany) wrote a remarkable trilogy, The Critique of Pure Reason, The Critique of Practical Reason, and The Critique of the Power of Judgment. In the first two works he advocated that pure reason teaches that human knowledge is based upon experience, whereas practical reason acknowledges that there are a priori (prior to experience) notions or thoughts in the mind, that are independent of experience, which state and underly the ideas of God, human liberty, and immortality.

To be sure, Kant has affirmed the fact that the Bible continually stresses, namely, the importance of rationally using one's mind! This must be motivated by a duty and love to merge knowledge with wisdom--the wisdom that comes only from God. It follows then that Christians must

63

Neil C. Roth

pursue with diligence, truth, and courage, the honest examination of their beliefs regarding not only matters of faith, but how that faith interfaces with experiential truth, regardless of who may be the discoverer of said truth.

The Apostle Paul, in a letter to co-worker Timothy urges him (and us) to: "Study (give diligence) to show (present) thyself approved unto God, a workman that needeth not to be ashamed, rightly dividing (handling aright) the word of truth" (II Timothy 2:15). This is surely a call to objective, rational Christianity, based upon God's truth and his ways of thinking, which are contrary to man's ways. Thankfully, even though his ways are not initially man's ways, we can, by the grace of God and the ministry of his Spirit, learn of Him and experience the "mind of Christ" (Philippians 2:5).

We are warned by philosopher Arthur F. Holmes that,

> Formal logic has limited power; it can neither establish the truth of the premises a deduction uses, nor wholly avoid the subjectivity of the philosopher, nor prove the logical necessity of free actions and unique events. Its primary value is as a negative criterion in exposing inconsistencies and fallacies, and positively in helping us see things as an ordered whole.[38]

We must not be tempted to shy away, however, from the use of our best logical thinking because of such commentary. With the help of the Holy Spirit, regenerate man is able to see and interpret life, death, and the future with the "hidden eyes of the spirit of Truth! Even Abraham of old, had eyes to see"... a city which hath foundations, whose builder and maker is God (Hebrews 11:10).

Characteristically, there are many pitfalls that plague us in thinking consistently and logically. Maylon H. Hepp warns of three types of these fallacies: (1) Semantical fallacies--when we are improperly or carelessly using a word; (2) Formal fallacies--when we draw invalid conclusions from our stated premises. For example, take this syllogism: Major premise: All human beings are warm-blooded (correct general premise). Minor premise: The dog is warm-blooded (correct specific idea). Conclusion: The dog is a human being (incorrect conclusion). (3) Empirical fallacies--This happens

You Are What You Think

when we generalize too quickly about possible relationships.[39] For example, we could surmise that since we have risen each morning at 4:30 a.m., and then later witnessed the rising of the sun and the delivery of our milk and paper, that we have been the causation of all three events. Beware of the dangers of reading in causation from cause and effect evidence (or from correlational studies).

This brings us to deciding on a suitable goal to pursue in our quest for true mental health. I am proposing that all persons need to be open to the evidence that accrues from all of life's experiences (empirical and experiential facts) and learn to integrate these truths into the higher rational and spiritual experience that is acquired only by faith in our Lord Jesus Christ, and in his special plan for our lives. This unique and subjectively "personal" experience with the Author and Finisher of all things, Jesus Christ, will not be void of the unifying and pleasurable emotions (headed by love), but will restore balance to one's perspective of life and the world (an environment of countless personal idiosyncrasies, which has become increasingly "thing," "it," and mechanically oriented).

Our central challenge as human beings is to face up to our key problem in life--that of not <u>lining up</u> with God and with his Word. Jesus said, "He that findeth his life shall lose it: and he that loseth his life for my sake shall find it" (Matthew 10:39). I am convinced, that among the many lessons this verse teaches, it warns that we will lose our eternal soul by not committing ourselves, body, mind, and spirit to the living Lord, Jesus Christ. Our mental commitment clearly implies that our minds will be open to God for instruction on how to face reality with responsibility and love.

Norman Vincent Peale describes the people who are joyless, unenthusiastic, and fearful, and labels them as being afflicted by <u>psychosclerosis</u>, or the hardening of thoughts and attitudes. He feels that a great many persons have lost their interest in life and their thinking has become hard and fixed.[40] Heaven will need (and can only) to help that individual who is bound by psychosclerosis, or, in the tired phrase, "Don't give me the facts, my mind is made up."

Now, before concluding this discussion on the origins of feelings and emotions, it should be understood that emotions, such as love, compassion, concern, affection, joy, anger, and jealousy, etc. need to be recognized within ourselves as strong motivators for certain forms of behavior. They

65

Neil C. Roth

can sometimes lead us into constructive, worthwhile experiences and pursuits. Or, they can cause us to "shift into neutral" and profit from periods of contemplation and reflection. What we wish to avoid, however, is the potential harm and destruction that may be inflicted on persons (and the environment) when the disunifying emotions of fear, anxiety, depression, bitterness, jealousy, and hate, etc. are allowed to rule our lives.

The development and possession of positive behavior control becomes critically important to us if we are to achieve emotional and spiritual maturity and have a redemptive influence in our world for Jesus Christ. The Apostle John said, "Beloved, if God so loved us, we ought also to love one another" (I John 4:11). If our rational or irrational thoughts about God, self, others, and life create the majority of our emotional reactions, it becomes then paramount that we learn <u>how</u> to think and <u>what</u> to think. Jesus said: "If ye keep my commandments, ye shall abide in my love; even as I have kept my Father's commandments, and abide in his love. These things have I spoken unto you, that my joy might remain in you, and that your joy might be full" (John 15:10, 11).

Do you see it? Our emotional experience (love, joy, peace; the emotions most sought after by all humans, but rarely experienced) is a by-product or result of walking with God in love and keeping the commandments! This is where Christian Rational Thought Psychology differs dramatically from all other man-oriented systems of psychology. In essence, C.R.T. Psychology is undergirded by the following general assumption:

> That man can learn, through C.R.T. Psychology, to challenge his emotionally, distressing satanic, and irrational thoughts, and replace them with positive and loving Christian rational thoughts that are in accord with the precepts and principles of the Living Word, Jesus Christ, as revealed through the written Word (the Bible). Thus, illuminated by God's Holy Spirit, and supported by the lessons learned from experience with self and others, the individual begins to experience a peace and joy that passeth all human understanding!

I hope you have sensed the critical need for straight thinking in our world of upset and chaos. Surely, rationalism is not enough to get at the

You Are What You Think

critical emotional and spiritual problems of our age. We desperately, as humans, need a source of authority that can be unquestionably relied upon. We need a truthful, valid and reliable guide against which to test the rationality and rightness of our thinking.

Praise God, we do not have to look further! We have that Guide and Authority in the person of God's Son, Jesus Christ and his Word, the Holy Bible. Only our Creator God, who knows "our frame" and the "intent" of our hearts, yes, our very destiny in life, can possibly know enough to set our thinking straight and guide us into Christian rational thinking in his own balanced and holy way.

In chapter four, we shall investigate the practical and specific underlying assumptions of C.R.T. Psychology and see how they are in accord with God's Word and his desired will for your life and mine. It is my prayer that our Lord will bless you in this quest for "straight thinking" and joyous "emotional control!" After all, <u>YOU REALLY ARE WHAT YOU THINK</u>.

FOOTNOTES

1. Doan, Eleanor L. The Speaker's Sourcebook. Grand Rapids: Zondervan Publishing House, 1960, p. 104.
2. Webster's New World Dictionary, College Edition. New York: The World Publishing Co., 1968, p. 533.
3. Marx, Melvin H., and Hillix, William A. Systems and Theories in Psychology, 3rd Edition. New York: McGraw-Hill Book Co., 1979, p. 83.
4. Coleman, James., Butcher, James N., Carson, Robert C. Abnormal Psychology and Modern Life, 6th Edition. Palo Alto, California: Scott, Foresman, and Co., 1980, p. VI - Glossary.
5. Hilgard, Ernest R., Atkinson, Rita L., and Atkinson, Richard C. Introduction to Psychology, 7th Edition. New York: Harcourt, Brace, Jovanovich, Inc., 1979, pp. 331-334.
6. Ibid, pp. 333-334.
7. Ibid, p. 334.
8. Jung, Carl G. Man and His Symbols. London: Aldus Books, 1964, p. 49.
9. Slater, E. T. O. "Genetics in Psychiatry." Journal of Mental Science, 1944, p. 90.
10. Abrams, R., & Taylor, M. A. "Unipolar mania: A preliminary report." Arch. Gen. Psychiatry, April 1974, p. 30.
11. Rosenthal, S. H. "The Involutional Depressive Syndrome." American Journal of Psychiatry, 1968, p. 131.
12. Crow, Lester D., Crow, Alice. An Outline of General Psychology. Totowa, N. J.: Littlefield, Adams and Co., 1966, pp. 73-74.
13. Goldstein, Michael J., Baker, Bruce L., Jamison, Kay R. Abnormal Psychology. Boston: Little, Brown, & Co., 1980, p. 278.
14. Ibid, p. 278.
15. Ibid, pp. 278-279.
16. Ibid, p. 279.
17. Ibid, p. 279-280.
18. Ibid, p. 282.
19. Kolb, Laurence C., Modern Clinical Psychiatry. Philadelphia: W. B. Sanders Co., 1973, p. 278.

You Are What You Think

20. Goldstein, Baker, and Jamison. op. cit., p. 291.
21. Kolb, Laurence C. op. cit., p. 299.
22. Goldstein, Baker, and Jamison. op. cit., pp. 278-279.
23. Ibid, p. 279.
24. Coleman, Butcher, and Caron. op. cit., p. 263.
25. Ibid, p. 261.
26. Ibid, p. 259.
27. Kolb. op. cit., p. 280.
28. Unger, Merrill F. Unger's Bible Dictionary. Chicago: Moody Press, 1961, p. 462.
29. May, Rollo. The Meaning of Anxiety. New York: W. W. Norton & Co., Inc., 1977, p. 158.
30. Ewen, Robert B. Theories of Personality. New York: Academic Press, 1980, p. 137.
31. Doan. op. cit., p. 221.
32. Harris, Thomas A. I'm OK--You're OK: A Practical Guide to Transactional Analysis. New York: Harper and Row, Publishers, 1969.
33. Doan. op. cit., p. 220.
34. Ibid, p. 220.
35. Tillich, Paul. The Courage to Be. New Haven: Yale University Press, 1952.
36. Ellis, Albert. Reason and Emotion in Psychotherapy. Secaucus, New Jersey, 1962, p. 36.
37. Maltz, Maxwell. Psycho-Cybernetics. New York: Pocket Books, 1960, pp. 70-75.
38. Holmes, Arthur F. Faith Seeks Understanding. Grand Rapids: Eerdmans, 1971, pp. 51-52.
39. Hepp, Myron H. Thinking Things Through. New York: Charles Scribner & Sons, 1956, Chapter 31.
40. Peale, Norman Vincent. Enthusiasm Makes the Difference. Englewood Cliffs, N. J., 1967, p. 50.

CHAPTER FOUR

THE FOUNDATION OF C.R.T. PSYCHOLOGY--GOD'S WORD!

"To the Bible men will return because they cannot do without it.
The true God is, and must be preeminently the God of the Bible."
-Matthew Arnold[1]

We are now set to embark on an exciting exploration into a land of thought and adventure that too few humans dare to experience. At this moment of writing, I am praying that you will become excited as we pursue truth together! I dare not mince words here, for to pursue truth, is to ultimately lead us to pursue the Author of Truth, our Creator and Father God, as revealed through his Son, Jesus Christ, our Lord.

As stated earlier, I am firmly committed to the belief that the majority of our emotional experiences (perhaps more than 90%) are a direct result of what we think about our life situations. In addition, personal experience, and observation of others, has confirmed this fact: that the individual can dramatically change and improve his physical, intellectual, emotional, social, and spiritual life by learning how to objectively evaluate the rationality of his thinking.

But, you may say, "I don't know anyone who has the last word on what to think or how to act!" Or, "How can I trust anyone for advice or counsel? All the experts seem to be confused about morality and life too." Rest assured, there is One to whom we can go for answers that are proven and sure. From generation to generation, God's Holy Word has stood against every onslaught of attack and has emerged as a "constant"

You Are What You Think

in a world of consistant change. You see, we are really talking about the Lord God Himself, "Jesus Christ, the same yesterday, today, and forever" (Hebrews 13:8). He was the one who said, "...before Abraham was, I am" (John 8:58). Praise God, our Lord ever liveth! He said, "I am He that liveth, and was dead; and, behold, I am alive for evermore..." (Revelation 1:18). And, because He lives, we can too! Jesus assures us that "He that believeth on the Son hath everlasting life" (John 3:36a).

Robert Browning, in his poem "Rabbi Ben Ezra," penned his faith in the constancy and love of God for mankind. He wrote (in stanza xxvii):

Fool! All that is, at all,
Lasts ever, past recall;
Earth changes, but thy soul and God stand sure:
What entered into thee,
That was, is, and shall be:
Time's wheel runs back or stops:
Potter and clay endure.[2]

To whom then, can we go to seek knowledge, wisdom, and rationality of thinking? To whom else but to God, Himself! One day, Jesus told some Jews, "You search the Scriptures, because you think that in them you have eternal life; and it is these that bear witness of me" (John 5:39, N.A.S.). He went on to say "For if you believed Moses, you would believe Me; for he wrote of Me. But if you do not believe his writings, how will you believe my words?" (John 5:46-47, N.A.S.) Here, we see Jesus authenticating the Mosaic authorship of the first five books of the Bible (known as the Pentateuch) and establishing his Person and Message as the principal themes of the texts of those writings" (See Genesis 3:15 and Deuteronomy 18:15).

It is with confidence, then, that we can rely upon the living Word of God, as revealed in the Bible, for rational, eternal, tried, and proven thinking that has come from the One who made us.

C.R.T. Psychology is premised on the belief that we can evaluate and challenge our irrational thinking by checking it with God's Word and seeing whether or not our thoughts are in line with his principles and precepts. In other words, is our thinking, feeling, and behavioral experience being interpreted correctly according to God's Word? Remember, if "you

71

are what you think," you can with God's help change your thinking and be someone else. Someone once put it this way, "You may not be what you think you are, but what you think, you are." Our Lord promises us that if we will commit ourselves to Him and his ways, we can become a new creation in Christ Jesus. The Apostle Paul affirms this by saying, "Therefore if any man be in Christ, he is a new creature: old things are passed away; behold, all things are become new" (II Corinthians 5:17).

As you may have already gathered, C.R.T. Psychology is premised on the unquestionable authority of the Word of God and his right to expect our commitment, love, and loyalty to his Person and to his will for our lives. I would refer you to the Appendix for a brief review of the spiritual tenets upon which C.R.T. Psychology is founded.

Years ago, in 1922, Dr. W. Graham Scroggie wrote an eloquent and scholarly book entitled Is the Bible the Word of God? In it, he describes the Bible as human, yet Divine. Why? Because Christ was human, yet Divine. Furthermore, the Bible is manifold, yet one: manifold in subjects, but uniform in its central theme--man's redemption.

Finally, he states, the Bible is ancient, yet modern, because even though some of its writings are over 3,000 years old, it is completely contemporary, as if it had just been penned! Dr. Scroggie closes his book by declaring:

> The Bible never leaves a man where it finds him, because it bestows privilege, opens up opportunity, and creates responsibility every time we consult its pages. Being of divine origin, it speaks with sovereign authority, and each of us turns aside from it at the cost of his present and eternal undoing. Let us take this precious Word to our bosoms and our business, and prove it to be more than sufficient alike for faith and practice.[3]

In order to rightly ascertain how to evaluate and challenge our irrational, destructive thoughts about life, we will need to look closely at what God has said about our thinking and our living. Obviously, the Bible will be the key reference during our inquiry. Paul, in writing to Timothy reminded him that his learning and development were largely influenced, as a child, by the Holy Scriptures which were able to make him wise through faith in Christ Jesus. Paul went on to say:

You Are What You Think

All scripture is given by inspiration of God (God-breathed), and is profitable for doctrine (teaching), for reproof, for correction, for instruction in righteousness: That the man of God may be perfect (adequate and complete), thoroughly furnished (equipped) unto all good works" (II Timothy 3:16, 17).

The Bible is not just another great book that ranks along side of other literary masterpieces. It surely is a literary masterpiece but much, much more! It is God's special revelation of Himself to man that reveals how man must think and live if he wishes to find fulfillment and happiness in this life and assure himself a place in heaven.

Dr. Billy Graham has so beautifully described the message of the Bible. He writes:

The Bible is concerned only incidentally with the history or a system of ethics. The Bible is primarily concerned with the story of redemption of God as it is in Jesus Christ. If you read the Scriptures and miss the story of salvation, you have missed its message and meaning. There have been those who have gone through the Bible and traced the story of Jesus:

In Genesis He is the Seed of the woman.
In Exodus He is the Passover Lamb.
In Leviticus He is the Atoning Sacrifice.
In Numbers He is the Smitten Rock.
In Deuteronomy He is the Prophet.
In Joshua He is the Captain of the Lord's hosts.
In Judges, He is the Deliverer.
In Ruth, He is the Heavenly Kinsman.
In the six books of Kings He is the Promised King.
In Nehemiah He is the Restorer of the nation.
In Esther He is the Advocate.
In Job He is my Redeemer.
In Psalms He is my All and in All.
In Proverbs He is my Pattern.
In Ecclesiastes He is my Goal.

In the Song of Solomon He is my Satisfier.
In the Prophets He is the Coming Prince of Peace.
In the Gospels He is Christ coming to seek and to save.
In Acts He is Christ risen.
In the Epistles He is Christ at the Father's right hand.
In the Revelation He is Christ returning and reigning.[4]

Perhaps you are not acquainted with the story of the dying Sir Walter Scott, who, when near his earthly end, said to his son-in-law, Lockhart: "Bring me the Book." "What book?" said the son-in-law. "The Book," said Sir Scott; "The Bible--there is but one." Literally tens of millions could testify of their trust and reliance on this Book for comfort, guidance, strength, and salvation if opportunity was given. But time and space will allow us just a few more words of commendation.

Gary R. Collins, author of <u>Search for Reality</u>, <u>Overcoming Anxiety</u>, and other fine works, has been concerned that psychologists have not been cognizant of the fact that the Bible alone presents a unifying philosophy of man that psychology could build upon. Dr. Collins holds that Kierkegaard's idea that man, in order to find God, has to make a blind "leap of faith" (because reasoning was limited in value), is not an accurate or tenable position for one to hold. He writes:

> The Bible, however, does not promulgate a 'leap of faith' philosophy. It demonstrates and promises God's forgiveness, guidance, protection, help, love, faithfulness, power, and mercy. It enables the believer not to plunge into the dark, but to put his hope confidently in something that is clearly spelled out for the Christian. Faith is not an irrational jump into an abyss; it is a complete dependence on a dependable and trustworthy God who has revealed Himself to mankind.[5]

Again, listen to what some very great Americans of the past have said about the Bible:

> <u>Abraham Lincoln</u>--In regard to the great Book, I have only to say that it is the best gift which God has given man.

You Are What You Think

George Washington--It is impossible rightly to govern the world without God and the Bible.

Andrew Jackson--The Bible is the rock on which our republic rests.

Thomas Jefferson--The Bible is the cornerstone of liberty.

Robert E. Lee--The Bible is a book in comparison with which all others are of minor importance. In all my perplexities and distress the Bible never failed to give me light and strength.

Woodrow Wilson--A man has deprived himself of the best there is in the world who has deprived himself of this, a knowledge of the Bible.

When you have read the Bible, you will know that it is the Word of God, because you will have found it the key to your own heart, your own happiness, and your own duty.[6]

It should be clear that many pages could be devoted to testimonies, on behalf of the Bible by great men, but one thing keeps coming out: the Bible is the Word of the Living God and its precepts and principles are valid, reliable, and eternal! Someone once said, "I have read many books, but the Bible reads me." Truly, the Bible is like a mirror into which we look and from it we see a shockingly accurate reflection of our true self. In reality, this Biblical reflection of self reveals the quality of our thought life and of our relationship with God and others. David said it so well: "Thy Word is a lamp unto my feet, and a light unto my path" (Psalm 119:105). When we read and heed the Word, we expose our self to God's blinding light of honesty and truth. The Apostle John said:

And these things write we (John and the Holy Spirit) unto you, that your joy may be full. This then is the message which we have heard of Him (Jesus Christ), and declare unto you, that God is light, and in Him is no darkness at all. If we say we have fellowship with Him, and walk in darkness, we lie, and do not the truth: But if we walk in the light, as He is in the light, we have

Neil C. Roth

fellowship one with another, and the blood of Jesus Christ, his Son, cleanseth us from all sin" (I John 1:4-7).

Put another way, when we allow ourselves to honestly and courageously face God's Truth (His light) about ourselves, then He will make his ways to be our ways, and his thoughts to be our thoughts. Fellowship (relationships) will improve with man but especially with God. Why? Because we are no longer willfully breaking that bond of fellowship with Him!

Furthermore, the Holy Spirit becomes our teacher of Truth, our Convictor of sin, our Comforter in time of sorrow and calamity, etc. (See John 14:26; 16:8-11; Romans 8:14-16; I Corinthians 6:19). The blood of Christ spoken of here globally refers to the giving of his life for us on the Cross as payment for our sin. The act of Calvary by Jesus Christ is effective, for as long as time shall be, to "cover" or "pardon" our sinful guilt before God.

We must be cautious, however, not to fall into the trap of saying or thinking that we have no sin (irrational, selfish thoughts before God). The Gnostics of Jesus' day were high pretenders of knowledge but soon found out that pretense does not mean possession (I John 1:6). The Apostle John affirms this truth when he declares: "He that saith, I know Him, and keepeth not his commandments, is a liar, and the truth is not in him" (I John 2:4). Now, honestly, how many persons really like to be thought of as a liar? Yet, we are just that when we do not seriously consider and heed the truth of God's Word.

John goes on with a positive affirmation by saying: "But whoso keepeth his Word, in him verily is the love of God perfected: hereby know we that we are in Him" (I John 2:5). Oh, if we could only realize that actualizing, personal liberty only comes when we fully obey God's laws. We would do well to view the laws of God, not as punitive edicts but as opportunities to be free. Truly, obedience to the law is the largest liberty that one can experience in life. Dr. J. R. Miller once said, "It is a great deal easier to do, no matter how hard it is, than to face the responsibility of not doing it."[7]

Continuing, someone once said that responsibility is our response to God's ability. How very true this is! God has not called us to be saints without providing all of the resources necessary for victorious success. The Apostle Paul reminds us of his encouraging encounters with the Lord by saying: "But my God shall supply all your need according to his riches in glory by Christ Jesus" (Philippians 4:19).

You Are What You Think

Our very special need regarding the development of Christian rational thinking is that of wisdom. James, a very pragmatic apostle, entreats us:

> But if any of you lacks wisdom, let him ask of God, who gives to all men generously and without reproach, and it will be given to him. But let him ask in faith without any doubting, for the one who doubts is like the surf of the sea driven and tossed by the wind. For let not that man expect that he will receive anything from the Lord (James 1:5-7, N.A.S.).

Have you ever wondered why people wish they could be better physically, emotionally, intellectually, and spiritually? I certainly have, and it seems abundantly clear that, since we are made in God's image, we are programmed to develop, mature, and grow in all areas of our life. We were created never to be content with the status quo.

In fact, Psychiatrist Victor Frankl describes the phenomenon of man's search for meaning as ultimately encompassing the dimension of the noetic, the realm of experience above and beyond the somatic and psychic. The noetic is a new dimension that allows man to not only take a stand toward the world but also toward himself. Inevitably, noetic tension occurs and will continue throughout life. It is essentially our continual realization that striving for excellence and perfection will never completely bring about the desired result. Hence, noetic tension, and sometimes anxiety, become the striver's common lot.[8]

It is apparent that some people seem to be psychologically and spiritually content staying just where they are for years and years. But, down deep, and most often, on the surface, they reveal keen disenchantment and frustration with life. As we get older, it becomes apparent that sometimes youth is wasted on the young. But what about life being wasted, period? The magazine, <u>Moody Monthly</u>, described modern living as "A senseless whirl which has been spelled in three words--hurry, worry, bury." Thankfully, we can do better than this! Clearly, the old saying, "Life is for the living" really applies to those who are willing to seize life, by faith and trust in God, and live it to and for his glory. True living begins when we are free to know. Then, we are free to <u>be</u> and <u>do</u>!

Neil C. Roth

OUR GOD IS THE LORD OF RATIONALITY.

The doctrine of God describes his unfathomable qualities and character. Included in those characteristics, which are related to his creation, are God's omnipresence (He is Spirit and hence not bound by time and space); Omnipotence (as creator of all things, all ultimate power and creativity resides in Him); and, Omniscience. Since God has created and knows man (and all things) as he is, He knows the necessary sequence of man's behavior and the act of man's free will.

God's foreknowledge (prophecy, etc.) is in itself not to be thought of as causative of man's behavior.

> Free actions do not take place because they are foreseen, but for God, they are foreseen because they do take place. Omniscience embraces the actual and the possible, but it does not embrace the self-contradictory and the impossible because these are not objects of knowledge.

So it is then, that

> Omniscience, as qualified by holy will, is in Scripture denominated 'wisdom.' In virtue of his wisdom, God chooses the highest ends and uses the fittest means to accomplish them.[9]

The Bible describes God's omniscience in unmistakable terms. We are bound to interpret God's knowledge in the light of our own knowing, but throughout this evaluative process, we remove all limitations and imperfections! Listen to the Word:

> O God, thou hast searched me, and known me. Thou knowest my downsitting and mine uprising, thou understandest my thoughts afar off. Thou compassest (searchest out) my path and my lying down, and art acquainted with all my ways. For there is not a word in my tongue, but lo, O Lord, thou knowest it altogether (Psalm 139:1-4).

You Are What You Think

Known unto God are all his works from the beginning of the world (Acts 15:18).

But the very hairs of your heads are all numbered (Matthew 10:30).

All things are naked and opened unto the eyes of Him with whom we have to do (Hebrews 4:13b).

There are numerous other scriptures that tell of God's omniscience and yet space compels us to let the above verses suffice at this time. Dr. S. J. Gamertsfelder, former president and professor of systematic theology at the Evangelical Theological Seminary said this regarding God's omniscience:

> God's perfect knowledge qualifies Him to be the judge of all the earth. It would be folly to attempt to hide anything from his all-seeing eye. But on the other hand, it is most comforting to know that a loving Heavenly Father knows our hearts, knows our sorrows, and all our needs as well as all the resources of our help. The doctrine of the divine omniscience is the source of purest joys and sweetest pleasures to all who delight to walk in the ways of the Lord.[10]

Furthermore, we cannot neglect to mention that our Lord is not the author of confusion, but of peace (rationality, as only God can give--I Corinthians 14:33). Peter emphasized that "He that believeth (trusts) on Him (Christ) shall not be confounded" (confused--I Peter 2:6b).

Truly, the Lord has provided the Christian with a spirit of love, of power, and of a "sound mind," and not a spirit of fear (II Timothy 1:7). Our God is the God of design and order, righteousness, love, and certainly justice. What else could we expect from the Lawgiver but laws that reflect his righteousness and holiness?

OUR LORD CALLS US TO BE RATIONAL.

Perhaps the most concise, total call-to-reason is found in Paul's letter to the Romans. He appeals to them (Romans 12:1), and to us, to commit ourselves completely to God and let Him work in us a work of divine grace, by and through his Holy Spirit. Then he states:

> And be not conformed (fashioned according; squeezed into its mold) to this world: but be ye transformed by the renewing of your mind, that ye may be able to prove what is that good, and acceptable, and perfect, will of God (Romans 12:2).

The call for mental (thinking) renewal is ultimately a call by God to us to save ourselves and others from self-destruction. If we persist on being conformed to the image of the world, we will flounder and perish. Jesus said the world and its lust would pass away, as well as those persons who pursue these things, over God and his Kingdom. As Dr. Grant Howard, Jr. put it: "To renew the mind is to be programmed by the Word. There is no life transformation apart from the renewing of the mind."[11]

Also, to submit to God's call means that we let Him begin to do his perfect work of regeneration in our spirits and minds. The result will be evidenced in our altruistic service to God and mankind. When we fail to master our selfishness, it soon masters us. When Jesus Christ is the Master of our self, then self is truly free to "become." Instead of glorifying self, we will then begin to glorify God! The proof: in changed attitudes and changed behaviors that are evidenced by our "out-living" of the "in-living" Christ!

The Bible is full of the notable calls of God to man to be reasonable and consider His immutable wisdom. Some of these gems are:

> Come now, and let us reason together, saith the Lord: though your sins be as scarlet, they shall be as white as snow; though they be red like crimson, they shall be as wool (Isaiah 1:18).

> Thou shalt love the Lord thy God with all thy heart, and with all thy soul, and with all thy mind, and with all thy strength: this is the first commandment (Mark 12:30).

> Apply thine heart (mind) unto my knowledge (Proverbs 22:17b).

> Be renewed in the spirit of your mind (Ephesians 4:23).

> Let this mind be in you, which was also in Christ Jesus (Philippians 2:5).

You Are What You Think

Come unto me, all ye that labour and are heavy laden, and I
will give you rest. Take my yoke upon you, and learn of me: for I
am meek and lowly in heart: and ye shall find rest unto your souls.
For my yoke is easy, and my burden is light (Matthew 11:28-30).

In all of the just-mentioned passages of Scripture, we hear the
unmistakable call of God to commit ourselves to his school of obedience
and discipline. After all, disciples are those who willingly agree to the rules
of discipline set down by an authority to whom they wish to submit. Lord
DeWar once said, "Minds are like parachutes--they only function when
open!"[12] So it is that our attitude and spirit must be open to the "teacher"
that is come from God, Jesus Christ, our Lord. He calls us to "learn of
Him!" To step into the yoke (wood stocks for controlling oxen) with Him
and learn from Him (after all, He goes with us through every experience).
"Lo, I am with you alway, even unto the end of the world" (Matthew
28:20b). How better else to learn God's truth than to learn it first hand in
his very presence. We will pursue this theme in a later section of the book.

OUR GOD IS THE LORD OF EMOTIONALITY.

Lest you think that Christian Rational Thought Psychology is only
interested in rational, straight, God-led thinking, let me assure you that
C.R.T. Psychology is equally concerned about the emotional life of every
human being. After all, our emotional responses affect the quality of living
in direct proportion to the quality of our thinking. The Lord created man,
and He saw that creation (man and woman) was "very good" (Genesis
1:31). Emotions and feelings are a part of man and God saw it then to be,
and sees it now as "very good" if our emotional responses are prompted
by his Holy Spirit and our obedience to his Word!

Throughout the Bible our Lord reveals his deep love for righteousness
and ominous hatred for sin and evil. But He is quick to qualify that He
loves, beyond comprehension, the sinner, but hates (allowing judgment
and spiritual death), the sin.

Since we are made in God's image, we can reasonably deduce that
we possess a limited but comparable emotional quality like unto his. The
Apostle Paul urges us to approach the Lord with courage and confidence so

Neil C. Roth

that mercy might be granted and grace imparted during times of need. But how could we possibly be able to approach a Holy Righteous God and live? (Remember, how God once said before Christ's advent, "There shall no man see me and live"--Exodus 33:20b). The answer is provided in Hebrews 4:15: "For we have not an high priest (Jesus Christ) which cannot be touched with the feeling of our infirmities; yet was in all points tempted as we are, yet without sin." It is clear that God, thru his Son, has feelings that are vastly sensitive beyond our own, but which generally approximate our own.

The greatest love ever expressed was (and continues to be) evidenced by God in the giving of his only begotten Son. John declares: "For God so loved the world (you and me) that He gave his only begotten Son, that whosoever believeth in Him (accepts Him as Lord of life) should not perish, but have everlasting life" (John 3:16). God's love extended from heaven to earth as Jesus Christ, his Son, shared with humanity what it truly meant to be a total, spiritual human being. Jesus, as noted earlier, was "touched with our infirmities" and continues to feel with us when we experience emotion; especially those emotions of distress or concern.

He too, while living here, felt and expressed deep feelings. Briefly, observe Jesus as an emotional being: The scene: Mary and Martha's brother Lazarus has died. Jesus comes four days after the death to view his good friend's body. He looked at Mary weeping and "...he groaned in the spirit, and was troubled, and said, Where have ye laid him? They said unto him, Lord, come and see. Jesus wept. Then said the Jews, Behold how he loved him!" (John 11:33-36).

This display of deepest emotion by our Lord should forever dispel the idea that God is harsh and square and only interested in commandments, obedience, and judgment. The marvel of it is that these values and actions exist because of his love, not independent from it.

When many of our Lord's own people, the Jews, would not receive Him and the message from God, Jesus was sorely distressed. He agonized, "O Jerusalem, Jerusalem, thou that killest the prophets, and stonest them which are sent unto thee, how often would I have gathered thy children together, even as a hen gathereth her chickens under her wings, and ye would not" (Matthew 23:37).

These experiences pale when compared with the spiritual and physical suffering that Jesus endured during the last week of his life. While in the Garden of Gethsemane, Jesus prayed to his Father:

You Are What You Think

> ...If thou be willing, remove this cup from me: nevertheless, not my will, but thine, be done. And there appeared an angel unto him from heaven, strengthening him. And being in agony he prayed more earnestly: and his sweat was as it were great drops of blood falling down to the ground (Luke 22:42-44).

The climax of the Passion Week was his crucifixion and death. After his cross was set into the ground, between the two thieves, Jesus spoke these most profound of all words--words of love: "... Father, forgive them: for they know not what they do" (Luke 23:34a).

But Jesus was not through, yet! The resurrection guaranteed that He would appear many times before He would rejoin his Father in Heaven. Jesus once met Peter and discussed with him the nature and quality of Peter's love for Him. "Lovest thou me?" "If so" (He went on), "feed my sheep" (John 21:15-17). Jesus was concerned about the quality of love that Peter felt for Him. Peter had not yet come to understand what true agape love was. "Yes Lord, I love you as a friend (Phileos)." Peter would later learn what agape love really meant. He, like his Lord, would lay down his life for his "friends." Needless to say, Jesus was and is vitally interested in quality emotion!

Many more examples of our Lord's emotional reactions could be cited in the Old, as well as in the New Testaments. Our Lord has stated that He had emotions such as delight (Isaiah 62:4); anger (Deuteronomy 29:20); jealousy (I Corinthians 10:22); and hate (Isaiah 61:8). Perhaps it is sufficient to say that our God, in the Person of the Father, Son, and Holy Spirit loves righteousness and you and me. On the other side, He hates unrighteousness, and will ultimately bring judgment on its followers.

Let us not forget that the Bible is essentially God's love letters to his people. John said, "Herein is love, not that we loved God, but that He loved us, and sent his Son to be the propitiation (penalty for our sin, who knew no sin) for our sins" (I John 4:10). Charles Wesley sensed the very heart of God's emotion when he wrote: "Jesus, thou art all compassion, pure, unbounded love thou art...." Needless to say, our God is the Lord of Emotionality!

Neil C. Roth

OUR GOD CALLS US TO BE EMOTIONAL.

In reality, God created us as we are, except for the fall that Adam and Eve experienced when they defied God's law. Yet, despite our sin, God's creative act of man was good and still is. Yes, our emotions are a part of the good if we can learn to control their expression. Pure emotion rises out of truth; whereas emotionalism is added on to it without being guided by reason.

Dr. E. Stanley Jones, famed scholar and missionary to India, said that when one came to Christ "It is the birth of a new dominant affection by which the God-consciousness, hitherto marginal and vague, becomes focal and dynamic."[13] This psychological definition of conversion puts the emotions in the center of conversion, not the will or the mind, although they both team-up to give the emotions a proper foundation.

Our Lord calls on us repeatedly to make sure we have a "new dominant affection" for Him and his church. In other words, God is waiting for us to transfer the center of our love from self to Him. Surely love comes through self-surrender! Can you imagine a real marriage of two people without it? When the inner self is held back, love is blocked. Our Lord calls us to love Him with all that we possess as persons and with all the enabling grace and blessing that He will give us as persons in the future.

It is so difficult, but we must learn to accept our feelings and emotions as a God-given gift and be thankful, as King David was, as he marveled at his own being. He said, "I will praise thee; for I am fearfully and wonderfully made: marvelous are thy works; and that my soul knoweth quite well" (Psalm 139:14).

Sidney Jourard, in his book <u>The Transparent Self</u>, convincingly urges the individual, and especially men, to begin to express their emotions more openly and freely lest a psychosomatic effect overtake them. How many sons, daughters, and wives would be refreshed and relieved to see their male provider break down and shed a tear or two? You and I know the answer! Feelings and emotions, under the control of the Holy Spirit are meant to be shared. When they are not, they become petrified and of no use.

Throughout the Scriptures, our Lord emphasizes, over and over again, his call for us to respond to life with the emotions that reflect his truth in our lives. The central emotion of God that He instills in the heart of the believer is love. The character and quality of our love is vitally crucial to

You Are What You Think

our salvation and relationships with God and others. God, through Jesus Christ, is calling us to love Him and others unconditionally, in-spite-of.

The story is told about the Christian farmer who affixed the words "God is Love" on the arrow of his weather vane located on the crest of the barn. One day, a neighbor came by and, upon seeing the sign on the vane, asked: "Why did you put those words on a weather vane. Is God's love that fickle?" "Why no," the farmer replied. "I only wanted to show that 'God is love' whichever way the wind blows!" God's love is "in-spite-of" the wind's direction.

Continuing, God's first commandment (see Exodus 20:3 and Mark 12:29-31) is uncompromising in its demand for "agape" love. As Rev. E. McChesney has said, "Love is the preeminent virtue inculcated and produced by Christianity. The whole law is summed up in love...."[14] We must always keep in mind that God's love can only be our possession as a result of his grace. Someone once defined God's grace in a fascinating acrostic: <u>G</u>od's <u>R</u>iches <u>a</u>t <u>C</u>hrist's <u>E</u>xpense. Another way of viewing God's grace in an acrostic is <u>G</u>od's <u>R</u>espect and <u>A</u>cceptance for our <u>C</u>haracter as <u>E</u>videnced. His grace accepts us wherever we are!

Truly his grace has provided us with the fruits of his Holy Spirit and love is the greatest (see Galatians 5:22 and I John 3:14) of his gifts to us. Paul emphasizes this when he said, "...The love of God is shed abroad in our hearts by the Holy Ghost which is given unto us" (Romans 5:5).

Also, our Father's love is the central motive and foundation of all moral thinking and behaviors. Rev. McChesney again comments: "Without this (love) all other motives fall short of furnishing the true stimulus of Christian living. As all sin roots itself in selfishness, so all virtue springs out of love."[15] Truly we learn to love Him "because He first loved us" (I John 4:19). This process is humanly visible in the child, who, when exposed to the love of his parents, learns to love-in-kind.

True love is perhaps more thoroughly dealt with in I Corinthians, Chapter 13, than in any other passage of holy writ. It is here where we learn that our former levels of loving were inadequate in God's sight. Our "if" and "because" love, which is full of conditions, is shown up for what it really is: A false love that attempts to use, manipulate, coerce, exploit others, and God Himself. In a later chapter, we will ponder true love and try to discover how it should interface with meaningful human and Divine relationships.

Neil C. Roth

To sum up this section, God has created us to experience emotions that are respondents of the influence of his Holy Spirit within our lives. These unifying, agape-like emotions, and resultant behaviors, are complex but can be identified as: "...love, joy, peace, longsuffering, gentleness (kindness), goodness, faith (faithfulness), meekness, temperance (self-control): against such there is no law" (Galatians 5:22, 23). The Bible also mentions emotions like compassion, sorrow, desire, pity, anger, hatred, malice, and many others that describe positive and negative human reactions to life.

Paul goes on to emphasize that the true Christian has "crucified the flesh with its passions and desires" (Galatians 5:24b, N.A.S.). In reality then, the Christian has a law higher than himself that he is observing. Lust is not being encouraged or pampered because we are now living our life in and by the Spirit of God! (See Galatians 5:25). It becomes clear that rationality, found only in Christ, becomes the genesis for appropriate emotional responses that are desired for the believer by our Creator-God. But, let us never forget, God calls us to respond to Himself, and to others, with deepest affection and commitment. What could be more emotional, and yet rational, than that?

THE PRECEPTS AND PRINCIPLES OF THE WORD: GOD'S RATIONAL THOUGHTS.

Now we come to the central theme of C.R.T. Psychology, namely: that we can learn to objectively evaluate the rationality of our thinking, greatly improving our emotional experience, by "matching it" up with the tried, tested and true precepts and principles as found in the Holy Bible, God's Word, and from truth that is derived from experience in life. These truths may include advice, counsel, learnings, circumstances, feelings, desires, etc., but are considered only secondary to the Word. These experiential truths will be discussed later on in this chapter.

You might ask, "What precepts and principles, as well as experiential truth, can I really count on as reliable for guidance in my quest for rational thinking, emotional stability, and happiness?" Frankly, all of God's Word is valid, reliable, and profitable for our counsel and admonition (see II Timothy 3:16, 17). There are, however, certain central precepts and principles that essentially encompass the entire message of Scripture. In addition, there is a body of experiential truth that has been discovered by many individuals throughout history (particularly by those in theology, philosophy, anthropology, sociology, and psychology) that interfaces well with the precepts and principles of the Word.

<u>What is a principle</u>? Webster states that a principle is "a fundamental truth, law, doctrine, or motivating force, upon which others are based."[16] The road sign that urges us to "drive carefully" reflects a principle, from which eminates the (sixth commandment) precept. The principle: life is precious, so guard it (Exodus 20:13). The Bible lists literally hundreds of them, an example of such being, that we are to respect and value our bodies because they are the temples of the Holy Spirit. Also, proper respect and treatment of them will bring glory to God (see I Corinthians 6:19, 20). This principle obviously applies to any physical abuse that would injure or debase God's human temple.

So it is then, that central principles of the Word are revealed in certain scriptures that offer viable attitudinal and behavioral guidelines to the believer. These principles are then to be used in evaluating the advisability and morality of certain responses to potential life-decisions and/or dilemmas. We shall investigate the "umbrella statement" of Christian ethics (I John 2:15-17), the Priority Principles, later in chapter five.

Now continuing, <u>what is a precept</u>? Webster says that a precept is, "A commandment or direction meant as a rule of action or conduct."[17] In other words, they are statements of what is right and wrong. A road sign that says "Speed 55 miles per hour" is reflecting a precept just as surely as the sixth commandment which says "Thou shalt not kill" (Exodus 20:13). Fifty-five miles-per-hour does not allow for any exceptions! Right is right and wrong is wrong with any precept, human or Divine.

The Word lists many precepts which detail the desired will of God for his children. It follows that if I am going to know God's desired will for my life, then I had better know his precepts (See again, Romans 12:2b).

The central precepts of the Word are summed up most adequately, in my opinion, by the Decalogue, a word adopted by the Greeks to designate the Ten Commandments. These were the moral and spiritual laws conveyed by God to Moses on Mount Sinai (see Exodus 20:1-7;

Neil C. Roth

Deuteronomy 5:6-21). It has been aptly said that "there are 35 million laws and no improvement on the ten commandments."

In addition, these commandments were fulfilled by Christ during his life on earth, his death and resurrection, and through his heavenly role as our Lord and Savior. Listen to Him speak:

> Think not that I am come to destroy the law, or the prophets: I am not come to destroy, but to fulfill. For verily I say unto you, till heaven and earth pass, one jot or one tittle shall in no wise pass from the law till all be fulfilled. Whosoever therefore shall break one of these least commandments, and shall teach men so, he shall be called the least in the kingdom of heaven: but whosoever shall do and teach them, the same shall be called great in the kingdom of heaven" (Matthew 5:17-19).

The Apostle Paul reiterates the fact of Christ and his sacrificial love for us, as being the central theme of the Bible. He said, "All the law is fulfilled in one word, even in this; Thou shalt love thy neighbor as thyself" (Galatians 5:14). How, except we experience the love of Christ within, could we love anyone in the way that God loves us, unconditionally, "in-spite-of our dirty, onery, mean, little selves?" Only because of God's grace!

To continue then, Christian Rational Thought Psychology is premised on the notion that these Biblically-based principles and precepts represent the soundest bases upon which we might begin to rationally, emotionally, and ethically improve the quality of our lives. These principles and precepts are essentially reflections of God's pure rationality and his concern for man, as well as for his entire creation. Man was, after all, as God's crowning creation, ordained to prudently manage the earth (replenish and subdue the earth) as a good profitable steward (see Genesis 1:26-28, and Luke 12:41-48).

If we humans can learn to obey the moral principles and precepts as stated by God, through Moses, and by Jesus Christ, revolutionary changes for good will occur in our personal lives, and throughout society, as we interrelate with it. Solomon reflected wisely when he said, "...the law is light..." (Proverbs 6:23); "He that keepeth the law, happy is he" (Proverbs 29:18b); and "In her (the law) tongue is the law of kindness" (Proverbs 31:26b). But how is this possible to be happy and joyful while keeping the

You Are What You Think

law? King David had discovered the secret. He declares: "Blessed (happy) is the man that walketh not in the counsel of the ungodly, nor standeth in the way of sinners, nor sitteth in the seat of the scornful. But his delight is in the law of the Lord; and in his law doth he meditate day and night" (Psalm 1:1).

Our Lord shared a precious truth regarding this love we could possess for truth. He exclaimed, "Blessed are they which do hunger and thirst (starving for) after righteousness (right standing before God): for they shall be filled (satisfied)" (Matthew 5:6). Note, that Jesus did not say we would be happy and contented if we sought after happiness, for the pursuit of personal happiness always ultimately brings about failure. Whereas, the pursuit of righteousness, or right standing with God (infers obedience to his precepts and principles) produces real happiness, a true by-product of truth and integrity.

Listen to David again, a real expert in lawkeeping, as well as lawbreaking!

> The law of the Lord is perfect (sufficient), converting the soul: the testimony of the Lord is sure (infallible) making wise the simple. The statutes of the Lord are right, rejoicing the heart: the commandment of the Lord is pure, enlightening the eyes. The fear of the Lord is clean, enduring forever: the judgments of the Lord are true and righteous altogether. More to be desired are they than gold, yea, than much fine gold: sweeter also than honey and the honeycomb" (Psalm 19:7-19).

Let us conclude this chapter by hearing from Dr. E. Stanley Jones, as he commented on his extended experience as a student of God's Word. He said:

> After thinking and talking about one subject for 60 years, one should be bored and should want a moral holiday, want to get away and think of something else. On the contrary, I was never so excited, so exhilarated, so full of surprise as now. Something new breaks out from him everyday, a surprise around every corner, horizons cracking, life popping with novelty and meaning--and value. The Truth is making me free--free to find more Truth and yet more Truth.[18]

Neil C. Roth

I will never forget the blessing and discovery experienced when I was privileged to attend a week of spiritual-life meetings with Dr. Jones during the early sixties. These meetings, held in the chapel at Cascade College in Portland, Oregon, revealed in Dr. Jones, who then was in his seventies, to be a man of exceptional spiritual zest and insight. He truly emanated a life that was "popping" with the joy of the Lord--the Truth, Jesus Christ, was making him free (and me too!).

FOOTNOTES

1. Brooks, Keith L. The Creme Book. Chicago: Moody Press, 1938, p. 11.
2. Poems of Robert Browning, Edited by Donald Smalley. Boston: Houghton-Mifflin Co., 1956, p. 286.
3. Scroggie, W. Graham. Is the Bible the Word of God? Chicago: Moody Press, 1922, p. 121.
4. Doan, Eleanor L. The Speaker's Sourcebook. Grand Rapids: Zondervan Publishing House, 1960, pp. 33, 34.
5. Collins, Gary R. The Rebuilding of Psychology. Wheaton, Ill.: Tyndale House Publishers, Inc., 1977, p. 125.
6. Doan. op. cit., pp. 36, 37.
7. Ibid, p. 175.
8. Frankl, Victor E. Psychotherapy and Existentialism. New York: Simon and Schuster, 1967, pp. 3-5.
9. Strong, Augustus Hopkins. Systematic Theology. New York: A. C. Armstrong and Son, 1893, pp. 135, 136.
10. Gamertsfelder, S. J. Systematic Theology. Harrisburg, Penn.: Evangelical Publishing House, 1921, p. 192.
11. Howard, Jr., J. Grant. Knowing God's Will and Doing It! Grand Rapids: Zondervan Publishing House, 1976, p. 36.
12. Doan. op. cit., p. 161.
13. Jones, E. Stanley. How to be a Transformed Person. Nashville: Abingdon--Cokesbury Press, 1951, p. 24.
14. Unger, Merrill F. Unger's Bible Dictionary. Chicago: Moody Press, 1961, p. 668.
15. Ibid, p. 669.
16. Webster's New World Dictionary. New York: The World Publishing Co., 1966, p. 1158.
17. Ibid, p. 1147.
18. Jones, E. Stanley. The Word Become Flesh. Nashville: Abingdon Press, 1963, p. 51.

CHAPTER FIVE

THE C.R.T. PERSON PRECEPTS
AND PRIORITY PRINCIPLES

> "One's love for God is equal to the love
> one has for the man he loves least."
>
> -John J. Hugo

C.R.T. CENTRAL PRINCIPLE--THE LOVE PRINCIPLE:
"SINCERELY RESPECT AND LOVE GOD, YOURSELF, AND OTHERS."

The central overriding principle upon which C.R.T. Psychology and Therapy rest is that of divine agape love as it is revealed in the Person of Jesus Christ. Do you remember these words of His, quoted earlier?

> Hear, O Israel; the Lord our God is one Lord: and thou shalt love the Lord thy God with all thy heart, and with all thy soul, and with all thy mind, and with all thy strength. This is the first commandment. And the second is like, namely this, Thou shalt love thy neighbor as thyself. There is none other commandment greater than these (Mark 12:29b, 30, 31).

> On the two commandments hang all the law and the prophets (Matthew 22:40).

You Are What You Think

The above verses truly sum up the meaning of the Ten Commandments (see Exodus, chapter 20). This principle, founded upon God and his love, helps us to see what God's standards for man are. It is apparent that if we were to fully obey this commandment, that we would love God as no other, concentrating on pleasing Him with unselfish deeds springing up from a heart made holy. This principle is God's call to be holy. It is given to us by Jesus, who <u>only</u> can qualify as the Source and Norm for our holiness.

In addition, our Lord Jesus' central passion was, and is the pursuit and acquisition of practical heart holiness that is characterized by "fervent" love for God and man. Paul reiterates Jesus' passion when he said: "For God hath not called us unto uncleanness, but unto holiness" (I Thessalonians 4:7).

Now, let us briefly consider God's Person Precepts, the Ten Commandments. They consist of two distinct, but related, classes of duties. The first four (Exodus 20:3-8) deal with man's duties to God; and the last six (Exodus 20:12-17) with man's duties to other human beings.

The first commandment is concerned with the fundamental issue of God and his existence. The philosophical proofs of God's existence are valuable insights for every individual to possess. They are usually given as the (1) Cosmological--Cause and effect (Acts 17:28); (2) Ontological--All men have an idea of God (John 1:9); (3) Teleological-Design and purpose in the world disclose an imminent intelligence and purpose (Romans 1:20); (4) Moral--Man's moral nature and sense of values as seen in conscience and sense of duty and obligation. It implies God as the Source and Guarantor. He also instills a notion of rightness and wrongness; and (5) Personal experience--"I know in whom I have believed" not "I think" (II Timothy 1:12). Without such an acknowledgment of God's existence we could not go further, because without God, and an obligation to please and obey Him, there would be no real moral impetus to keep the last six commandments.

The commandments essentially convey that we are to respect and love God and, as a result, we are to love and respect people. But, more importantly, our Lord has entrusted us with the most sacred trust of all, his life and love. As an indication of his glory, He has given us a mirror reflection of Himself--the Ten Commandments! Put into the positive, they read like this:

Neil C. Roth

Commandment	Exodus 20	The C.R.T. Person Precepts
No. 1	vs. 3	Please love me solely for I am your creator and God, and I sincerely love you.
No. 2	vs. 4,5	No substitute god is necessary--I am your all in all and will meet all your needs.
No. 3	vs. 7	Speak of, and to me with love and respect.
No. 4	vs. 8	Communicate and fellowship with me--I want to hear from you regularly.
No. 5	vs. 12	Respect and love your mother and father.
No. 6	vs. 13	Respect and love all other persons--life is sacred.
No. 7	vs. 14	Be faithful in marital, and in all other human relationships.
No. 8	vs. 15	Be trustworthy with the resources and possessions of others.
No. 9	vs. 16	Be truthful in all thought and conversation.
No. 10	vs. 17	Be content with what God has given you.[1]

These C.R.T. precepts are a paraphrase of the real text in Exodus, chapter 20. Now look at the actual commandments. They are as follows:

Decalogue--Exodus 20

1. Thou shalt have no other gods before me (vs. 3).
2. Thou shalt not make unto thee any graven image, or any likeness of anything that is in heaven above, or that is in the earth beneath, or that is in the water under the earth. Thou shalt not bow down thyself to them, nor serve them: for I the Lord thy God am a jealous God...(vs. 4, 5a).
3. Thou shalt not take the Name of the Lord thy God in vain; for the Lord will not hold him guiltless that taketh his Name in vain (vs. 7).
4. Remember the Sabbath Day, to keep it holy (vs. 8).
5. Honor thy father and mother (vs. 12).
6. Thou shalt not kill (vs. 13).
7. Thou shalt not commit adultery (vs. 14).
8. Thou shalt not steal (vs. 15).
9. Thou shalt not bear false witness against thy neighbor (vs. 16).

You Are What You Think

10. Thou shalt not covet thy neighbor's house, thou shalt not covet thy neighbor's wife, nor his manservant, nor his maidservant, nor his ox, nor his ass, nor anything that is thy neighbor's (vs. 17).

The Commandments have been charmingly put into verse by an unknown author:

Commandment	Exodus 20	The Ten Commandments in Rhyme
No. 1	vs. 3	Thou no gods shalt have but me.
No. 2	vs. 4,5	Before no idol bend the knee.
No. 3	vs. 7	Take not the name of God in vain.
No. 4	vs. 8	Dare not the Sabbath day profane.
No. 5	vs. 12	Give to thy parents honor due.
No. 6	vs. 13	Take heed that thou no murder do.
No. 7	vs. 14	Abstain from words and deeds unclean.
No. 8	vs. 15	Steal not, for thou by God are seen.
No. 9	vs. 16	Tell not a willful lie, nor love it.
No. 10	vs. 17	What is thy neighbor's do not covet.[2]

The commandments are, in essence, God's person precepts. At the bottom line God is saying that respect, trust, and love are the glue that holds relationships intact. Each commandment echoes forth the call: "be faithful" to God and to others! If we can but comprehend that our Lord has issued the human race an invitation to commit themselves to Him, and to each other in order to preserve themselves from committing the ultimate folly of individual and mass extermination. All of God's laws, when broken, have unavoidable consequences associated with their transgression.

Satan, who appealed to Adam and Eve to doubt God's Person and Word, led them to believe that God's laws really would keep them from experiencing the best in life. Satan promised instant fulfillment to them in every sphere of life without obligation to maintain integrity, or responsibility in relationships. Satan said to them, and surely to us, "love things and use people." The Lord calls upon us to <u>love people</u> and <u>use things!</u>

Neil C. Roth

Satan claimed that it was foolishness to be bound to God's "grievous" laws. "After all," he said, "why be in bondage to God's silly rules when you are really already 'gods yourself?" "And, why should 'gods' have to be in servitude to any law?" "Everyone knows that a moral code is only for servants and slaves!" The first man and woman were enamored by their own lust for what Satan promised. They would be invincible and live, even though they were told by their Creator that they would surely die if they ate the fruit from the tree in the middle of the garden (see Genesis 3:1-4).

W. H. Auden describes our dilemma regarding the observance of God's holy law by stating: "Let us love one another, or die!" In effect, Satan drew a circle around himself and shut God out. God has lovingly drawn an infinitely bigger circle that can include all persons who accept his love.

Dr. Francis A. Schaeffer comments on God's command, that we love all men, by stating:

> All men bear the image of God. They have value, not because they are redeemed, but because they are God's creation in God's image. Modern man, who has rejected this, has no clue as to who he is, and because of this he can find no real value for himself and other men....This is, of course, the whole point of Jesus' story of the good Samaritan: Because a man is a man, he is to be loved at all cost.[3]

God loves us not on the basis of who we are, but because of who He is! "God is love," John declares, and "he that loveth not knoweth not God but everyone that loveth is born of God and knoweth God" (I John 4:7b, 8).

Furthermore, God's person precepts are but a reflection of his character which is holiness personified. They remind us of how we might have been before the moral fall of man. But, more importantly, God's precepts reveal to us our absolute inability to totally obey them without complete commitment to the greatest truth in life, that being: the laws of God can only be kept if God's Son, Jesus Christ, abides within our hearts through the work and ministry of his precious Holy Spirit! Jesus Christ was, and is the personified fulfillment of all the law (Matthew 5:17), not its destroyer. The Bible states, in the support of Jesus' claim of divinity, over and over, that Jesus was God's only Son, and is co-equal with the Father. Jesus

You Are What You Think

proclaimed: "I and my Father are one" (John 10:30). Perhaps one of the most representative scriptures denoting relationship is that where, upon the baptism of Jesus, God the Father speaks from out of heaven saying, "Thou art my beloved Son, in whom I am well pleased" (Mark 1:11b). "Before Abraham was, I am" (John 8:58b).

When asked by Thomas regarding where the way of truth and knowledge was to be found, Jesus replied: "..I am the way, the truth, and the life: no man cometh unto the Father, but by me" (John 14:6). That Jesus can be viewed as One of divine authority is a matter of personal knowledge and faith. For certainty, once a person looks into the life and ministry of Jesus, and begins to <u>try on</u> his spiritual principles in daily living, there remains no doubt as to his Lordship and Authority over our lives. "For Christ is the end of the law for (unto) righteousness to everyone that believeth" (Romans 10:4). So, Paul could exclaim to all that "...the law is fulfilled in one word, even in this, thou shalt love thy neighbor as thyself" (Galatians 5:12).

The one word that Paul refers to in the above scripture is "love." But who is the author of love? Surely it is God Himself, the <u>Living Word</u> mentioned in John 1:1 and the <u>Loving Word</u> mentioned in John 1:4, 9, 12, and 14. John was also quick to declare that "The law was given by Moses, but grace and truth came by Jesus Christ" (John 1:17). "In this," John goes on to say, "was manifested the love of God toward us, because that God sent his only begotten Son into the world, that we might live through Him" (I John 4:9).

Wonderfully, when we love God with all of our being, the last six commandments are automatically kept. Without love, the law becomes impossible to keep. Paul, in writing to the Galatians, describes how the law cannot be perfectly kept because our human nature (the flesh) is weak. He states: "Wherefore the law was our schoolmaster to bring us unto Christ, that we might be justified by faith" (Galatians 3:24). By faith, the keeping of the law becomes possible. With love, the law becomes automatic! These precepts, when viewed through faith and love, are no longer an obligation, but to be effortlessly experienced as we walk in sweet fellowship with the Lord Jesus Christ. This "effortless" keeping of the law is that rest that remains for the true people of God (see Hebrews 4:9-11).

There is no doubt that God, the Father, ordained Jesus' work on the earth and was extremely delighted by it (see Matthew 3:17). Listen to Paul's description of God's view of his Son!

> Wherefore God also hath highly exalted him, and given him a name which is above every name: that at (in) the name of Jesus every knee should bow, of things in heaven, and things in earth, and things under the earth; and that every tongue should confess that Jesus Christ is Lord, to the glory of God the Father (Philippians 2:9-11).

What principles for my life and practical living can we learn from this agape love that the Bible repeatedly describes? C.R.T. Psychology is premised on the idea that love, in its highest meaning and application, is seen exemplified in Jesus' person and life. This is not to say that many humans, from earliest history to the present, have not shown sincere love to their families and to others: but Jesus' love was marked by a quality that was openly acknowledged as supreme and totally pure.

This remarkable fact can perhaps be best illustrated by his statement that: "Greater love hath no man than this, that a man lay down his life for his friends" (John 15:13). Jesus made good on that statement and did lay down his life for you and for me. "No greater love than this?" you ask. "Many persons have become heroes and martyrs!" Yes, true. But God's love was their motivation. A careful reading of <u>Fox's Book of Martyrs</u> will convincingly reveal this quality of loving commitment.

Also, how many of these, apart from those who were real Christians, prayed to their Heavenly Father as they were facing death, and asked, "Forgive them; for they know not what they do" (Luke 23:34a). The centurion, and those who were there with Jesus at Calvary were remarkably impressed and shaken! "...Truly this was the Son of God" (Matthew 27:54), they exclaimed!

Even Napoleon, conqueror of the then-known world, acknowledges his Lordship. "If Socrates would enter the room, we should rise and do him honor. But if Jesus Christ came into the room, we should fall down on our knees and worship Him."[4] Why are people everywhere so impressed with

You Are What You Think

Jesus? Because He gave and He forgave! These qualities still are, and always will be the marks of a true Christian, eager to emulate and please his Lord.

A vital part of God's love, and true Christian love on the human level, is that it be, honest. The Bible declares that above all else God calls upon us to be truthful. (Truth is a central theme of the precepts and principles in God's Word!) What has a man or woman left when they have not integrity?

In addition, our Lord calls on us to face his Truth: the Truth that reveals Him as Creator, Lord, and King of the earth, and all that dwell therein (not to mention his Lordship of the universe); the Truth about ourselves that confirms that we cannot be, or do anything eternal without Him in our lives; the Truth that his ways will produce fruitful meaning and purpose in life, and ultimately a permanent home in heaven, as opposed to despair and judgment if we choose not to obey his ways.

In the present context, we see God urging us to hearken to the wisdom of loving his righteousness and hating iniquity. The Apostle Paul describes God's evaluation of Jesus' key passion by stating, "Thou hast loved righteousness, and hated iniquity, therefore God... hath anointed thee with the oil of gladness above thy fellows" (Hebrews 1:9). Truth, and its twin-brother righteousness (using truth in love), in the heart and mind of the believer, does bring about a remarkable emotional by-product of joy and gladness, just as Jesus experienced! The idea that truth can, and will make us free is not difficult to prove. It is best tested and confirmed by personal experience. Our Lord issues this challenge: "...Prove me now herewith, ...if I will not open you the windows of heaven, and pour you out a blessing, that there shall not be room enough to receive it" (Malachi 3:10). Knowledge and truth do dispel all forms of personal, and sometimes social, darkness. Jesus' words ring clear with appeal as He promises: "Ye shall know the truth, and the truth shall make you free" (John 8:32).

By truth He must mean much more than just the possession of spiritual knowledge, however important that may be. He answers our questions by returning us to the fountain of love. Paul is speaking:

> Though I speak with the tongues of men and of angels, and have not charity (love), I am become as sounding brass, or a tinkling cymbal. And though I have the gift of prophecy, and

Neil C. Roth

understand all mysteries, and all knowledge; and though I have all faith, so that I could remove mountains, and have not charity (love), I am nothing (I Corinthians 13:1,2).

Talk about the dynamite of the Gospel; this passage is inherently explosive! Frankly, we think we understand what love really means, that is, the love that our Lord is describing here through Paul. If you think that true love has only to do with our human relationships, failure will be your portion and reward. <u>True love</u> must begin first and foremost with our redemptive relationship with our Lord Jesus Christ. Then, from this love, the God of love, proceeds our unconditional love for his Word, his children, and his creation.

Bishop Gerald Kennedy once said that, "we will never learn to say yes to the best until we have learned to say no to the worst." God is calling us to say YES to his righteousness (his Word and Will) and NO to sin and iniquity! The Bible is clear here: to go against God's Word is sin. Of a truth "the carnal mind is enmity against God" (Romans 8:7a) and brings death (Romans 8:6). Sin is false, foolish, futile, and downright fatal. Lowrey states that, "Sin is deadly. It must, therefore, be destroyed, or it will destroy. Any remedy that does not take primal account of sin, and aim at its absolute abolition, is insufficient, if not spurious![5]

Do you seek after God's righteousness? Do you enjoy walking with the Lord in fellowship sweet? Do you guard your relationship with God by knowing, obeying, and praying to the Living Word, Jesus Christ? Vital questions to be sure! But, do you know, that what a person really loves he will <u>seek</u> after. We usually do what we want to do, and think what we wish to think, and lovingly pursue our own will! Yes, we also <u>enjoy</u> what we truly love. People enjoy sin for a season, not realizing that its consequences will be as bitter as they imagined. Furthermore, we tend to <u>guard</u> what we love. It is like the dog with a bone: He will guard it tenaciously unless he is given something better! People protect what they value and prize.

We have not reached the crux of the matter, however, until we understand that the Biblical standard for holy, pure love is heart-focused. To vitally grasp the principles of holy living, a brutal honesty must pervade our being. Paul lays it on the line as he says: "Examine yourselves, whether ye be in the faith; prove your ownselves" (II Corinthians 13:5a). The Apostle is urging us to be sincerely sure about the most important matter

You Are What You Think

in life: Is our love and affection being given and committed to the right Person? And then, is it being demonstrated to all persons, in His way? Will you, right now, pray this prayer with me, a prayer so necessary if we are to find and experience the living and loving God in our lives?

> Search me, o God, and know my heart: try me, and know my thoughts: And see if there be any wicked way in me, and lead me in the way everlasting" (Psalm 139:23, 24).

By this time, we have become aware that God's Holy love is what He yearningly wishes for his children to possess--a love for his Truth and righteousness. Obviously, we humans, in our unregenerate condition, do not fathom how to feel and convey love for God and his righteousness. For one thing, we are incapable, in our unregenerate state, to comprehend true love because of our spiritual blindness (see Romans 1:21). The Bible says that we "all have sinned and come short of the glory of God" (Romans 3:23), and that "the wages of sin is death; but the gift of God is eternal life through Jesus Christ our Lord" (Romans 6:23).

Let me continue by sharing this point; before we are made free from sin and its consequences (when we yield ourselves totally to Christ as Lord and Master), we naturally will follow after those goals in life, maintain attitudes, and adopt behaviors that are self-seeking and contrary to God's righteousness and truth. We are lost in the darkness, struggling and falling because we are fearful to approach the Light. This fear is because the Light will reveal who we really are. Jesus said, "For everyone that doeth evil hateth the light, neither cometh to the light, lest his deeds should be reproved" (John 3:20). Remember that word integrity? But Jesus continues by declaring, "But he that doeth truth cometh to the light, that his deeds may be made manifest, that they are wrought in God" (John 3:21). The difference in attitude can only be explained by the lure of the Light!

Paul declared that:

> To be carnally minded (the mind of the flesh) is death; but to be spiritually minded (the mind of the Spirit) is life and peace. Because the carnal mind (mind of the flesh) is enmity (hostile

Neil C. Roth

toward God) against God: for it is not subject to the law of God, neither indeed can be (Romans 8:6, 7).

Do you see the picture? We need a radical change in our perspective and knowledge of God and his ways! And this can only happen if we allow the Holy Spirit to teach us to recognize the irrational, carnal ideas and attitudes that cause us to walk in despair and dishonesty before God and our fellows.

Join me as we look now at the main passage of scripture that sets off the C.R.T. Priority Principles. It is of critical importance that these be understood if Christian rational thinking and behavior are to be realized. Let us not forget, however, that the overriding central principle still stands and that is LOVE: Love God, his Word, his righteousness, his people, his creation (see Matthew 22:40). But how can we test our love and discover its genuineness? Here it is, then--LOVE NOT THE WORLD!

"Now," you say, "You've blown me away by saying that!" "I'm in the world, why can't I enjoy and appreciate what God has created and provided?" Well, obviously, God has charged us to be caretakers and stewards of his creation, and to be thankful for his provisions. After all, He surely created the world with an aim to please man, for it does in so many exciting ways. So, what is meant by "love not the world?" Let us look at this passage in its entirety and see. John is speaking:

> Love not the world, neither the things that are in the world. If any man love the world, the love of the Father is not in him. For all that is in the world, the lust of the flesh, and the lust of the eyes, and the pride of life, is not of the Father, but is of the world. And the world passeth away, and the lust thereof: but he that doeth the will of God abideth forever" (I John 2:15-17).

On the one hand, this passage reveals the central principle of God's love in the believer, and not a "love" for the world: Or, on the other hand, its exact opposite--the world love that robs the individual of God's love and favor, and which leads to that ultimate separation from God and heaven.

The "love of the world" spoken of is, in reality, a spirit inherent in man that is self-seeking and God-ignoring! It is the same spirit that Paul spoke

You Are What You Think

of in Romans, chapter eight, verse six. Yes, it is a carnal spirit that John alludes to here: A spirit that philosophically is tied to the godless hedonism of our age that cries out, "Eat! Drink! Be merry! For tomorrow you may die." I put "may" in the statement because it seems that most persons somehow think they will escape dying, even though they know everyone else will. "Perhaps," they say, "God will allow a Hollywood happy-ending with my life!" The stark truth is: the world and its carnality (lust) are doomed! They will all fail and pass away. Look around you. The world order is failing now and will continue to do so (see Romans 1:18-32); but, again hear Paul as he describes the extreme wickedness of the last days in which we are living:

> This know also, that in the last days perilous (grievous) times shall come. For men shall be lovers of their own selves, covetous, boasters, proud, blasphemers, disobedient to parents, unthankful, unholy, without natural affection, trucebreakers, false accusers, incontinent (without self-control), fierce, despisers of those that are good, traitors, heady (reckless), high-minded (self-conceit), lovers of pleasures more than lovers of God; having a form of godliness, but denying the power thereof: from such turn away. For of this sort are they which creep into houses, and lead captive silly women laden with sins, led away with divers lusts, ever learning, and never able to come to the knowledge of the truth (II Timothy 3:1-7).

Wow! Nothing is left out. What a graphic picture of the day in which we live. Everybody is pictured and the scenario is "Love the world, baby, for it's all we've got!" Perhaps you have heard that a ship is safe in the ocean as long as the ocean is not in the ship. It also follows that the Christian is only safe in the world so long as the world is not in him. Without a doubt, the attitudes described are all potentially fatal and each are mentioned in our "love not the world" passage in I John.

Let us look now at the three characteristic attitudinal thrusts of loving the world. Each of these worldly thrusts exhibits an almost total disregard (at heart) for the rights of others, and ultimately, an elevation of one's own so-called rights and lusts. The love of the world is essentially an ignoring of moral and ethical boundaries that the law of Christ (passed on to men in moral and civil laws and mores) instills in the believer's heart and mind.

Adam Clark, in his commentary on the Bible, describes the passage, "For all that is in the world" to mean "all that it can boast of, all that it can promise, is only sensual transient gratification, and even this promise it cannot fulfill; so that its warmest votaries can complain loudest of their disappointment."[6]

The C.R.T. Priority Principles are, in fact, a further elaboration of the commandments and the C.R.T. Central Principle of love that was stated at the beginning of this chapter. Jesus' words to his disciples, during the Sermon on the Mount, provide a philosophical framework for the three Priority Principles. He said, "Seek ye first the kingdom of God and his righteousness; and all these things shall be added unto you" (Matthew 6:33). The Priority Principles get at isolating man's abortive attempts to satisfy himself with artificial materials, activities, and values. Lust and pride can never permanently satisfy, but Jesus Christ can and will add unto us pleasures forevermore _if_ we will seek Him preeminently!

It would be well to remember that Jesus has condemned the flesh (carnal spirit) in that it always chooses evil, and cannot see, or enter into the kingdom of heaven. Furthermore, the flesh is disqualified: volitionally (Ephesians 2:2, 3); emotionally (Romans 8:5-8); and intellectually (I Corinthians 2:14).

Let us now proceed to our discussion of the C.R.T. Priority Principle No. 1. Figure 4 presents the salient aspects of these principles.

<u>C.R.T. Priority Principle No. 1--The "Provision" Principle:</u>
<u>Flee Lust--Respect your Body--Trust God for Needs</u>

THE LUST OF THE FLESH (I JOHN 2:16)

What is lust? In a moral and ethical sense (in which it is being used in this passage), "lust is used to express sinful desire--sinful either in being directed toward forbidden objects, or in being so violent as to overcome self-control, and to engross the mind with earthly, carnal, and perishable things."[7] Webster defines lust as: "A desire to gratify the senses, bodily appetite."[8]

You Are What You Think

Biblically speaking, the world lust encompasses all of these

"Seek ye first the kingdom of God,
and his righteousness; and all these things
shall be added unto you" (Matthew 6:33).

Love of the Father
(I John 2:15-17)

The Kingdom of Heaven
(In the world, but not of the world)

SPIRITUAL PRIORITY PRINCIPLES

1. PROVISION	2. POSSESSION	3. POSITION
• Flee lust (lust or love).	• Treasures in Heaven.	• Love for God, self, others.
• Respect Body.	• Good steward.	• Servant model--saved to serve, not to be served.
• Trust God for needs.	• Seek God first and foremost and He will provide material blessings according to his will!	• Trust in God, not self. • Being--orientation.

"There is a great gulf fixed" (Luke 16:26).

Love of Satan

Kingdom of the World

CARNAL PRIORITY PRINCIPLES

Lust of Flesh	Lust of Eyes	Pride of Life
1. PROVISION	2. POSSESSION	3. POSITION

Neil C. Roth

- Sensuality without bounds or restraints.
- Exploitation.

- Covetousness.
- Materialism.
- Mismanagement.
- Thing and having-orientation.

- Prestige.
- Pride.
- Power.
- Self-seeking.

Figure 4 C.R.T. PRIORITY PRINCIPLES

meanings, and more, depending on the attitude and motivation of the person. I do not believe that the lust of the eyes, as used here, could be inferred to mean a lust for power. That meaning is reserved for our third attitudinal thrust, the pride of life. In contrast, the lust of the flesh does describe human sensuality, in any form, that goes unbridled with little concern for moral or ethical bounds, self-respect, or mutual respect. Adam Clarke describes "The lust of the flesh" as "sensual and impure desires which seek their gratification in women, strong drink, delicious viands (meats), and the like."[9] This kind of attitude is typically exploitive and manipulative of other persons. It is supported by the mass mind, that secular humanism has created, that cries out: "If it feels good, go for it. After all, everyone is doing it!"

In our day, lust is being pandered for all it is worth by the mass media. The movie and television industry, spurred on by the rank and totally immoral Playboy ethic (the Hedonism of Rome's day) has attempted to legitimize lust as the proper attitude for all to hold. As a result, we are now seeing our culture blindly "getting into bed" with ancient Rome, Sodom, and Gomorrah.

We rather stupidly ask, "Why are marriages failing so often?" or "Why did my mate of thirty years have an affair?" The answer is greatly associated with lust (also, communication breakdown with God and spouse), and when we yield to it without exercising constraint, or considering the effects of our actions on others or self. Lust is essentially always an urge to circumvent God's moral boundaries. Its by-products will always be damaging in every way simply because a relationship is never quite the same once infidelity has been experienced. Our memories hold these past experiences, and even later when we are enjoying a sound sexual relationship with our mate, the past memories are prone to surface and

You Are What You Think

haunt us with comparisons of the present. Make no mistake, lust is sin, and sin, like the knife, leaves a scar. That scar is MEMORY!

I once had a client who was perplexed with her marriage because of past memories. She loved her husband but could not put her former sexual escapades out of her mind while having sex with her husband. This is not an uncommon experience and most assuredly confuses and troubles many potentially good marital relationships.

Characteristically, lust is essentially a craving to be filled and a yearning for provision. We clamor for bread, drink, sex, activity, excitement, etc., and fail to see that our bodies are really vessels that God wishes to use for his glory and purposes.

Regarding sex, this powerfully potent drive is part of God's "good" creative act, and has its rightful place within marriage. Dr. Howard Hendricks has described God's purpose for sex as three-fold. First, propagation of the race as seen in "Be fruitful and multiply" (Genesis 1:27-28); Second, for the prevention of fornication (I Corinthians 6:18-20); and Third, to promote mutual love and pleasure in the marital relationship (Hebrews 13:4; Genesis 2:24). But apart from marriage, sex is a by-product of lusting.

Karl Menniger, in discussing lust, comments on its damaging role in fostering rape on the streets and adultery in marriage.

> Rape, is characteristically less a sexual act than a form of assault and mayhem--a form of hurting, debasing, and destroying another person for power drive satisfaction. That's sin! Adultery, likewise, is less 'sinful' for its sexual content than for its violation of trust and integrity.[10]

In effect then, rape, as an act, is primarily a quest for power fostered by a strong sense of personal inferiority and insecurity. Similarly, adultery is based upon the false assumption that two insecure, unfulfilled persons can, by emotional and physical copulation, allay their inadequacies. Tragically, nothing is ever gained but the stark realization that one's integrity and self-respect have been traded for a brand, burned-in-deep, labeled DISLOYAL!

What are God's sexual standards for singles? He declares that all sexual activity, apart from marriage, is lust that has become sin. All persons (singles) are instructed to abstain from fornication (Acts 15:20); to not commit our bodies to it (I Corinthians 6:13); and that we should not once be named as fornicators (Ephesians 5:3). Celibacy, or abstinance is God's standard for all who are unmarried, Christian or non-Christian!

Paul reiterates this principle when he said:

> ...It is good for a man not to touch (sexually) a woman. Nevertheless, to avoid fornication, let every man have his own wife, and let every woman have her own husband...for it is better to marry than to burn (I Corinthians 7:1, 2, 9b).

It is clear from experience that Paul, and countless thousands of single people, have either chosen to be single, or are single by virtue of limited opportunities to marry. Then again, Paul testified that his celibacy was a more expedient way to live so that the ministry could be better attended. The crucial point here is: Single persons can and must renounce sexual thoughts or activities because sex apart from marriage can never be anything but lust. Illicit sex is a perversion of what God intends to be just one small facet of the relationship experienced between the marriage partners.

Much has been written recently about the "normalcy" and innocency of masturbation. To my alarm, some Christian professionals are espousing such views. In my opinion, masturbation, even though it may seem "normal" because so many practice it, is another way to express the "lust of the flesh!" Those who practice it during their youth are potentially setting themselves up for less-than-satisfying sexual relationships in marriage. Why? Because the first learned behavior becomes part of one's mind-set. This mind-set includes scenarios like: "If normal sex with my spouse doesn't work out, I can always masturbate." Or, consider the millions of young men and women who have been raised on <u>Playboy</u> or <u>Playgirl</u>-type magazines. Without a doubt, these publications are pandering prurient stimulation so that lust will be created and magazines sold. The by-product, however, is the creation of an entire generation of persons who are attempting to satisfy a marriage-bound urge through erotic stimulation, lusting, and masturbation.

Hence, witness the many clients who have asked, "Why does my spouse have to read erotic magazines before we attempt sex in order to

You Are What You Think

get stimulated. Am I not appealing enough?" This is a tragic, but not uncommon experience these days for many! The point is: Masturbation is no less a sin than adultery, fornication, or rape. It reflects an attitude of "lusting" and deception. It is deception because of one's attempt to pervert God's normal provision for sexual fulfillment through marriage!

Furthermore, as a psychologist, I am not convinced that homosexuality is anything more, or less, than the perversion of the normal sex urge. It gets started rather naturally in youth when boys are thrown in with boys, and girls with girls. When puberty signals heterosexual urges, the adolescent is typically, rightly hindered by society from heterosexual activities. Hence, former patterns of youthful genital exploration, possible masturbation, and innocent group exploration (like pre-school children playing doctor and nurse) may lead to homosexual practices. The homosexual might have tried to establish heterosexual relationships, but failed due to possible personality weaknesses or lack of "social-stimulus value" to members of the opposite sex.

The deviant outcome is predictable, for in order to satisfy sexual needs, four choices are open to the potential homosexual: abstinence, masturbation, intercourse, or mutual stimulation. The later activity is chosen because it offers more than just mutual orgasm. It offers a quasi relationship with another human being that is falsely seen as analogous to the one experienced in marriage. Let it be clearly understood, however, that the homosexual is produced, not by nature, but due to directed attention and choice! I have witnessed many homosexuals change because of their conversion to Jesus Christ. The change came when they normalized and redirected their perverted sex urges through the power of Christ in their lives. Praise God, all crookedness can be made straight by His grace! (See Romans 1:20-32).

Listen again to Paul:

> Know ye not that ye are the temple of God, and that the Spirit of God dwelleth in you? If any man defile (destroy it with lust) the temple of God, him shall God destroy; for the temple (Your body) is holy, which temple ye are (I Corinthians 3:16, 17).

Neil C. Roth

God's Word is crystal clear on the matter. We will pay a stiff penalty if we continue to follow after lust as our god. We stand to lose our health through abuse and disease; genetic mutation, broken relationships with God and men, and possible death, all because of physical lusting, abuse, and perversion!

Also, the lust of the flesh applies to the sin of gluttony, as well. Gluttony is the habit of eating too much. Going a bit further, it is the habit of ingesting excessive and/or harmful quantities of food, drink, and drugs into the system.

Jesus' first temptation in the wilderness was associated with a legitimate need--to eat. Satan offered Him bread if He would turn the stone to bread. Jesus responded: "Man shall not live by bread alone, but by every word of God" (Luke 4:4b). Satan urges Jesus to yield to what Wayne Oates calls the "instant syndrome!" That is, let us forget that bread is to be earned and baked, and somehow fantasize that we can shortcut reality and make bread from stones! Jesus would not yield to this temptation to take a shortcut to satisfaction. Yes, He was terribly hungry. Who would not be after forty days of fasting? As Dr. Oates has said, "The basic hungers of a person are fertile sources of fantasy and temptation to take shortcuts to turn fantasies into reality without work or discipline."[11]

In other words, our Lord has an infinitely better plan for meeting our bodily needs than through the medium of lust. Why? Because lusting to fulfill our bodily craving will not bring satisfaction but it will bring us a whirlwind of sadness, bitterness, and woe. Lusting is irrational because it is contrary to God's plan and will for humans and it is selfish, utterly disregarding the other person and one's respect for self.

Jesus went further and said that if a man (or woman) would harbor sexual lust in his heart for another, that, in effect, adultery had already been committed (Matthew 5:28). So we cannot say to ourselves, "It's alright if I look, but don't touch." If by looking you mean lusting, then challenge these irrational, sinful thoughts and replace them with God's pure rational thoughts. We really cannot ask God to help us out of lustful situations unless we help ourselves not to get into them in the first place. Keep out of Satan's territory!

In the positive vein, our Lord is clearly stating "Respect your bodies and use them to glorify Me and do My will." As mentioned earlier, He

You Are What You Think

ordained marriage, and sex was an integral part of his "good" creation. But sex and sensuality must not be confused with lust. Lust is sensuality that disregards the bounds of marriage or the boundaries of mutual and self-respect. "Respecting" is God's principle of managing the urge of lust that grips every human being. By respecting, I mean that we learn through God's Word and his enabling Holy Spirit, to value the person (obviously ourselves first) and view each relationship within the bounds of God's moral law, and his highest law governing relationships, loving another as ourselves.

Paul was very concerned about the fidelity and genuineness of Christian testimony. He declares:

> I keep under my body (discipline it) and bring it into subjection (make it a slave): lest that by any means, when I have preached to others, I myself should be a castaway (rejected as cracked pottery, put on the shelf) (I Corinthians 9:27).

What is the lesson to be learned? It is: that God calls upon us to rationally respect our bodies and understand their rightful purposes. He will honor and bless sensuality within the proper bounds of respectful relationships that are condoned by Scripture. Again, the need to show respect for all persons is primary and essential, and we are not to quit being men or women who sense physical and emotional feelings. As Margaret Mead once said, "We must learn to accept our sexuality and not be ashamed, but proud of the fact we are a male or female."

It is therefore apparent that God wishes for us to express his message and love through the vehicle of our personalities which, in this life, will be shaded by our maleness and femaleness. But God is calling for us to flee fornication, but not only of the body, but more importantly, of the spirit. Our "instant syndrome" minds are to be totally purified from the lust of the flesh by God's Holy Spirit.

Peter was concerned about this when he called upon us to be holy persons, even as God who calls us is holy. And how was this to be evidenced? In all manner of conversation (Living--I Peter 1:15). Then he says,

Neil C. Roth

> Seeing ye have purified your souls in obeying the truth through the Spirit unto unfeigned love (respect and concern) of the brethren, see that ye love one another with a pure heart fervently: Being born again, not of corruptible seed (lust and selfishness), but of incorruptible (truth and honesty, by the word of God, which liveth and abideth forever (I Peter 1:22, 23).

Do you realize what has been said? The Lord will provide all of our physical needs (see Matthew 6:25-34) and help us to move from lust to respect when we obey the Truth--his Truth, with the Holy Spirit's help.

Now let us briefly review this principle. The "Provision" Principle states that: It is irrational and fatal to be "lusting" after physical fulfillment when God's way for providing our physical fulfillment is through "respecting" and loving God, ourselves, and others; thus, as a by-product, physical and spiritual satisfaction will be achieved within the proper moral boundaries that are set according to God's Word.

May I ask, where are you in your life with regard to the Provision Principle? Lusting or respecting? Paul's words are ever before us: "Be not conformed to this world, but be ye transformed by the renewing of your mind, that ye may prove what is that good, and acceptable, and perfect, will of God" (Romans 12:2). It really boils down to a choice of lust or love!

C.R.T. Priority Principle No. 2--The "Possession" Principle: Seek God First and Foremost, and He will provide Material Blessings According to His Will

The "Possession" Principle entails the quality of our love for things and how we attempt to use them. The "lust of the eyes" that John speaks about (I John 2:16) is describing an attitude that man has about his real and desired possessions. Again, Adam Clarke interprets the "lust of the eyes" to mean: "Inordinate desires after finery of every kind, gaudy dress, splendid houses, superb furniture, expensive equipage, trappings, and decorations of all sorts."[12]

The lust for things is clearly seen in our world and is aptly described by Eric Fromm as the "having" orientation.[13] This urge to accumulate

You Are What You Think

material goods is vigorously encouraged by the materialistic order in which we find ourselves.

In his penetrating study, entitled <u>Freedom of Simplicity</u>, author Richard Foster discusses the fallacious attitudes that people hold toward material goods.

> Misery arises when people try to make a life out of provision. While it is an essential ingredient in the good life, it is by no means the only ingredient, nor is it even the most important one. So often the biblical teaching on provision has been taken and twisted into a doctrine of gluttonous prosperity. All the subtle, and sometimes not so subtle, coaxing to "love Jesus and get rich' reflects our failure to see the biblical limitation upon things. Incarnated into our theology are covetous goals under the guise of the promise of God.[14]

Madison Avenue, obviously, and our "buy now, pay later" monetary system are exceedingly difficult for some to resist. A.B.C. radio newscaster Paul Harvey recently philosophised about this instant debt syndrome into which our nation has fallen. He stated: "When your outgo exceeds your income, the upshot may be your down-fall."

Out Lord warns us of the folly of yielding to the "lust for material things." Listen to Jesus speak:

> Lay not up for yourselves treasures upon earth, where moth and rust doth corrupt (consume), and where thieves break through and steal: But lay up for yourselves treasures in heaven, where neither moth nor rust doth corrupt (consume), and where thieves do not break through nor steal: For where your treasure is, there will your heart be also (Matthew 6:19-21).

Here we see a contrast made between earthly and heavenly treasures. Surely, Jesus warns us of the idiocy of acquiring treasures that we cannot ultimately keep, and also warns us against the danger of losing our soul, as well as our wealth, if we value it over loving God.

Furthermore, His third major temptation dealt with possessions. Satan said to Him "All these things (the kingdoms of the world) will I give thee,

Neil C. Roth

if thou wilt fall down and worship me" (Matthew 4:9). Of course, Jesus set him straight immediately, "Get thee hence, Satan: for it is written, thou shalt worship the Lord thy God, and Him only shalt thou serve" (Matthew 4:10). Jesus already was the Creator and real owner of all things. But, as a diligent antagonist, Satan continues to try and shift our attention from the Divine purpose (as he tried to do with Christ) and induce us to detach our will from the Father's will and become "lustfully and materially" independent.

But Jesus counters Satan by saying: "Seek ye first the kingdom of God, and his righteousness; and all these things shall be added unto you" (Matthew 6:33). Here Jesus deals a death blow to the attitude and spirit that characterises the carnal "lust of the eyes." Instead of the greedy accumulation and selfish use of our possessions, God calls us to seek one of his top priorities for our lives first. That priority is linked to the principle that people are infinitely more important than material things! This principle is a derivative from the first commandment: namely, that God is more important than anything that He has created. Hence, laying up treasures in heaven is personally acknowledging that our love of, respect for, and obedience to God must always take preeminence over possessions. As Paul said, "That in all things He might have the preeminence" (Colossians 1:18b).

So, we see, God is calling us to view Himself, ourselves, and others (in a proper spiritual and physical sense), and our relationships, as the key values of life. Only then, can our view of our possessions be premised on: "what are my material requirements to fulfill God's will in my life," and "how can I learn to become a good steward of these possessions?"

Upon realizing the preceeding truth, we can then move from a "having" to a "being" orientation.[15] This occurs when "persons" capture your love and attention supremely. In addition, we begin to see others, as well as God, as a "thou," instead of an "it."[16] You see, the crass, selfish love of things ultimately demeans other persons, as well as oneself. Truly, the proper Christian use of money and wealth is the only advantage in having it!

Furthermore, the Lord is calling on us to become good stewards of that which He has entrusted to our care. Jesus said, "unto whomsoever much is given, of him shall be much required: and to whom men have committed

You Are What You Think

much, of him they will ask the more" (Luke 12:48b). John Wesley, in commenting on stewardship said, "Make all the money you can, save all you can, and give all you can." Interestingly, at the end of life, Wesley was as poor as when he entered the world. Close to the end of his days he wrote: "I left no money in my will, because I had none."[17]

Dr. Oswald J. Smith gives us some insight on this subject: "I have learned that money is not the measure of a man, but it is often the means of finding out how small he is."[18] The Bible warns us about a cancer of the spirit that can totally corrupt our soul and reduce our integrity: "For the love of money is the root of all evil" (I Timothy 6:10a). This love or "lust of the eyes" for things does not bring us independence but slavery to "things!"

When Christ rules our hearts, however, a positive reading of the preceding verse will be: that the love of the right use of money is the root of much good! True independence from material servitude comes when we submit ourselves to the God beyond gods. It follows that we can only discover our innermost selves when we are willing to trade our priorities for His. Jesus' words need no improvement or embellishment:

> If any man will come after me, let him deny himself, and take up his cross, and follow me. For whosoever will save his life (have his own way) shall lose it: and whosoever will lose his life for my sake shall find it. For what is a man profited, if he shall gain the whole world, and lose (forfeits) his own soul? Or what shall a man give in exchange for his soul (Matthew 16:24-26)?

Henry Ford once said: "If money is your only hope for independence, you will never have it. The only real security that a man can have in this world is a reserve of knowledge, experience, and ability."[19] Mr. Ford displayed a keen and proven insight but he missed the critical point regarding true security. To be sure, true security is based upon all the things he mentioned, but upon much, much more! Here it is again: C.R.T. Priority Principle No. 2--the "Possession" Principle: Seek God first and foremost, and He will provide material blessings according to his will.

Someone once put it this way: "It's good to have money, and the things that money can buy, but it's good, too, to check up once in a while to make

Neil C. Roth

sure you haven't lost the things that money cannot buy."[20] In reality, there is no man so poor as he who has only money!

C.R.T. Priority Principle No. 3--The "Position" Principle: We are Saved to Serve--Not to be Served "The Pride of life" (I John 2:16)

Now we come to the "Position" Principle. What is this "pride of life" that John spoke of (I John 2:16)? In essence, it is a collage of many human behaviors that is premised on the carnal attitude, unrighteous pride. Those afflicted crave after prestige and power and are usually seen manipulating and exploiting others to bolster their sense of pride. Benjamin Franklin once said that "the proud hate pride--in others."[21] The task, though easy to say, is to detect pride in ourselves!

Unrighteous pride is that spirit that seeks favor and honor among men in order to elevate oneself. Webster calls it: "an overhigh opinion of oneself; exaggerated self-esteem; conceit. The showing of this in behavior; haughtiness; arrogance."[22] Adam Clarke, our previously used commentator, describes "the pride of life" to mean "Hunting after honours, titles, and pedigrees; boasting of ancestry, family connections, great offices, honourable acquaintance, and the like."[23]

Obviously, there is a self-less pride that is wholesome and proper--a pride for one's accomplishments, one's family, one's country. Someone once said, "Always hold your head up, but be careful to keep your nose at a friendly level." But for the Christian, this righteous pride has deeper roots. Deep down we acknowledge that God is the provider of personal talent and resources. In effect, our pride rests in God and in His grace to us.

Unrighteous pride, however, is a destructive force in human life. Hear Soloman as he shares from his years as King of Israel and sampler of all that life could offer:

> Pride goeth before destruction, and an haughty spirit before a fall (Proverbs 16:18).
> Everyone that is proud in heart is an abomination to the Lord: though hand join in hand, he shall not go unpunished (Proverbs 16:5).

You Are What You Think

When pride cometh, then cometh shame (Proverbs 11:2a).
An high look, and a proud heart...is sin (Proverbs 21:4).

These words from a very learned and coy man cannot be dodged! Pride is a very deadly and perverse sin. Hear another, the Apostle James: "...Wherefore He (the Lord) saith, God resisteth the proud, but giveth grace unto the humble" (James 4:6).

How revealing it is that Jesus was tempted on this very thing. Satan told Him to cast Himself down from the pinnacle of the temple and then to command the angels to save Him from death. What folly, this was, for Satan knew Jesus would not be tempted by the fantasy that nature's laws could be ignored and, more importantly, that He could possibly strike a bargain with Satan to serve him. After all, Jesus, and his Father, God, had created Satan (then Lucifer), Son of the Morning. Dr. Wayne Oates cogently sums up this point by saying:

> In essence, this (the three temptations of Jesus) is a trilogy of fantasies which are common to mankind. To come to terms with them as one faces the demands of adult life is a time of testing and trial. The alternative to consecration to the God of Reality is to make a Faustian pact with the god of deception and especially self-deception. Such an alternative is an "approach-avoidance" of the sufferings and disciplines required for a clear-headed sense of realism. It permits a person to live in a world of his own, dreaming rather than 'being.'[24]

We must challenge our pride, and its irrationality, and learn to walk in this world as servants, "being" instead of "dreaming!" This does not mean bondage. For service can never become slavery to the one who truly loves. But wait! Are you tempted to think that somehow you are favoring God by serving Him? As Victor Nyquist declared, "He honors you by allowing you to serve Him!"[25] Jesus reminds us again, "Whosoever shalt exalt himself shall be abased; and he that shall humble himself shall be exalted" (Matthew 23:12).

117

Neil C. Roth

WE ARE SAVED TO SERVE--NOT TO BE SERVED.

Jesus showed us servanthood at its very best while here on earth. In all matters, He glorified his heavenly Father, not himself. He sought his Father's favor--not the favor of men. All that He said and did promoted the dignity and priceless worth of the individual and servanthood. He spoke words like:

> ...Thou shalt love thy neighbor as thyself...(Mark 12:31).
> Therefore all things whatsoever ye would that men should do to you, do ye (help others) even so to them: for this is the law and the prophets (Matthew 7:12).
> If any man desire to be first (with God), the same shall be last of all, and servant of all (Mark 9:35b).

"Why," you ask, "should we serve others at all?" "What possible good can come from this behavior?" Listen again to Jesus: "Give, and it will be given to you; good measure, pressed down, shaken together, running over, they will pour into your lap. For by your standard of measure it will be measured to you in return" (Luke 6:38, N.A.S.). This was, and is Jesus' standard of stewardship and giving.

What is it that will "pour into your lap?" Namely, God's richest commendation and blessing! For, it follows that as we give of ourselves to others it is as though we have given directly to God. In their timely book, entitled, Healing Love, Shostrom and Montgomery make a critical point:

> A key to the healthy expression of strength is that the personal power that is experienced is used not only in behalf of his or her own well-being, but also as a service to facilitate the well-being and happiness of others. Thus the power of the actualizing Christian is used to edify or build up others, rather than dominate, intimidate, or exploit them.(*) It is a power made gentle by Christ's love and insulated by the virtue of humility.[26]

---

* See Shostrom, Everett, Man, the Manipulator. Nashville: Abingdon, 1967, for excellent reading on this subject.

You Are What You Think

How wonderful it is when man's "Pride of life" spirit is made over into a gentle spirit reflecting God's love and His control, while being kept humble by the presence of the Christ within! How privileged we have become to experience such a heavenly treasure in an earthen vessel! Clearly, the Christian life is vitally summed up in the word LOVE. An "outgoing love that results in concrete deeds of service is the fruit of one who is being led by the Holy Spirit."[27]

Where do you stand with regard to these critical priority principles? Dr. Clarke states that lust and pride began here and will end here (the world passeth away, and the lust thereof); and that they neither come from or lead to God. Lust and pride are "continually fading and perishing but he that doeth the will of God--that seeks the pleasure, profit, and honour that comes from above, shall abide forever, always happy through time and eternity, because God, the unchangeable source of felicity, is his portion"[28]

Jesus' words are self-explanatory: "For where your treasure is, there will your heart be also" (Luke 12:34).

<u>Chapter Review at a Glance</u>

C.R.T. Central Person Principle--the Love Principle:
"Sincerely respect and love God, yourself, and others."

C.R.T. Person Precepts

1. Please love me solely for I am your creator and God and I sincerely love you.
2. No substitute god is necessary--I am your all in all and will meet all your needs.
3. Speak of and to me with love and respect.
4. Communicate and fellowship with me--I want to hear from you regularly.
5. Respect and love your mother and father.
6. Respect and love all other persons--life is sacred.
7. Be faithful in marital and all other human relationships.
8. Be trustworthy with the resources and possessions of others.
9. Be truthful in all thought and conversation.

10. Be content with what God has given you.

C.R.T. Priority Principles

1. Flee lust--Respect your body--Trust God for needs (the "Provision" Principle). Lust or Love!
2. Seek God first and foremost and He will provide material blessings according to His will (the "Possession" Principle).
3. We are Saved to Serve--not to be Served (the "Position" Principle)!

FOOTNOTES

1. Doan, Eleanor L. The Speaker's Sourcebook. Grand Rapids: Zondervan Publishing House, 1962, p. 155.
2. Ibid, p. 52.
3. Schaeffer, Francis A. The Church at the End of the 20th Century. Downer's Grove, Illinois: Inter-Varsity Press, 1971, p. 134.
4. Doan. op. cit., p. 33.
5. Taylor, Richard S. A Right Conception of Sin. Kansas City: Nazarene Publishing House, 1945, p. 21
6. Clarke, Adam. Clarke's Commentary. Nashville: Abingdon, 1959, p. 908.
7. Unger, Merrill F. Unger's Bible Dictionary. Chicago: Moody Press, 1961, p. 671.
8. Webster's New World Dictionary, College Edition. New York: The World Publishing Co., 1968, p. 874.
9. Clarke. op. cit., p. 908.
10. Menninger, Karl, M.D. Whatever Became of Sin? New York: Bantam Books, Inc., 1973, pp. 163-164.
11. Oates, Wayne E. The Psychology of Religion. Waco, Texas: Word Books, Publisher, 1973, p. 188.
12. Clarke, op. cit., p. 908.
13. Fromm, Eric. To Have or To Be? New York: Harper & Row, 1976.
14. Foster, Richard. Freedom of Simplicity. San Francisco: Harper and Row, Publishers, 1981, pp. 9-10.
15. Fromm. op. cit
16. Buber, Martin, I and Thou. New York: Scribner's, 1958.
17. Wesley, John. The Journal of John Wesley, edited by Percy Livingstone. Chicago: Moody Press, 1951, p. 409.
18. Doan. op. cit., p. 166.
19. Ibid, p. 167.
20. Allee, G. Franklin. Evangelistic Illustrations. Chicago: Moody Press, 1961, p. 258.
21. Doan. op. cit., p. 202.
22. Webster's New World Dictionary. op. cit., p. 1156.
23. Clarke, op. cit., p. 908.

Neil C. Roth

24. Oates. op. cit., p. 189.
25. Doan. op. cit., p. 224.
26. Shostrom, Everett L. and Montgomery, Dan. Healing Love. Nashville: Abingdon, 1978, p. 91.
27. Ibid, p. 106.
28. Clarke. op. cit., p. 908.

CHAPTER SIX

THE C.R.T. SEVEN CARDINAL INSIGHTS FOR LIVING

"What the country needs is dirtier fingernails and cleaner minds."
-Will Rogers[1]

Perhaps it is extremely presumptuous of me to proclaim that I have special "insight" into the topics of this book and of this chapter. At best, we all have limited insight, in varying degrees, that is perhaps best described by Paul. Listen: "For now we see through a glass darkly, but then (when we see the Lord in Heaven) face to face" (I Corinthians 13:12a). Webster defines insight as: "The ability to see and understand clearly the inner nature of things."[2] Thankfully, it is the Lord who gives us insight and wisdom, and He knows how I have asked Him for these qualities throughout my Christian life. James gives us the procedure to follow: "If any of you lack wisdom (who does not?), let him ask of God, that giveth to all men liberally, and upbraideth not (without reproach); and it shall be given him" (James 1:5).

Since becoming a Christian I have tried to keep before me the following admonition by Thomas à Kempis, author of the classic, The Imitation of Christ. He said: "To have a low opinion of our own merits and to think highly of others, that is wisdom. All men are frail, but thou shouldst reckon none as frail as thyself."[3] I have, with God's assistance, attempted to be open to the learnings that come from experiencing my own shortcomings, and successes. But also, there is a whole world from which we must redemptively learn. Surely, if we do not heed the lessons

Neil C. Roth

learned by our contemporaries, and those who have gone before, we will be rightly doomed to repeat their mistakes. None of us have enough time in life to constantly keep on "reinventing the wheel!" For life is far too precious and too brief for constant repetitions of that futile exercise. It is a one-way street and we are not coming back. W. E. Channing said: "Life is a fragment, a moment between two eternities, influenced by all that has preceded, and to influence all that follows."

So, please understand that these "insights" are really learnings from my life experience that have become critically important and vital! By digesting them into your mind and behavior (along with the precepts and principles of God's Word) your life can, and will be radically changed for the best.

C.R.T. CARDINAL INSIGHT NO. 1--IF YOU WILL TO CHANGE, YOU CAN!

Do you believe that you are not happy, successful, or fulfilled because you cannot be? If you think this way, you are not alone. Millions of people are bound because they are thinking "I cannot" when really what binds them is "I will not!" These "I cannot" persons say to themselves: "Attitudes are more important than facts." But, are they? Karl Menninger thinks not! He declares that "attitudes are facts." In my opinion, it is more difficult to say "I will" than "I can." "I can" is always preceded by "I will!"

Ironically, some people sometimes think they have a strong will, when it is really a strong "won't." Tragically, most people are binding themselves, as surely as with a chain, by refusing to acknowledge truth and wisdom. Remember, that our Lord will not change your will against your will. He has given you a free will to choose His will. This principle applies to all of life. We are told to "refuse not Him (Christ) that speaketh. For if they "men" escaped not who refused him that spake on earth, much more shall not we escape, if we turn away from Him that speaketh from heaven" (Hebrews 12:25).

Surely, when God calls upon us to forsake sin and repent, our wills are vitally involved. After we have deeply sensed our sin (Isaiah 6:5; Luke 5:8), and have experienced the deep emotion of godly sorrow that worketh for repentence (II Corinthians 7:10); it is then that our wills must be

You Are What You Think

operative! For at the center of repentance (or, change of any kind) is that earnest determination to forsake our evil ways, and, to quote Dr. Billy Graham: to <u>want</u> and <u>will</u> to "change one's attitudes toward self, toward sin, and God; to change one's feeling; to change one's will, disposition, and purpose. Only the Spirit of God can give you the determination for true repentance."[4] But before repentance, or change of any kind, can become a reality, we have to sense within ourselves serious discontent or frustration with our condition or situation!

Fortunately, we are not alone in this process of willing, for there is always that greatest affirmer of the soul, the blessed Holy Spirit, supportively reassuring! As the great saint and preacher, Daniel Steele, once wrote: "When this glad evangel resounds within, love to God springs up responsive to his great love to me. This is a new motive power. It reinforces the ethical feeling, the sense of obligation to right action."[5]

Surely, even when we know a thing to be right, how difficult it is to pursue it when there is no strong drawing toward it. The lust for appetites and passions (the love of the world) that are diabolical constitutes a painful and debilitating warfare between the flesh and the Spirit, entailing upon the latter a sense of degrading bondage. "I see the right, and I approve it too; I see the wrong, and yet the wrong pursue. But this new motive makes it easy to obey the law, because we love the lawgiver."[6]

Continuing further, it is important to remember: if we enjoy doing a thing, we will pursue it. More seriously yet, if we really love a thing (person, activity, thing) we will not only pursue it, but nurture it, and defend it, and guard it! Why? Because we <u>will</u> it (or desire it)! Those who contend for and ultimately become Olympic stars are not generally from the genius class. They are, however, a <u>disciplined class</u>! They have willed to become and disciplined their wills to win!

Jesus calls us to discover real contentment, joy, and peace by coming to Him for spiritual regeneration. If you are "fed up" with how you are, and experience a deep thirsting for that "something much better and refreshing" in life than just existing "till being undertaken," Jesus offers this invitation: "Let him that is athirst come. And whosoever <u>will</u>, let him take the water of life freely" (Revelation 22:17b).

The above invitation was the last that Jesus gave to men, and it describes the potential bestowal of the greatest possession ever offered by God to

Neil C. Roth

men--Himself! He is the Water of Life that can, if willfully accepted, well up like a fresh, bubbling spring, unto everlasting life!

Shostrom and Montgomery, in their book <u>Healing Love</u>, describe the person who is stuck in a rut using ego defensive strategies (like rationalization, projection, undoing, etc.) that were hopefully going to produce ease, freedom, and joy in his living. The opposite result occurred, however--tenseness, rigidity, and futility. These defenses (or self-defeating behaviors) are learned and can be extinguished, if we will them to be. The authors comment: "We can begin to reverse the process. That is at once the burden of responsibility and the potential for joy for all human beings. There is light at the end of the tunnel! There is hope for the troubled, entangled, and imprisoned individual."[7] But, needless to say, this light is not reached without risk and pain! They continue by saying:

> We may have to experience the real travail of owning our feelings and learning to express them honestly to others before we begin to enjoy the celebration of restored meaning in our lives. Every way of being stuck can be understood as an overt or subtle distortion of man's existential calling: to love himself, others, and God wholeheartedly. This is where it becomes important to realize that praying about our life situation must be combined with the courage to do something about it. Otherwise our "prayers" are only a form of avoidance--a flight into fantasy and magical thinking.[8]

The owning of our feelings, and learning to express them, is important in order to clarify how we feel. But, the redeeming, viable by-product of this process is to identify the irrational thinking that prompted the feeling response. Furthermore, the "overt or subtle distortion" referred to is, in essence, our <u>will</u> saying <u>no</u> to God's "come unto Me!"

Remember that choice, not chance, determines human destiny. If you know some change is needed in your life, why not decide now to do so, and will it, as God's constraining love fills your life! Clearly, love must first be viewed as an attitude, not an emotion. It is an attitude that says, "I will, I can!" Paul's word reaffirms the possibilities: "I can (and will) do all things through Christ (in him) which strengtheneth me" (Philippians 4:13).

You Are What You Think

C.R.T. CARDINAL INSIGHT NO. 2--YOU CAN STOP BLAMING AND ASSUME RESPONSIBILITY!

The natural selfish bent of man (or the unregenerate, carnal nature) sets him up to be sorely prone to "pass the buck" when anything goes wrong. Our first parents, Adam and Eve, started this most destructive human practice by passing the blame for their sin from man, to woman, to serpent (see Genesis 3). Today, we place blame for our problems on our parents, the environment, the government, the communists, our fixated complexes, and most recently, the Iranians.

With the exception of those legitimate complaints stemming from criminal activities or neglect, the human family (especially Americans), are suing each other with unprecedented fervor. We sue for a host of dubious reasons: all the way from mental cruelty to canaries, to a fly in the cereal box! In fact, a woman recently sued her husband for rape within their marriage!

We are all for justice, but juries (we make up our juries) have decreed judgments, and awarded settlements, that sometimes defy any reason, except that we Americans rather sadistically like to see the bankrobber get away with his money (really our money) or the claimant win over XYZ Corporation and show the "big brass who is really in control!"

Whatever happened to accepting responsibility for one's actions? Well, the truth is that no one, excepting precious few courageous and honest persons, have thought it to be a good idea. Afterall, who wants to have that awful egg on his face? Of a truth, if we are really wanting to grow as persons, we have no other alternative than to stop blaming and assume responsibility for who we are, where we have been, where we are now, and where we are going with our lives!

Surely, a convincing case can be made for the sometimes tragic influences that one's environment has on our human development. We are, in the main, a product of all the experiences that have gone on before this very moment. But, can we evade responsibility by continually shifting all the blame to other causes and influences? I think not, and more importantly, our Lord thinks not! Jeremiah quoted the Lord, who said: "But everyone shall die for his own iniquity" (Jeremiah 31:30a). Paul said, "For all have sinned and come short of the glory of God" (Romans 3:23).

Neil C. Roth

These words are undoubtedly pointing to personal responsibility for our thoughts, words, and deeds. Listen to a wise man, King Solomon: "For God shall bring every work into judgment, with every secret thing, whether it be good or whether it be evil" (Ecclesiastes 12:14). But if you lack total confidence in an earthly king, hear the King of Kings! Jesus said,

> For there is nothing covered, that shall not be revealed; neither hid, that shall not be known. Therefore, whatsoever we have spoken in darkness shall be heard in the light; and that which ye have spoken in the ear in closets shall be proclaimed upon the housetops" (Luke 12:2, 3).

Everyone of us will bow to Christ, one way or another: with assurance, love, and adoration for Him or with fear and expectancy of His eternal judgment and damnation! Hear Paul: "So then every one of us shall give account of himself to God" (Romans 14:12).

Paul states these truths not only to warn us of our accountability before God, but to warn us of the inherent dangers and pitfalls of judging any other human being. Jesus said: "Why dost thou judge thy brother?" Only our Lord has the qualifications to judge. If this be true, how can we justify passing blame on others when our eye may have a beam in it (see Matthew 7:3).

Consider this question: Does our very nature condemn us to be continually blaming and criticising others? Yes, it does, unless we become willing and ready to stop our blaming. Paul said, "If we would judge ourselves (our own thoughts, words, and deeds), we should not be judged" (I Corinthians 11:31). Praise the Lord, there is hope for all of us if we learn to accept responsibility for ourselves and begin the joyful, and yet sometimes painful, process of examining our motivations, thoughts, and actions in the light of God's precepts and principles.

In addition, to stop blaming means we will commit to not binding others or ourselves to some past, present, or future attitude or action. It becomes essential for us to ask the Lord for forgiveness of any sin that surrounds prior times of our life. Then, it is of paramount importance to our emotional and spiritual health, to accept his forgiveness as final and not continue to swim in the sea of guilt. When we protract our guilt, we

You Are What You Think

are in effect not forgiving ourselves! In reality, we are saying "Yes, I know that the Lord has forgiven me (we can cite verses like I John 1:9; Ephesians 4:32, etc.), but after all, my judgment is a slight bit more insightful about my character than is our Lord's! So, in reality, we keep perpetuating guilt because of faulty, irrational thinking.

Our greatest example of a truly forgiving spirit, is the Lord Jesus. Paul urges us to be: "Forbearing one another, and forgiving one another, if any man have a quarrel (complaint) against any: even as Christ forgave you, so also do ye" (Colossians 3:13). Without stretching the meaning of Paul's words, I believe Christ's intent was not only to have us forgive another person, but ourselves, as well.

Just a word more on what I call "event-binding" of attitudes and behaviors. With others, and ourselves, we suffer quilt and blame others and ourselves for what we have done in the past. You might say "Ex-convicts are unreliable and not to be trusted!" If you should hold such an attitude, how can the individual, who once failed but paid his debt to society, ever escape the bondage of your binding him to his past behaviors? How can he change if you will not allow him to? Statements like: "you've always been this way," or "why can't you ever do anything right," or "I'll forgive her criticism of me, but I'll never forget," really mean that you are not willing to let another person grow without the chains of the past binding him.

We also bind ourselves by saying to ourselves such irrational things as: "I failed once, so I dare not risk trying again, because, after all, I might fail again." Or, "I must be inadequate, dumb, and inept because everyone tells me so." The truth is that we often bind ourselves to the past because of what others are saying or doing. Their behavioral responses become our models! But before you continue to be bound, realize that others are also in bondage to their past faults and failures and are, more often than not, projecting onto you their guilt and blame. These persons are seldom willing to forgive themselves and accept responsibility.

Another side to "event-binding" of our past is to "think and believe" messages like: "I can't be happy because of what happened!" or, "I must continue to be sick because of this trauma or tragedy in my life." We are most prone as humans to catastrophize events into "permanent-effect" status. Truly, most behaviors (events) are the result of our attitudes (learnings

Neil C. Roth

and thoughts about them) and they can be changed. The consequences of events in life may be unalterable, however.

Paul assures us that no event in life should emotionally shipwreck us if we meet God's standards for His family membership. He proclaims: "For we know that all things work together (are synchronized together) for good to them that love God, to them who are the called according to his purpose" (Romans 8:28). Then, we can be assured that God will not allow our lives to be capriciously manipulated by events. He has a desired design for our lives, and He will integrate the good and the bad experiences, so that His good might be experienced in the end. Note, this promise only holds *if* we truly love God (remember the Central Principle on loving God). The acid test for the reality of this principle is found in I John 4:20 where "loving one's brother" must be the "up-front" evidence.

Furthermore, we will "survive" all of life's tragedies *if* Christ is our Lord and Savior. By survival, I mean the soul, (your personality) will be eternally safe. Paul explains: "Who shall separate us from the love of Christ? Shall tribulation, or distress, or persecution, or famine, or nakedness, or peril, or sword? Nay, in all these things we are more than conquerors through him that loved us" (Romans 8:35, 37). Paul's list of potential perils is certainly inclusive of the full range of earthly possibilities, and yet, God's love, through Christ, makes such a victory possible!

Paul's look at the future should interest us, because we must eventually live there, too. Proper planning is necessary in life, but telling ourselves, "I will not be happy or fulfilled until some hoped-for future event comes about, is a self-induced paralysis. Rather, we must learn to live fruitfully, happily, and responsibly in the "now" for that is where our life exists. In fact, the moment of now is past the moment you think about it! The now is, more accurately stated, a period of time that encompasses prime opportunity and attitudinal readiness.

The past being gone, with the exception of the attitudinal memory of it, should, when reviewed, grant us new insights and perceptions on how we might improve the quality of our lives. Cautiously, we must not dwell too much in the future so that we lose sight of, and touch with, the ethos of the Great Commission: physical and spiritual ministry to hurting "flesh and blood" people!

You Are What You Think

True freedom will only be ours when we finally commit ourselves to courageous self-judgment and a willingness to accept its concomitant self-discipline. The most free are undoubtedly those who are under self-control and being led by God's Spirit. You are free to jump off the cliff, take heroin, or rob a bank but, once done, you lose your freedom. God's laws cannot be broken without incurring the natural consequences of the act. Whatsoever you <u>will</u> to sow with thoughts, words, or deeds, will bring about that predictable reeping of inevitable consequences. The Bible is clear when it states that our sin will surely find us out! Sowing and reaping is "for real." "Be not deceived; God is not mocked: for whatsoever a man soweth, that shall he also reap" (Galatians 6:7).

Obviously, our behaviors toward other people are vitally important if relationships are to be meaningful and loving. By learning to see other persons, as well as yourself, as in the process of becoming, then, the blinders of ignorance, and the binders of attitude can be removed so that growth can begin. It is wise to remember that we are all at different levels in our development! This truth should force us to realize how vitally we all need special understanding, patience, and love from other persons! For, without this understanding, the negative inhibitors may be activated anew. Frankly, so many people have missed learning some extremely vital lessons (developmental tasks)* which they should have learned at the so-called teachable moment. Consequently, they now have to live out their days with learning handicaps that are frustrating and debilitating.

When we judge, blame, or criticize, do we truly understand all of the causes of another's behavior and their attendant ramifications? I think not, and certainly God says not! Sir Thomas Browne, in commenting on this, said: "No man can justly censure or condemn another, because indeed no man truly knows another."[9] The Bible is clear on this point: we are to concentrate on knowing ourselves! David said, "Search me, O God, and know my heart" (Psalm 139:23a). We can be sure that our Lord will reveal to us what He sees within our true self, for in reality we do not read God's Word – it reads us! The only people on earth that God can help are those who are willing to change, and who are ready to assume responsibility for who they really are as persons. But never forget, you are not alone in this!

---

* See <u>Developmental Tasks</u> <u>and</u> <u>Education</u> by Robert J. Havighurst. New York: McKay, 1952.

Neil C. Roth

Remember that responsibility is your response to God's ability. You must learn to accept the marvelous provisions of God.

With confidence, you can stop blaming and assume responsibility NOW and become free.

C.R.T. CARDINAL INSIGHT NO. 3--YOU CAN LEARN TO CONTROL YOUR THINKING AND EMOTIONS!

If we are willing to change and are ready to stop blaming ourselves, others, and past, present, or future situations, then we become ready to begin learning how to control our thinking and emotions. As we approach this preliminary process of evaluating ourselves, and what we think, the Holy Spirit will sensitively be our teacher and guide. Paul knew from experience that it would become necessary for us to bring "into captivity every thought to the obedience of Christ" (II Corinthians 10:5b). Do you remember Romans 12:2? "Be not conformed (fashioned according) to this world (see I John 2:15-17 for review): but be ye transformed by the renewing of your mind...." Our growth, faith, and salvation are the direct result of how and what we think.

Dr. Martin Luther King, Jr. once pointed out the importance of straight thinking in his sermon, "Strength to Love." He said, "One day we will learn that the heart can never be totally right if the head is totally wrong." He is aptly describing the content of this book, namely: we are what we think! If we desire quality, loving behavior in ourselves and others, then the quality of the sensory stimulation (via the media, associates, etc.) must be seriously evaluated and monitored. We would not eat garbage (unfortunately, some do in our world) but we purposely choose sensory stimulation and activities that undermine and pervert rationality, goodness, and decency! Oh, how we need a grand garbage day pickup of all the things that hinder our spiritual progress!

Our world, our nation, our home--yes, we all need straight thinking, right now! Rationalism is not enough, for it is partial, or it may pervert the truth. Also, fantasy and rationalism are essentially twin brothers who mutually appease one another! What is needed is a tested source of authority upon which we can rely for straight answers that guide and help

You Are What You Think

us to live straight. Praise God-that authority is God's Word, the Holy Bible. The central Person of the Bible, Jesus Christ, is the only One who can effectively guide our thinking in a redemptive, balanced, holy way.

If C.R.T. Psychology and Self-therapy (see chapter 8 for C.R.T. Self-Therapy) is going to help you, the following three assumptions must be seriously considered and hopefully accepted.

First: you must have an objectively, positive attitude toward the veracity and authenticity of the Biblical record and be open to God's truth and pray for wisdom to understand it. Mark Twain once said: "It's not what I don't understand in the Bible that bothers me. It's what I do understand!" Remember, faith comes to us by hearing, and hearing from God's Word (see Romans 10:17). The real test of the Bible's veracity and credibility is best found in the lives of God's people who are in love with its Author!

Our second assumption is: that you must be open to accepting God's Truth, and be willing to act upon its precepts and principles with faith and trust in their promised outcomes or consequences. God only rewards faith. If you should have doubts, you are not alone. Take them to God in prayer and ask Him, as did the New Testament father of the sick child, "Help thou mine unbelief" (Mark 9:24b). Browning wrote encouragingly for the doubters when he said: "There lives more faith in honest doubt, believe me, than in half the creeds."[10] God's Word is true, and as you grow in your knowledge of it, its truths will be confirmed over and over.

Assumption three states: that after confirming the Truth of the Bible, and its precepts and principles, then be sincerely open to accepting the Person of the precepts and principles, Jesus Christ, as Lord and Savior of your life. Right now, you can accept Him if you really want a new life and, a reliable, loving friend to walk with.

Then, comes the task of growing in the nature and nurture of the Lord Jesus Christ. His Holy Spirit begins to teach us new, and sometimes old, truths and, as our self-concept, attitudes, thinking, and behavior are being modified into God's image, the very mind of Christ is being grafted into our souls. The result: the Lord begins to govern the ways we think, feel, and act.

Derek Bok, "famous" for Bok's Law, gave utterance to an oft-forgotten principle: "If you think education is expensive, try ignorance."[11] Forgive my poetic license here, but could we not accurately say: "If you think the Christian life is costly to live, try following Satan!"

133

Neil C. Roth

David Gerrold once stated in Starlog, "Half of being smart is knowing what you're dumb at." We have spent considerable time and space looking at the precepts and principles of God's Word. These were presented as the CONSTANTS against which to match the rationality of our intentions, thoughts, and behaviors. These are the standards, just as a ruler is a standard of measurement, as also the Bureau of Standards in Washington, D.C. a final authority on measurements.

But, we must realize that there are many obstacles to clear thinking that can block our rationality. Philosopher Harold Titus cites prejudice, propaganda, the pressure of public opinion, and the blind acceptance of authority as culprits who block our search for truth. He does, however, feel that habits, even though many are needed and useful, hinder us when we face new or unfamiliar experiences.[12] The man who said "we first make our habits and then our habits make us" knew something of the bondage to which we can fall victim!

Gladly for us, we can learn to challenge the poor habits that blind and inhibit, and learn to rethink those irrational ideas that caused the habits to be formed in the first place. Titus (like Hepp, p.99) explains the many fallacies in thinking that violate the principles of logic and consistency.

The <u>semantical</u> <u>fallacies</u> have to do with the careless or improper use of words. Words, for example, may shift in meaning as we proceed with our discussion.

The <u>formal</u> <u>fallacies</u> cause us to draw invalid conclusions from our premises. We may make an assertion about all the members of a group when the premises permit us to speak of some only.

The <u>empirical</u> <u>fallacies</u> arise due to our hasty generalizations. Because one event came after another, we may wrongly insist that there is a direct causal relationship.[13]

The above ideas suggest that we have much to learn about communication, interpretation, and thinking specifically! Improving one's vocabulary, keeping interpretations tentative, and basing our thoughts upon rational and consistent bases will greatly enhance the hoped-for success of our developmental pilgrimage through life.

You Are What You Think

Dr. Albert Ellis, mentioned in an earlier chapter as the developer of Rational Emotive Psychotherapy, has suggested that there are twelve irrational thoughts that people frequently think cause them emotional distress. The Rational Emotive Therapy of Ellis seeks: to assist the client in uncovering his persistent irrational idea/s; and to challenge them with rational thoughts; and after achieving insight, change thinking and emoting for the better, on the strength of reason and insight. Also, the individual is encouraged to set behavioral objectives that lead to changed behavior.

Below, the twelve irrational thoughts[14] are presented with my commentary regarding the validity of the R.E.T. irrational thoughts in the light of Biblically, oriented C.R.T. Psychology. These R.E.T. irrational thoughts are most helpful to survey as one analyzes thinking and emotional responses. It is imperative for the Christian to realize that they must not be completely accepted as some kind of logical panacea. Why? Because nothing in life is as simplistic as it may seem, especially in this area. The key problem with these twelve irrational thoughts is that they are based upon a very pragmatic, behavioristic humanism that espouses the idea that man has the ability to save himself by hard work and insight. C.R.T. Psychology holds that humanistic values come from God and receive their meaning from His redemption, and that these values are clearly described by divine revelation. In addition, C.R.T. Psychology opposes an egotistical humanism that rules out God and man's responsibility to Him as his Lord and Savior.

I am convinced that blatant, secular humanism, characterized by cultural relativity, hedonism, and agnosticism accounts for much of the moral dilemma our world faces today. In effect, selfishness (sin) is luring millions into its subtle trap. Life is to godless humanism <u>all</u> <u>time</u>, no eternity! Christian humanism, on the other hand, derives its power from: a clear vision of God that gives sanctity to all of life; total commitment to God, as well as to men; and a perennial renewal that comes from resensitizing our minds to God's will and ways (see Romans 12:2).

Agnes Allen has an interesting law which states: "Almost anything is easier to get into than out of."[15] As a nation, we have fallen for conceited humanism like an opossum falls for highways. (In my area, the slow opossum is frequently killed on our highways. A standard joke is: "Why did the 'possum get killed?" "Because he forgot the road flares for his pouch! Ouch!)

135

Neil C. Roth

Now let us look at the R.E.T. irrational thoughts of Ellis. Under each one, the C.R.T. position is briefly discussed.

TWELVE IRRATIONAL IDEAS OF RATIONAL EMOTIVE THERAPY
--Dr. Albert Ellis

WITH CHRISTIAN RATIONAL THOUGHT POSITION OF AGREEMENT OR DEVIATION

1. We must be loved by everyone and everyone must approve of everything we do.

   C.R.T. Position: We must acknowledge and receive the love that Christ has for us (John 3:1-36) and have Him confirm our behavior as pleasing or not. But no man can please everyone on the human level. We should, however, try to show true love and respect to everyone. If it is accepted--great! If it is not-- pray for the individual and try again!

2. We must be thoroughly competent, adequate, intelligent, and achieving in all possible respects.

   C.R.T. Position: Only Christ could claim such qualities, but Christians are challenged by God to be conformed to Christ's image and never accept the standard of mediocrity. "I can do all things..." (Philippians 4:13).

3. Certain acts are wrong or wicked or villainous, and people who perform them should be severely punished.

   C.R.T. Position: God is a moral God and we are created as moral beings. The Bible is full of God's past, present, and future judgments because of man's sin. The Bible speaks for punishment for sins of all kinds. It also speaks of forgiveness for sins. We hold that if appropriate punishment is not consistently given for crimes committed, no deterrent is sensed and crime increases. The Bible, if followed, could help us to discover anew the standards of proper punishment and forgiveness.

You Are What You Think

If boundaries are not set and consistently reinforced with appropriate consequences, no society can survive for long.

4. It is a terrible catastrophe when things are not as we would like them to be.
   C.R.T. Position: Agree that this thought is irrational.

5. Unhappiness is the result of external events and happenings that are forced on us and that we have no control over.
   C.R.T. Position: Agree that this thought is irrational.

6. We should be greatly concerned about dangerous and fearful things and must center our thinking on them until the danger is passed.
   C.R.T. Position: Agree that this thought is irrational.

7. It is easier to avoid difficulties and responsibilities in life than to face them.
   C.R.T. Position: Agree that this thought is irrational.

8. We need someone or something stronger than ourselves to rely on.
   C.R.T. Position: The individual absolutely needs Christ in his life as Lord and Savior in order to successfully live a fulfilled, rational, happy life. Afterall, Christ is the Author of Truth, rationality, and love. "For in Him we live, and move, and have our being" (Acts 17:28a).

9. Because something greatly influenced us in the past, it must determine our present behavior; the influence of the past cannot be overcome.
   C.R.T. Position: The consequences of sin leave their mark on the individual: negative attitudes, bad habits, genetic effects, environmental disabilities, disease; all effect us. Of greatest negative influence is Satan who woos us to lust and sin. If Satan is Lord, then our past cannot be successfully overcome. Christ is the answer!

Neil C. Roth

10. What other people do is vitally important to us, and we should make every effort to change them to be the way we think they should be.

    <u>C.R.T</u>. <u>Position</u>: As Christians, we are to be vitally interested in seeing them find Christ and be changed by the renewing of their minds and through commitment to Christ as Lord and Savior.

11. There is one perfect solution to every problem, and if it is not found, the result will be terrible.

    <u>C.R.T</u>. <u>Position</u>: For the Christian, God's desired will is of prime importance, and when not fulfilled, can lead to less than positive results and often to spiritual, emotional, and physical bankruptcy.

12. One has virtually no control over his emotions; he is their victim and cannot help how he feels.

    C.R.T. Position: Many emotional reactions are the by-product of stress and organic etiologies. We can, in large measure, control the life-stress factors by rational thinking, but need medical and Divine help for many of the organically caused emotional reactions.

C.R.T. Psychology and Therapy is formulated on a similar philosophical and methodological base as R.E.T. Psychology but features several important distinctions:

1. C.R.T. is Biblically-oriented and relies on the precepts and principles of the Word of God as constants.
2. The motivation to change thinking and behavior comes not only from within man himself (a will to change), but more importantly, from God Himself in the Person of Jesus Christ. You see, the physician of our soul must never become man, but to many, he already has. Dr. Thomas Szaaz warns us "that the psychiatrist displaces the priest as the physician of the soul."[16] Christ is the Great Physician and man merely an ally for God's purposes.

You Are What You Think

3. That immoral intentions, thoughts, and behaviors are sins, and that sin, that spirit of unbelief and rebellion against God and His law, is irrational thinking, and more: it is our willing to be above God and His laws.

For this reason, sin is more than irrationality and must be dealt with as sin.

Figure 5 portrays the C.R.T. Model of the Human Mind which describes the various qualitative functions that occur within the brain, centering in the cerebral cortex. Although simplistic in design, the model points out the differences of thinking and behavior that are by-products of the individual's loyalty to lust or love, unrighteousness or righteousness, Satan or Christ.

Perhaps comparing this model's awareness zones with Freud's Model of the Mind would be instructive. The C.R.T. zone of conscious awareness is partially analogous to Freud's id and ego. The C.R.T. zone of unconscious awareness is somewhat comparable to Freud's superego. Freud's pre-conscious mind and the C.R.T. zone of impending conscious awareness are essentially the same function.

Our brain is more than a computer, however. It is the home for our personality, or soul (psyche), and has the capacity to exert willful behavior. Man's will, and his brain, need to be placed under the expert and loving control of the Creator, Jesus Christ. Remember that the brain, like a chain, is only as strong as its weakest think! This is why C.R.T. Psychology holds that your thinking needs to be challenged by the Word of God (see precepts and principles, chapters 5 & 7), and if not found to be in accord with His Word, then you have the responsibility to challenge and renew your thinking.

Dr. Charles L. Allen, prominent southern minister and author, said: "Put God and others first, get something into your mind greater than yourself. In so doing, you lose yourself, selfishness is blotted out; instead of making ourselves miserable by what we do not have, we begin to gain the blessed thrill of what we can give."[17]

Next, comes commitment of yourself to rational Christian living through allegiance to Jesus Christ and His Word. Then you will be ready to discover the next C.R.T. cardinal insight. But remember, YOU CAN LEARN TO CONTROL YOUR THINKING AND EMOTIONS!

139

Neil C. Roth

Cerebral Cortex

> (ZONE OF CONSCIOUS AWARENESS (CA)
>
> (Lust or Love)
>
> Often jointly controlled
> <u>(see James 1:8)</u>
>
> <u>Spiritual Mind</u>...Rational thinking & loving behavior. Jesus Christ is Lord and Savior.
> <u>Carnal Mind</u>...Irrational thinking & selfish behavior. Satan is Lord and destroyer.
>
> ---
>
> (ZONE OF IMPENDING CONSCIOUS AWARENESS) (ICA)
> Often experienced in anxiety states or impending insight
>
> ---
>
> (ZONE OF UNCONSCIOUS AWARENESS) (UA)
> Often revealed by dreams, visions, hypnosis, therapy, conviction by Holy Spirit
>
> STORED MEMORIES OF OUGHTS AND SHOULDS
> (Temperamental Residuals and Carnal Nature)
>
> Voice of Spirit of Satan   Voice of Holy Spirit
>
> <u>CONSCIENCE</u>
>
> <u>Double-Mindedness</u>   <u>Single-Mindedness</u>
>
> God-Satan conflict over   Doubts settled; God-shaped blank
>   values & morality.   filled.
> Unrest because of   Peace & joy in Christ & Holy Spirit.
>   God-shaped blank
>   unfilled. (Source of
>   major psychosomatic
>   stimulation).

<u>The Locus of the Human Psyche is in the Brain</u>
<u>Control Center--the Cerebral Cortex</u>
<u>The Body is Simply a Receptor</u>
<u>of Cognitive Stimulation from the Brain</u>

Figure 5 C.R.T. MODEL OF THE MIND

You Are What You Think

C.R.T. CARDINAL INSIGHT NO. 4--YOU CAN FIND YOUR LIFE BY LOSING IT!

What a paradox this insight is! Can you imagine finding something by losing it? Yes, Jesus says just that:

> Then said Jesus unto his disciples, If any man will come after me, let him deny himself, and take up his cross, and follow me. For whosoever will save his life shall lose it: and whosoever will lose his life for my sake shall find it. For what is a man profited, if he shall gain the whole world, and lose his own soul? or what shall a man give in exchange for his soul (Matthew 16:24-26)?

Our Lord is calling upon us to choose Him and his Kingdom above every other priority in life. The steps are deceptively simple. We are to just say no to sin and no to making self number one (no longer lusting after the carnal world priorities); and then, yes to Christ! This yes, in reality, means elevating the Lord Jesus Christ to His rightful position as number One--Lord and Savior (loving God with all that is within our frame, no longer lusting after the carnal world)!

Wayne Oates describes this unique relationship of faith as "fidelity to a Person--Jesus Christ!" He states that "A demonstrated relationship of trust demands consistent persons for the identification of the growing person."[18] Our Lord is consistently consistent!

Richard Foster, author of <u>Celebration of Discipline</u>, and more recently, <u>Freedom of Simplicity</u>, joyfully exclaims:

> It is wonderful, this losing of one's self through a perpetual vision of the Holy. We are catapulted into something infinitely larger and more real than our petty existence. A blazing God-consciousness frees us from self-consciousness. It is freedom. It is joy. It is life.
>
> I cannot stress enough how essential this quality is to true simplicity of life. It is the only thing that will allow us to hold the interest of others above self-interest. It saves us from self-pity. It lifts the burden of concern over having a proper image. It frees us from bondage to the opinions of others.[19]

Neil C. Roth

Jesus goes on and describes this paradox in question: You can find your life by losing it! Perhaps, thinking of sowing and reaping will clarify Jesus' meaning. The farmer's seed is planted and it must die before it is ready to be resurrected into new life and produce fruit. A contradiction? Humanly speaking, yes! But remember, our Lord is the Creator and with Him nothing is impossible except--yes, one thing is impossible for God to do: He cannot do our deciding for us! He cannot repent, believe, or obey for us! He does lead, convict, convince, encourage, admonish, chastise, and bless us by, and through, His precious Holy Spirit. But, obviously, we must do our part and that is to die upon our own cross.

Soren Kierkegaard once said: "Purity is to will one thing." Our salvation is found in finally discovering that it is not "I" but Christ! Paul states it like this: "I am crucified with Christ: nevertheless I live; yet not I, but Christ liveth in me: and the life which I now live in the flesh I live by the faith of the Son of God, who loved me, and gave himself for me" (Galatians 2:20). The Apostle is emphatic--Jesus lives in him and helps him control every facet of mind, soul, and body. How? By Christ's marvelous Spirit of love.

But Paul provides us more insight as he speaks to the Church at Rome:

> Knowing this, that our old man (and old woman) is crucified with Him (here is our crucifixion of self), that the body of sin (its effectual power over us) might be destroyed (done away with) that henceforth we should not serve sin. For he that is dead (hath died to sin and self) is freed (justified) from sin (Romans 6:6, 7).

Truly then, to lose ourselves means we must step aside as the "preeminent person" and pledge our loving allegiance to the Preeminent Christ. Why should we do this? Simply, because our old nature cannot serve or please God. The Bible states: "The natural man receiveth not the things of the spirit of God...neither can he know them..." (I Corinthians 2:14).

In addition, the Bible teaches that we must crucify the old man, not patch him up! You see, God is not in the reformation business. He is only interested in regeneration as a change-agent! If we do not lay our egos aside, then God will lay us aside. But, praise God, there is absolutely no risk in abandoning ourselves to God! For in reality, nothing that we lose

You Are What You Think

by yielding to Christ is worth keeping. Fortunately, only when we die to all there is about us, can we then begin to live with Christ in us.

God is satisfied with His plan of redemption--namely that Christ's sacrifice on the Cross settled the sin question! We should be satisfied with what satisfies our heavenly Father. A man once said: "Born once, die twice; born twice, die once!" To be born again means we die out to self and become renewed by God's Spirit. When born-again, you will find that God will give new vision and understanding (II Corinthians 4:6); a new heart full of love (Jeremiah 31:33); and a completely changed will, with new determination and motives (Hebrews 13:20, 21).[20] You can find your life in Christ, if you will lose it. Be reminded though, God's Word warns that the direction we are going when death overtakes us, we will be going forever!

C.R.T. CARDINAL INSIGHT NO. 5--YOU CAN LEARN TO FACE REALITY WITHOUT FEAR!

Have you ever wondered why so many millions continue to choose attitudes and behaviors that are so self-destructive and irrational? For one thing, the individual's reluctance to accept responsibility, coupled with faulty thinking regarding existential matters, all contribute to this confusing dilemma. At this very moment, millions could be saying, "Let me off of this train of life for I am bored, unfulfilled, and most of all fearful!"

Certainly being fearful can largely explain boredom and futility in the lives of many. In a deeper sense, however, the fear of facing reality squarely is essentially the product of the fear "to be!" Fulfilling one's true destiny and potential can never be life's prime goal until the real self is actualized in Jesus Christ. It is He only who can call us "to be" and equip us with the courage to courageously take charge of our "being." (See chapter one, for more discussion on fear).

The Apostle Paul reaffirmed our total dependency upon Jesus, as our source of personhood, when he declared to the Athenians on Mars Hill: "For in Him we live, and move, and have our being; as certain also of your own poets have said, for we are also his offspring" (Acts 17:28). Jesus

143

echoed forth the same existential claim when He proclaimed: "I am the way, the truth, and the life: no man cometh unto the Father, but by me" (John 14:6).

That our very existence comes from God should not need to be proved to anyone. We exist because He exists. "Show me where God is and I'll believe in Him" said the atheist to the Christian. "Show me where He is not" declared the Christian, "and I'll become an atheist!" Furthermore, we bring nothing into the world: we surely will take nothing out. While here, we are recipients of God's blessing and benevolence (evidences of His being), adding only our individual talents to the God-given resources to produce our intriguing but flawed technology. It only takes some natural disaster, or a dramatic climatic deviation, to again remind us that we depend solely upon our heavenly Father for all of life, <u>including</u> existential meaning!

Just after our Lord told Thomas that He (Jesus) was the example to follow (the way), the source of all knowledge and wisdom (the truth), and the source of all energy and sustenance (the life), Philip asked Him to show the disciples the Father, Himself (God, the Father)! This question was probably prompted by Jesus' statement that no person could come to the Father except through Him. Apparently, this was evidence of Philip's deep yearning to find the ultimate reality, God! Jesus would not deny him, or the disciples, closure on this most vital question that man can ask. He affirms that "...he that hath seen me hath seen the Father..." (John 14:9).

Of paramount importance is the wondrous fact that Jesus Christ, being ultimate Reality (God, Himself), has invited us to become his children of the Light. Surely, fear resides in the unknown dark recesses of vague, yet remote experience. Jesus said, unequivocally, that He would enable us to walk through life without fear. Why? So, that we might show others an infinitely, more excellent way of living. God has chosen men and women, like you and me, to lovingly represent Him to other persons. We are also to be a "cut above" in character. Our character is made up by what we stand for, whereas our reputation is gaged by what we fall for. Christ has called us to stand for something-Him and His Kingdom! If we do not, we are likely to fall for anything that the kingdom of this world may have to offer.

John describes our human love as being made perfect by God's love: all so that we might have a holy boldness here, as we witness of Jesus before all

You Are What You Think

men, and, before God in the day of judgment. Beyond all explaining, we are made perfect in the love of Christ which instills in us a holy courage to fearlessly face life squarely. "There is no fear in love; but perfect love (the love of Christ) casteth out fear" (I John 4:18a).

The source of ultimate fear in all men is the dread that no one really loves us. My dear daughter, Laurie, always so sensitive to the anxious and lonely, wrote a beautiful song called "All Alone."

Praise God, we are loved by Him. We are not alone! Our task is to learn to believe and trust God's Word which is based upon the theme that we are deeply loved by Him! Brammer and Montgomery, in Healing Love, chose "perfect love casts out fear" as their primary thesis. They reflected: "This healing love causes the joyful expansion rather than the fearful constriction of the human personality....When we feel deeply loved, understood, and accepted in the core of our being, then our fears are healed changes and we find ourselves on the road to actualizing."[21]

The word actualization is a commonly used adjective which describes a process of human psychological, and spiritual growth and development which moves toward becoming one's best self. Ultimately, our best self is that self constructed in the image of Jesus Christ through the witness and empowerment of the Holy Spirit.

When Christ truly inhabits our soul, we can face life realistically and without fear for the very first time. To be sure, the greatness of our fear shows us the littleness of our faith in Him who loves us! This newfound freedom from fear also means that we can shed our ego-defensive devices that have been developing over a long while. The fear of reality is the taproot of all of our ego-defenses, and once severed, our basic integrity emerges like a breath of fresh, clean air. Some common ego-defenses are: rationalization, projection, undoing, compensation, fantasy, displacement, repression, reaction formation, identification, insulation, denial of reality, etc.

When we link ourselves to Christ, we no longer have to fear failure. Oh yes, we would wish to do our best, but realize that God looks at our intentions and obedience, not on our success-ratios. Thus, rather than fearing to fail, we use our failures to positively build upon. By failing (and sometimes often), we learn to assess life honestly, realizing that mistakes are normal happenings in life (Murphy's Law!). The Christian's greatest

Neil C. Roth

tribute to Christ is not in never failing, but in rising up, with His help, everytime we do fail! Hence, the ego-defenses of rationalization, projection, and compensation are gradually replaced by our honest and courageous acceptance of who we really are: fallible, imperfect human beings who have no need to be afraid of anything, because we are loved by our Creator and energized by His Holy Spirit!

Just a word here about perfectionism, that nemesis of nearly all humans. We often lay on ourselves this "trip" of being perfect because prideful self is exerting its will. In the perfection that Jesus calls us to, God is at the center. E. Stanley Jones said, "Since every self-centered person is automatically self-frustrated, so every perfectionist, always living in a state of self-reference, is automatically frustrated."[22]

Jesus offers men grace and power to move on to His perfection. His perfection, for us, is a relative perfection, "relative to something higher than itself, God--it can be realized and yet not realized. The bud may be perfect as a bud, but not perfect as a flower. Ours is to be a growing perfection, growing forever,"[23] being perfected in Christ's love.

The same is true when we experience guilt, hostility, inferiority feelings, or disappointments. Remember that Jesus Christ meets us where we are as real persons! His perfect love, in the form of His Holy Spirit, gives us the existential courage to face our sin, inadequacies, and frustrations forthrightly and honestly. This is all experienced without defensiveness or fear of being ostracized by our Redeemer.

A wise man once declared that "the only thing worse than a quitter is the man who is afraid to begin." Are you afraid to entrust your life with the only One who loves you without condition? William Booth, the founder of the Salvation Army, once remarked that "the greatness of a man's power is the measure of his surrender." The surrender he refers to is that which surrounds our courage to place our past, present, and future life into Christ's hands. It means that we truly trust Him for the physical, intellectual, emotional, and spiritual resources to face life (reality) with courage and love.

Furthermore, life, like a mirror, never returns to us more than we give. William James, the great English psychologist, once said that: "The great use of life is to spend it for something that will out-last it." Praise God, because He lives, we can face tomorrow (reality)! Because He lives all fear

You Are What You Think

is gone! Thankfully, our relationship with the living Christ will outlast this life, but our courage to trust Him will remain as an eternal memorial to His redemptive and regenerative love!

The first stanza from Frances Ridley Havergal's poem "Reality" captures the majesty of our Lord's unfolding Being:

Reality, reality.
Lord Jesus Christ Thou art to me!
From the spectral mist and the driving clouds,
From the shifting shadows and phantom crowds
From unreal words and unreal lives,
Where truth with falsehood feebly strives;
From the passings away, the chance and change,
Flickerings, vanishings, swift and strange,
I turn to my glorious rest in Thee,
Who are the Grand Reality!"[24]

So, with assurance, you can learn to face reality without fear! David, King of Israel, echoed with confidence this great conviction: "The Lord is my light and my salvation; whom shall I fear? The Lord is the strength of life; of whom shall I be afraid" (Psalm 27:1)? No one, when the Grand Reality is actualized in our hearts!

C.R.T. CARDINAL INSIGHT NO. 6--YOU CAN LEARN TO LOVE AND BE LOVED!

Shostrom and Montgomery have proposed a definition for the highest level of New Testament love called Agape. They state, "This could be translated as spontaneous, altruistic love that involves unselfishly willing the highest good of another. It is a love that cherishes, affirms, and respects the uniqueness of another person."[25] Their definition emphasizes the key insights necessary to the achieving of love in every sector of one's life. To be sure, love is a learned response: "We love him, because He first loved us" (I John 4:19).

Similarly, we learned to love other humans because other humans showed us love. Parents, siblings, friends, all were ambassadors of God's love to us in varying degrees of quantity and quality. The characteristic

Neil C. Roth

of selfishness was revealed to us, in its true egotistical light, by love. Of profound influence, of course, is the realization that Jesus Christ (God's Son) supremely loves us and backed it up with His life. This highest example of divine altruism overwhelms the most calloused individual who has become disenchanted with the futility of selfishness and pride. Without question, our doubts are finally dealt with at the foot of the cross when we identify with Jesus as our own personal redeemer! For as Christ loved us above every other thing, so we must learn to love Him above all things! He must be our Lord over all or else He is not Lord at all!

Through His example, we can learn what the fruits of His Spirit really mean in a human life. Jesus, by in-living our lives will produce an out-living quality that will, by nature, be loving, agape style. Tragically, many who claim Christ, do not evidence a religion that is forbearing, tender, kind, and patient with others. Without these graces, can we say that we are His? Some people, claiming to be followers of the Way, seem to preserve their religion in vinegar. Under the general label of love, Paul described the evidence of Christ's indwelling Spirit to be seen in behavior (as well as attitudes) characterized by "love, joy, peace, longsuffering, gentleness (kindness), goodness, faith, meekness, temperance (self-control): against such there is no law" (Galatians 5:22, 23).

Can you imagine a land without law? This could only happen if all people were in Christ! We can lift up duty as our prime motivator in life, and do things sometimes quite well. But only Christ's love, shed abroad in our hearts, can motivate us to live beautiful lives. The song, "Let the Beauty of Jesus be Seen in Me," expresses a reality that is worth the claiming if only we will! His beauty, a collage of love's attributes, will make us sensitive to the sorrows and pains of our fellow human beings. Unfortunately, some men claim to hate vice so much that they easily forget to love others as themselves.

How then, can we learn to love as we ought? First, by realizing that Christ loves us as persons and wants nothing less than His best for our lives. His best encompasses salvation, which includes renunciation of self and sin, acceptance of Himself as Lord and Savior, and obedience to His Word and Spirit. Also sanctification, which includes our growth and development in all sectors of our being as we are influenced and led by His Spirit. In addition to being born of the Spirit, it entails being filled

You Are What You Think

with the Spirit. It is, in reality, being filled with all the fullness of God! In essence, sanctification is as much God's will for Christians as is salvation His will for the unsaved. Paul prayed that our Lord, "The very God of peace sanctify you wholly; and I pray God your whole spirit and soul and body be preserved blameless unto (at) the coming of our Lord Jesus Christ" (I Thessalonians 5:23).

Here then, is the acid test of our love for Christ and others: that we keep ourselves pure and unspotted from the love of this world (I John 2:15-17), and learn to live and love in and through God's Holy Spirit. The Apostle Paul confirms the enablement by saying, "Faithful is he that calleth you, who also will do it" (I Thessalonians 5:24). Do what? Sanctify you wholly! God will not abandon you but will continue to "Make you perfect in every good work to do His will, working in you that which is wellpleasing in His sight, through Jesus Christ; to whom be glory for ever and ever" (Hebrews 13:21).

The Golden Rule, which urges that we should do unto others as we would have them do unto us (Matthew 7:12; Luke 6:31) is, in reality, another statement of loving our neighbor as ourselves. Paradoxically, we can only begin to appreciate ourselves, as God intends, when we are transformed into persons that are born of the Spirit of God (John 3:5), and filled with the Spirit of God (Acts 5:32; Ephesians 5:18). Then, and only then, can we move toward actualizing God's love to others, in the finest sense of God's intention. So, at this point, when Christ overwhelms our wills, we can extend to others the agape love that "cherishes, affirms, and respects the uniqueness of another person."[26]

Up to here, we have been talking about the pre-conditions of loving as Christ intends. But, once prepared, then we must practice loving, for ungiven love will soon turn into narcissistic love, and breed pride and lust anew. Hildebrand wrote pointedly: "In order to receive love, we must be mature enough to give it. If we find ourselves demanding love without being able to express it in return, we are emotionally ill."[27]

E. Stanley Jones strongly feels that true agape love is firmly rooted in our hearts when we can say "we" instead of "I" or "they." He explains:

Neil C. Roth

The center of the Christian faith is a "we" relationship.(*)
Up to the New Testament the relationship of God with man
was "I"--"They." God commanded; they obeyed. The relationship
was through law. Then came the Incarnation. God literally sat
where we sat. He identified Himself with man until at the cross
that identification became complete--He became identified with
our sins, "became sin for us." There the "I"--"they" merged into
the "we"--completely. The relationship was not through law, but
through love.[28]

This "we" relationship that exists between God, Jesus, and ourselves
leaves us no alternative than to view all human relationships in the same
light. Nothing goes right when we say "I" or "they." The family, or married
couple are still feuding when "I" reigns. The problem of blaming cripples
our potential freedom when we proclaim "they are at fault!" Dr. Jones tells
the story of a boy who pumped the pipe organ by hand behind the scenes.
He said to the organist after the church service,

'We played well today, didn't we?' And the organist in disdain
said, 'We? I played well.' The next Sunday the organist sat down
to play, pressed the keys, but nothing happened. The organist
sat there nonplussed and helpless when a voice from behind the
curtain said, 'Is it we or I?' When the organist said 'we' the music
went on.[29]

Truly, if we deny the "we" vertically with God, or the "we" horizontally
with men, we will not long be able to tolerate the "I." We must master the
"I" or it will master us!

Acrostically speaking, Christ's love is <u>L</u>ife's <u>O</u>nly <u>V</u>iable <u>E</u>xperience,
without which we shall dry up and die. Love is a statement of sowing
and reaping--doing unto others--losing ourselves to find ourselves--being
crucified and resurrected with Christ!

---

* Jones refers to Jesus' prayer to His Father in John 17:21: "That they all may be one;
as thou, Father, art in me, and I in thee, that they also may be one in us: that the
world may believe that thou hast sent me."

You Are What You Think

Yes, you can learn to love by "being" with Love, Himself--Jesus Christ! Then He, through His Spirit, will teach and lead you in the art of loving. Someone put it this way:

God is the source of love.
Christ is the proof of love.
Service is the expression of love.
Boldness is the outcome of love.[30]

C.R.T. CARDINAL INSIGHT NO. 7--YOU CAN LEARN TO BECOME A PROBLEM--SOLVER!

Our final C.R.T. Cardinal Insight deals with the practical action phase of our living. But before we could arrive at this step, we had to have some crises-oriented cognitive, volitional, emotional, and spiritual foundations laid down! We will to change, stop blaming others, and assume responsibility for our own attitudes, thoughts, emotions, and actions. Then, we learn to control our thinking and emotions by submitting ourselves to the ministry of the precepts and principles of the Living Word. In obedience to the Lord, we realize that we can only save our real self (soul--life) by losing it in Christ Jesus. Praise God, we learned that with Christ in our hearts, we can face reality without fear or the use of destructive ego-defensive strategies. Then, we are freed to begin learning how to love as Jesus loved, without fear and reluctance, but with confidence and courage.

Our day is not the only day of accountability. Men have always looked for examples of holy living that were more than just talk. The saying, "The proof is in the pudding," in some form or another, has probably always been around in the world. And such proof of our true character and commitment to Christ can be only evidenced by the loving quality of our deeds before men! Paul expressed this idea to the Corinthian Christians by saying: "Ye are our epistle written in our hearts, known and read of all men" (II Corinthians 3:2). Imagine your attitudes and deeds being broadcast on every billboard and newspaper front page--yes, epistle known and read!

The vital bottom-line question is, "How can I get off dead center and be an active, loving, witnessing, and joyful Christian?" I am thoroughly

Neil C. Roth

convinced that the secret is to be found in your attitude toward yourself, God, others, and the perplexing problems, whatever they might be. Once we learn to see ourselves as God's children, who are in the process of wholistic growth and development, and soon view others in the same light (that is, in the process of becoming--not all are Christians), then we will learn to view life and its problems as an opportunity, not as a handicap. In fact, Henry J. Kaiser, of World War II shipyard fame, echoed this idea by stating: "Problems are only opportunities in work clothes."[31]

The Apostle Paul reminds us of a very cogent principle when it comes to dealing with life's challenges. He said: "Be not overcome of evil, but overcome evil with good" (Romans 12:21). In essence, it is always infinitely better to light a candle rather than to curse the darkness. When we are through blaming and ready to go to work on our problems, the first critical step has been taken. When we shed our sin and change the spiritual direction of our lives, the second major hurdle is encompassed. But what about the weights that all so easily beset us (see Hebrews 12:1)?

These problems (weights) are usually associated with ignorance, or lacking skills, and can be dealt with and solved if we develop a plan of attack. Assuming you <u>will</u> to change and improve, the next step is to realize that change will not come easily. It is hard work to move from one negative habit, or attitude, to those which are positive.

Centuries ago, Aristotle observed, "We are what we repeatedly do." This insight, though not surfacely profound, should shed some light on the fact, that in order to adequately move from hindrance to freedom, we must be willing to break old, carnal ways by replacing them with new, spiritual ones. Indeed, Paul was a possibility thinker when he said, "I can do all things through Christ which strengtheneth me" (Philippians 4:13).

With Christ as our prime Motivator, we can begin to dream big dreams that are centered on solving the problems of our life experience. Robert Browning, in his poem "Andrea Del Sarto, put it so beautifully: "Ah, but a man's reach should exceed his grasp, or what's a heaven for?" Frankly, I do not believe we are ready to solve our personal, or world problems, until we allow God to challenge our being with a dream of what could be! Truly,

You Are What You Think

the degree of a man's success in life is directly related to the quality and scope of his dreams. Jesus is waiting right now to have us share our dreams with Him. He said, "Whatsoever ye shall ask in my name, that will I do, that the Father may be glorified in the Son. If ye shall ask anything in my Name, I will do it" (John 14:13, 14). Of course, He will cause them to be in the first place if we are seeking His perfect, desired will for our lives.

About 770 B.C., Joel, a prophet of the Lord to Judah, voiced these words of the Lord:

> And it shall come to pass afterward (after Christ's resurrection from the dead), that I will pour out my spirit upon all flesh; and your sons and your daughters shall prophesy (witness to God's grace), your old men shall dream dreams, your young men shall see visions" (Joel 2:28).

If these signs seem somewhat symptomatic of psychosis, please do not be alarmed! When we are fully under the control of God's Spirit, we are not possessing the spirit of fear, which is an overriding characteristic of psychotic reactions. Praise God, we do possess the spirit "of power, and of love, and of a sound mind" (II Timothy 1:7a). So, we need not withdraw from receiving all the fulness of God's Spirit for fear that we will be viewed as "wierdos" or the like. Our behavior, if fully under God's control, will always adorn the Gospel of Christ. That is, Christ living in you will cause you to live like Him in every loving and rational way.

Now, when attempting to solve any problem, keep these principles in mind:

1. <u>Every problem has a potential solution</u> whether it be physical, intellectual, emotional, or spiritual in nature.
2. Remember, your desire and belief (you can <u>will</u> to change!) that <u>you</u> <u>can</u> <u>change</u>, coupled with God's confidence in you and commitment to assist, sets the stage for changing--solving your problem/s.
3. <u>Relax</u> (tension does not help!) and <u>pray</u> to Jesus Christ for help in analyzing your problem and for His perfect solution. Rely upon God's help as reflected in the 73rd Psalm: "Thou shalt guide

Neil C. Roth

me with thy counsel" (vs. 24a). In most cases, the Bible already contains His answer to your prayer. Check the concordance of your Bible for topical references that center on your specific problem. Program your mind with His Word!

4. <u>Plan your work!</u> Assemble the pertinent information you need to evaluate the best course of action. Do not fail to include all pertinent possibilities (seeing competent advisers or counselors can be helpful here). Also, remember to check out your personal opinions or judgments against facts (as reflected by the Word of God, testimony of others, experiential confirmation, etc.), and be sure your information is valid, reliable, adequate, and rational. Also, it is always wise to be tentative in your interpretations until enough data is available for confirmation. Honest doubt is not heresy but simply reflects an attitude of openness and potential for growth. Remember, too, that we humans have a tendency to generalize in terms of extremes!

By "planning your work" I mean, set some realistic short and long-term goals that will provide you with an adequate structural and procedural framework to base your goal description upon. Nobody ever hit anything without aiming at it! Surely, if you have not decided on where you are going, you are lost before you start. Confine yourself to the possible. E. Stanley Jones says: "A great many make themselves miserable with worries about goals which they cannot attain. They have laid on themselves the task of setting the whole world right and when they cannot do it, they are frustrated and worried. Confine yourself to the accomplishable tasks around you and <u>accept the discipline of the possible</u>."[32]

Dr. Jones is not denouncing long-range planning or God-given dreams of a better world, but is saying we must work with what we are, what we have, and where we are. Jesus promised "He that is faithful in that which is least is faithful also in much" (Luke 16:10).

List these goals, and procedures to fulfill them, on paper. This will help you clarify your thinking and provide a reference for later consultation. This objectifies your problem or goal. When

You Are What You Think

our problems or goals remain subjective, we fail to deal with them forthrightly.

5. As you process your thoughts, <u>keep objective and listen to your intuition and insight</u>. God's Holy Spirit works through these mediums to reveal His truth and will.

6. <u>Work your plan, now!</u> Set your mind and heart on immediate action. Eld once said, "Knowing what our goal is and desiring to reach it doesn't bring us closer to it. Doing something does!"[33] The first two letters in the word goal are "GO." The Bible is continually urging us to act now because we may not have an earthly tomorrow.

   The wise Benjamin Franklin once remarked that "You may delay, but time will not." The Lord is calling us to be participators, not spectators; redeemers of time and persons, not destroyers; problem-solvers, not problem-makers!

7. <u>Keep praying for God's direction and will</u>! Sometimes progress will be slow but keep in mind that it has little to do with speed but much to do with direction. Emerson said, "Aim at the unattainable so that your work will have an ideal direction even though it never achieves perfection."[34]

8. <u>Practice</u> <u>consistently</u>! Any action, when consistently repeated, tends to be reinforced and becomes habit. Bad habits are extinguished by practicing behaviors that are the building blocks for new positive habits. Keep in mind that it is easier to prevent bad habits than to break them. But with Christ's help, you can change. It was Aristotle who said, "The hardest victory is the victory over self." With that victory won, through and in Christ, the fringe problem-areas will give way one by one to positive growth in all areas of our lives!

   Someone once declared, "I cannot explain the wind, but I can hoist a sail." You can hoist your sail--become a Problem-Solver! With Jesus Christ at your side--you and He are a majority!

Neil C. Roth

CHAPTER REVIEW AT A GLANCE

(Insight Hierarchy)
The Seven Cardinal C.R.T. Insights

1. If you <u>will</u> to change, you <u>can</u>!
2. You can <u>stop blaming</u>, and <u>assume responsibility</u>!
3. You can learn to <u>control your thinking and emotions</u>!
4. You can <u>find your life by losing it</u>!
5. You can learn to <u>face reality without fear</u>!
6. You can learn to <u>love and be loved</u>!
7. You can learn to <u>become a problem-solver</u>!

FOOTNOTES

1. Doan, Eleanor L. <u>The Speaker's Sourcebook</u>. Grand Rapids: Zondervan Publishing House, 1962, p. 291.
2. <u>Webster's New World Dictionary</u>, College Edition. New York: The World Publishing Co., 1968, p. 756.
3. Doan. <u>op</u>. <u>cit</u>., p. 283.
4. Graham, Billy, <u>Peace with God</u>. Garden City, New York: Doubleday and Co., Inc., 1953, p. 118.
5. Steele, Daniel. <u>Love Enthroned</u>. Salem, Ohio: Reprinted by Rev. H. E. Schmul, 1961, p. 18.
6. <u>Ibid</u>., p. 19.
7. Shostrom, Everett L. and Montgomery, Dan. <u>Healing Love</u>. Nashville: Abingdon, 1978, p. 66.
8. <u>Ibid</u>., p. 66.
9. Doan, <u>op</u>. <u>cit</u>., p. 73.
10. "In Memorium" by Lord Alfred Tennyson. <u>Poetry of the Victorian Period</u>, Edited by George Benjamin Woods. Chicago: Scott, Foresman, and Co., 1930, p. 81.
11. Dickson, Paul. <u>The Official Rules</u>. New York: Delacorte Press, 1978.
12. Titus, Harold H. <u>Living Issues in Philosophy</u>, Third Edition. New York: American Book Co., 1959, pp. 36, 37.
13. <u>Ibid</u>., p. 37.
14. Ellis, Albert. <u>Reason and Emotion in Psychotherapy</u>. Secaucus, N. J., Lyle Stuart, 1962, pp. 60-88.
15. Dickson. <u>op</u>. <u>cit</u>.
16. Szaaz, Thomas. <u>The Myth of Psychotherapy</u>. Garden City, N. J.: Doubleday/Anchor Press, 1978, p. 32.
17. Allen, Charles L. <u>God's Psychiatry</u>. Old Tappan, N. J.: Fleming H. Revell Co., 1953, p. 80.
18. Oates, Wayne E. <u>The Psychology of Religion</u>. Waco, Texas: Word Books, Publisher, 1973, p. 281-282.
19. Foster, Richard J. <u>Freedom of Simplicity</u>. San Francisco: Harper & Row, Publishers, 1981, p. 96.

Neil C. Roth

20. Graham. op. cit., pp. 137, 138.
21. Shostrom and Montgomery. op. cit., pp. 68-70.
22. Jones, E. Stanley. Growing Spiritually. Nashville: Abingdon-Cokesbury Press, 1953, p. 8.
23. Ibid, p. 8.
24. Havergal, Frances R. Poem: "Reality," Edited by Caroline M. Hill. The World's Great Religious Poetry. New York: MacMillan Co., 1923, p. 325.
25. Shostrom and Montgomery. op. cit., pp. 68-69.
26. Ibid, p. 69.
27. Allee, G. Franklin. Evangelistic Illustrations. Chicago: Moody Press, 1961, p. 242.
28. Jones, E. Stanley. How to be a Transformed Person. Nashville: Abingdon-Cokesbury, 1951, p. 257.
29. Ibid, p. 258.
30. Doan. op. cit., p. 154.
31. Ibid, p. 202.
32. Jones. How to be a Transformed Person. op. cit., p. 163.
33. Doan. op. cit., p. 112.
34. Ibid, p. 112.

CHAPTER SEVEN

TEN C.R.T. PROGRESS PRINCIPLES FOR PRACTICAL CHRISTIAN LIVING

> "No man has ever been greater than he
> longed to be, though some have been
> greater than they realized."

We are nearly ready to look closely at the ten C.R.T. Progress Principles of the Christian life. But before we do, allow me to make several observations regarding man's psychological and spiritual states, as reflected by the Word of God.

It is essential to understand that our Lord is vitally interested in our emotional health. The Scriptures are replete with numerous indications of God's concern in this regard. He spoke through Isaiah and gave us perhaps the greatest promise regarding emotional stability ever uttered. "Thou wilt keep him in perfect peace, whose mind is stayed on thee: because he trusteth in thee" (Isaiah 26:3).

Later in the book of Isaiah, God said, "Look unto me, and be ye saved, all the ends of the earth: for I am God, and there is none else" (Isaiah 45:22).

As we begin to peruse together the C.R.T. Progress Principles, please keep in mind the psychological, as well as, the spiritual implications of our study. For, clearly the successful maintenance of our mental health is directly related to the degree of our concentration upon the precepts and principles of God's Word.

Neil C. Roth

Peace can only be won when we are letting His ways totally infiltrate our being. But, more importantly, we must singularly see Him, without hint of defection from loyalty or love. An impossible dream? Yes, if we do not thoroughly commit ourselves to the rigorous discipline that the to-be-discussed C.R.T. Progress Principles will demand of us! When we finally submit to disciplining ourselves, God will then join us and share our burden of existential adjustment. D. L. Moody once said that "The Holy Spirit is God at work." Put another way, our Lord has said: Peace will come when you discipline your thinking and learn to trust me, and my precepts and principles, without hesitancy.

In addition, it must be strongly noted that the Christian life is much more than law or rational thinking. Indeed, our ability to keep the law is flawed by our very nature. Earlier, the Apostle Paul was quoted saying: "For all have sinned, and come short of the glory of God" (Romans 3:23). Paul was, himself, once burdened by the sin nature (the love of the world as a result of this nature) and discovered that only the "new birth" in Jesus Christ could bring him victory over this sin and its powerful hold on his attitudes. The process of being "born-again" (this is Jesus' way--see John 3) is sequentially stated again in the book of Romans:

> That if thou shalt confess with thy mouth the Lord Jesus (acknowledge Jesus as Lord), and shalt believe in thine heart that God hath raised him from the dead, thou shalt be saved. For with the heart man believeth unto righteousness; and with the mouth confession is made unto salvation. For the scripture saith, whosoever believeth on him shall not be ashamed. For whosoever shall call upon the name of the Lord shall be saved" (Romans 10:9, 10, 11, & 13).

Some may say, "From what am I to be saved?" Surely, from our narcissistic selves and the futility of continuing to try to live a fulfilled, meaningful, and joyful life apart from Christ. Without being "born" into the family of God through faith in Jesus Christ, our future identities are doomed for banishment. The words of Jesus are unmistakable on this point: "For God so loved the world (you and me), that He gave his only begotten Son that whosoever believeth in Him should not perish, but have everlasting life" (John 3:16). Later in the chapter, Jesus says" "He that believeth on the Son hath everlasting life: and he that believeth not the Son shall not see life; but the wrath of God abideth on him" (John 3:36). Existence! Identity! Eternal separation from all that is good! God! Awesome thoughts, yet how tritely we ponder their true meaning!

The word, "believe" used here means more than just mental assent to a code of ethics and morality. It means obedience to God's Word and loving Him with our total being. To help us succeed as "new-borns," Christ has promised us His Holy Spirit, our Comforter. For, without His marvelous enablement, we could not possibly keep the law or really hope to be able to think rationally about eternal truth. Paul reminded us that the letter of the law kills us (why? Because we cannot perfectly keep it!), whereas the Spirit of God gives life to the law (see II Corinthians 3:6). In other words, God's incarnate love is encouraging us to keep His Holy Law.

Jesus Christ came into this world to cancel out the effective power of Satan over men's minds. Satan's power was dealt a death blow at the crucial event of all time, the crucifixion of our Lord. Jesus did not bear the cross--He used it! John reminds us:

> For this purpose the Son of God was manifested, that He might destroy the works of the devil. Whosoever is born (begotten) of God doth not (habitually and willfully) commit sin, for His seed (the Holy Spirit) remaineth in him: and he cannot sin, because he is born of God" (I John 3:8b, 9).

But praise God, Jesus did not remain dead. Earth's saddest and most joyful days were just three days apart, for He arose from the dead on that third day, victorious over death, sin, and the devil!

Do you fathom what God has done for us through Jesus Christ? When we are willing to let Christ become Lord of Lords, and King of Kings, then we shall experience His Holy Spirit; affirming our new birth in Christ by His gentle witness. At this point, the appeal of sin begins to wane for us. When tempted (and we will be), the love of Christ constrains us to see beyond the immediate lustful gratification and we joyfully resist willfully falling again into habitual sinning. This is not to imply that we

Neil C. Roth

cannot sin! We could, and unfortunately, sometimes do. But, as we grow into spiritual maturity and learn to appreciate the rationality, truthfulness, and blessing that flows from God and His Word, we become advocates of the rational Living Word and opponents of the irrational spirit of sin that once afflicted us.

A vital point to clearly understand is that Christ's love constrains us to be faithful to Him and His Word (II Corinthians 5:14). If we should sin, we then should, with godly sorrow, confess our sins. Fortunately, He promises again and again to forgive our sins, and to continuously cleanse our hearts and minds of all unrighteousness (I John 1:9) if we ask Him to!

Continuing, a vital principle of the Christian life is to be found when we walk in obedience and honesty before God. The Apostle John discovered this truth to be the key to mental and spiritual health. He said:

> If we say that we have fellowship with Him, and walk in darkness, we lie, and do not the truth: but if we walk in the light, as He is in the light, we have fellowship one with another, and the blood of Jesus Christ His Son cleanseth us (continually) from all sin" (I John 1:6, 7).

So, it is when we walk in His Spirit, and obey His precepts and principles, we will enjoy fellowship with God and with His children. Truthfully, the destruction of Satan's power is complete in our life as long as we "pay attention" to our Lord! If we are not diligent in our pursuit of God, and not watchful unto prayer, we could become fair game for temptation, lust, and sin once more. Let us not despair! The love of Christ, through His Holy Spirit will continue to convict us of those sinful drifts of motivation and attitude, and prompt us, through love, to repent and again walk in the light of His Presence.

We must keep in mind that to possess the indwelling Spirit of the Lord is not only a condition, but a relationship that is fostered through intimate fellowship and communication. Ellen Goreh and George Stebbins jointly wrote a hymn that expresses this special relationship. The first stanza reads:

You Are What You Think

In the secret of His presence,
How my soul delights to hide!
Oh, how precious are the lessons
Which I learn at Jesus side!
Earthly cares can never vex me,
Neither trials lay me low;
For when Satan comes to tempt me,
To the secret place I go,
To the secret place I go.

For a step-by-step description of the spiritual condition of man and his pilgrimage of spiritual and moral development, please refer to the C.R.T. Model of Man in Figure 6. By following through the sequence of the stages, one can ascertain his own spiritual level at this particular time of life. In addition, the C.R.T. Characteristics of Man (Figure 7) might provide some useful insights regarding

----

(Bondage to Satan)

Narcissism-to-Conditional Love (if, because) For Others and Self. Irrationality--Ignorance or avoidance of God's Precepts and Principles.

I	II	III
Innocent Child	Carnal Man	Carnal Man
Before age of accountability reached--not under condemnation (John 1:9).	Searching for faith in self and others.	Living by faith in self.
Extremely vulnerable to outside stimuli.	Tender to God and Satan (Rom. 8:6, Rom. 1:20-32).	Controlled by conflicting forces: Satan--dominant. Holy Spirit--convicting of sin. (Rom. 8:6, Rom. 1:20-32)
	Age of accountability reached--now under condemnation.	Mature and set in ways.
	When awareness of "right" and "wrong" condemns the soul.	Life characterized by: Emptiness Futility Fear Conditional Love

Neil C. Roth

Spark of the Divine (John 1:9) Knowledge of moral values undeveloped.	Pliable. Motivators: Lust of flesh, Lust of eyes, Pride of life. (I John 2:15-17) See chapter 5-- "Love of the world" discussed. Uses ego defenses like: rationalization, projection, reaction formation, etc.	Rigid. Motivators: Lust of flesh, Lust of eyes, Pride of life. (I John 2:15-17) See chapter 5-- "Love of the world" discussed. Uses ego defenses like: rationalization, projection, reaction formation, etc.
Death brings safety and abiding with God. (No verses, but rationally inferred)	Death brings judgment and final condemnation. (John 3:18-26, Romans 6:23) Conditional love.	Death brings judgment and final condemnation. (John 3:18-26, Romans 6:23)
Stage I	Stage II	Stage III Note: can by-pass level III by experiencing NEW BIRTH.

Figure 6 THE CHRISTIAN RATIONAL THOUGHT MODEL OF MAN

(Freedom in Christ)

Unconditional (in-spite-of) Love for God, Self, and Others.
Spiritual <u>Rationality</u>--Knowledge and Acceptance of God's Precepts and Principles.

You Are What You Think

IV	V	VI
Spiritual Man	Spiritual Man	Glorified Man

IV — Spiritual Man

II Corinthians 5:17

Born again by faith in Jesus Christ. Holy Spirit has begun His work. (John 3:3-16, Rom. 10:9, 10)

Carnal nature. Irrational mind still a burden. (Romans 7)

Warfare constant due to: struggling with allegiance to Christ and seeing life rationally. Love of Christ constraining. (II Cor. 5:14; I John 3:1)

Love still unstable but lessons being learned.

Stability variable. (I Peter 2:2)

FAITH GROWING

Sometimes uses ego defenses.

Honest about self. Pliable.

Death or the rapture brings glorification. (I Cor. 15:51-58; I Thess. 4:13-18)

Stage IV

(center vertical text:) CRISES AND GROWTH 12: 1, 2.

V — Spiritual Man

II Corinthians 5:17

Born again by faith in Jesus Christ & filled and controlled by the Holy Spirit. (Rom. 12:1, 2)

Carnal nature subdued by Holy Spirit in concert with will of man. Divine rationality and loves becomes the central driving force (constraining love of Christ--II Cor. 5:14) of the personality.

Spirituality growing and committed to God. (I John 1:5-10; 2:1-5; 2:15-17; 3:8-11; 4:13-18)

SANCTIFIED WHOLLY (Romans 8:9, 10)

God's law of love enthroned in heart.

Courage to face reality resulting in honesty, courage, and sincerity.

Death or the rapture brings glorification. (I Cor. 15:51-58; I Thess. 4:13-18)

Stage V.

VI — Glorified Man

With Christ for evermore. (I Thess. 4:13-18; I Cor. 15:51-58)

Translated to Heaven through death or the rapture.

Stage VI

Figure 6 (Continued)
THE CHRISTIAN RATIONAL THOUGHT MODEL OF MAN

Neil C. Roth

1. Man has basic physical, psychological, and spiritual needs.
2. Man is impinged on by deistic and satanic forces, characterized by righteousness (rationality, love, altruism, good) and unrighteousness (irrationality, fear, hate, deceit).
3. Man is, by nature, carnal (self-centered) and potentially spiritual (God and other-centered).
4. Man is prone to laziness, expediency, and irrationality.
5. Man is subject to physical, intellectual, and spiritual laws, which are immutable and punitive when violated.
6. Man has a free will; is not completely stimulus-response bound; and can choose actions and attitudes toward life.
7. Man begins to die physically at height of maturation; the soul never dies.
8. Man's accuracy and objectiveness of sensory perception depends upon past, present, and future interpretations of real or imagined biases or prejudices, and the quality of his sensory receptors.
9. Man seeks meaning and purpose in life.
10. Man's soul (psyche) is a "God-shaped vacuum" which, in order to be satisfied, requires filling by the Spirit of God.
11. Man seeks immortality; is spiritually dead from time of recognition of accountability and loss of innocence.
12. Man can be transformed into a new person by Christ through the Holy Spirit.
13. From the time of New Birth, man is assured of a place in heaven with God; otherwise, will spend eternity in Hell with Satan and his angels.

Figure 7 C.R.T. CHARACTERISTICS OF MAN

the qualities found in humans, to relate to your analysis of the C.R.T. Model of Man material. Also, many concepts may have been used with which you might be unfamiliar. Do not panic! With Bible in hand, you can work through them with relative ease. If questions, arise, you should not hesitate to ask for assistance from a Christian friend or minister who is familiar with the Word.

You Are What You Think

After carefully evaluating the C.R.T. Model of Man, which stage do you feel you occupy at this time? Surely, the most important consideration that you can ponder is: Are you a born-again child of God? Do you know that, if you would die at this moment, your soul would be with the Lord in Glory? If your answer is no to these two questions, would you be willing to bow your head and ask the Lord Jesus Christ to come into your heart and save you from the sin nature, and to forgive your past sin. Then, ask Him to make your life over into a new creation, and to fill you with His precious Holy Spirit. Do it now, and see God radically change your life into an experience of fulfillment, joy, and praise. (Praise God, if you have just become a "born-again" Christian!)

If you already are a born-again child of God, may you be sensing a greater desire to grow more in the nurture and nature of our Lord. Why not, right now, pray for such growth, as the Lord gives you wisdom and light.

Charles H. Spurgeon, the British preacher, was reported to have prayed this prayer each evening before retiring: "Oh Lord, never let me be, what I cannot be forever." How terribly irrational it is for us to hang onto a spiritual condition that will not allow us to receive God's best for us here, in this life, and throughout eternity. Claim your inheritance!

As hopefully a born-anew (or at least seriously considering the option) person in Jesus Christ, you should be aware that without the Holy Spirit in your life, the keeping of God's Word is difficult, at best, if not impossible! He will speak to you through the Word, through experiences, through other persons, and just to you in your heart and mind. The Holy Spirit will instruct, convince, convict, empower, comfort, encourage, affirm, enthuse, and lead you unto all truth and righteousness. Plan now, to learn to live and walk in God's Spirit. Paul said, "For as many as are led by the Spirit of God, they are the sons of God" and he further states: "The Spirit itself (Himself) beareth witness with our spirit, that we are the children of God" (Romans 8:14, 16).

C.R.T. PROGRESS PRINCIPLES OF THE CHRISTIAN LIFE

To this point, we have learned that what God has to say to us through His Word is sensible and rational. Generally speaking, the non-Christian views God's Word and ways as foolishness, however, we need to remember that such attitudes are largely due to ignorance of God's ways and, of course, personal sin. Paul declared: "For the preaching (word) of the cross is to them that perish foolishness; but unto us which are saved, it is the power of God" (I Corinthians 1:18).

How wonderful it is to realize that God does not call us to follow Him without the empowerment or the instructions. He has blessed us with both His Spirit and His Word. So it is, that the following C.R.T. Progress Principles reflect the hundreds of scripture passages and verses that espouse the root ideas of these Principles. As in almost every area of life, certain rules must be observed if we are to succeed. So, in order to grow properly, God's immutable rules must be obeyed if we are to enjoy spiritual health. Peter prayed, "But grow in grace, and in the knowledge of our Lord and Savior Jesus Christ" (II Peter 3:18a). Without further delay, let us investigate the relevancy of the Progress Principles to Christian Rational Thought and to victorious Christian living.

C.R.T. PROGRESS PRINCIPLE NO. 1--READ AND STUDY THE BIBLE DAILY!

The Bible is the Christian's textbook and contains the spiritual food that you spiritually will need to prosper and develop. Peter told us that we should "...desire the sincere milk of the Word...", so that we could thereby grow (I Peter 2:2).

As His children, we are to study the Word to find out what God wants of us as Christians. Paul urged Timothy to "Study to show thyself approved unto God, a workman that needeth not to be ashamed, rightly dividing (handling aright) the word of Truth" (II Timothy 2:15). How can we possibly share the precious Truth with others unless we can properly understand and evaluate what God is saying through His Word? Knowledge is only acquired when we study a subject diligently. Do not be content to "discover" and "land on it" (my Columbus method of typing) but get into the depths of the Word and study it book by book, verse by verse.

You Are What You Think

I would heartily recommend that you start your Bible study with John's Gospel; then move on through I John, Romans, and Ephesians. By the way, do not forget the Old Testament, for its books contain the marvelous record of God's first redemptive steps for the human race. Begin in Genesis, and work your way through the Old Testament, while maintaining systematic reading of a New Testament book. Remember, that redemption through Jesus Christ is the key theme to watch for in your study. Also, it is wise to obtain a good Bible commentary to illuminate your Scriptural understanding. Resist the temptation to quit just because you do not understand everything you are reading. Time, effort, and maturity, plus God's assistance, will help illuminate the fuzzy areas. According to the Lord, we learn by adding precept upon precept; line upon line...here a little and there a little (see Isaiah 28:10). This learning method has not been improved upon through our day by anyone! Praise God, we have the Holy Spirit who interprets the Truth (God's Word) for us so that we might understand!

A good rule while reading is to: get everything out of it; do not read anything into it, and, let nothing remain unread. Also, underline those scripture verses that stand out to you and try committing them to memory. Then, they really become your's forever!

Rev. F. B. Meyer once wrote describing how to read the Bible. He said:

> Read the Bible, not as a newspaper, but as a home letter. If a cluster of heavenly fruit hangs within reach, gather it. If a promise lies upon the page as a blank check, cash it. If a prayer is recorded, appropriate it, and launch it as a feathered arrow from the bow of your desire. If an example of holiness gleams before you, ask God to do as much for you. If the truth is revealed in all its intrinsic splendor, entrust that its brilliance may ever irradiate the hemisphere of your life.[1]

Attitudinally, approach your study of God's Word expectantly, surrendering to its truth, and planning to implement its message. The Word will then redirect your will, enlighten your mind, elicit proper emotions, and quicken your total personality!

Neil C. Roth

In a treasured Bible, my now-departed saintly grandmother wrote these words of Dwight L. Moody: "This Book will keep you from sin. Sin will keep you from this Book." May David's resolve be ours, but be clear on this issue--it is really the Christ of the Book that can keep us from sin. David declared to the Lord: "Thy Word have I hid in my heart, that I might not sin against thee" (Psalm 119:11).

Aristotle once said, "Wicked men obey from fear; good men, from love." Christ alone, by His love, can help us to obey His words! Let us always remember that God's Word is the "sword of the Spirit" and is an integral part of the Christian's protective armor. Without a doubt, we need God's armor in order to stand against the wiles of the devil. (See Ephesians 6:10-18). Plan to read and study the Bible daily!

C.R.T. PROGRESS PRINCIPLE NO. 2--PRAY WITHOUT CEASING!

Prayer is talking with God, not to God! We need to pray so that we can share with God our praise and adoration for Him. Indeed, He created us to have fellowship with Him and prayer is the means. We are commanded by the Word to be in a continual state of prayer (see I Thessalonians 5:17); which means, that we are to be continually sensing God's Spirit, and talking to Him in the Spirit. Someone once remarked: "If you are going to be prepared, you will need to be pre-prayered!" How vitally true, for we can only receive God's affirmation, and confirmation of His leading, if we precede every decision with prayer! So many times we pray, "Lord bless my decision," rather than "Lord, please assist me in arriving at Thy will in this matter!"

Note how our Lord Jesus Christ always prayed to His Father before making decisions or taking actions. Follow Doctor Luke's Gospel through and check Jesus' prayer life out! You will find that He prayed all night before calling the twelve disciples (Luke 6:12); He prayed before feeding the five thousand (Luke 9:16); He prayed, and then was transfigured before Peter, James, and John (Luke 9:29); and so on through Luke and the Gospels. Jesus practiced and lived a life of prayer. The saying, "He stands best who kneels most," fits our Lord to a tee!

You Are What You Think

The crucial fact is: If Jesus needed to pray, as God's Son, we need it immeasurably more. Seriously, Luke 11:1-13 is a "must" to read on prayer. Christ urges us to pray; to ask Him for leading, blessing, and, most importantly, for the Holy Spirit in our lives. A note of caution here: Answers to our prayers are keyed to God's timing, not ours! Sometimes, no answer is truly the answer! Someone once said: "Prayer is to ask not what we wish of God, but what God wishes of us." Charles Trumbull said it so accurately: "Prayer is releasing the energies of God. For prayer is asking God to do what we cannot do."[2] It is essentially linking our inadequacies to His sufficiency!

Psychologically, to speak to God in prayer has a redemptive cathartic effect; that is, a similar sense of relief that comes when we confess a need or sin to someone who cares and understands (a friend, counselor, minister, etc.). As our Creator, our Lord knows that "getting our concerns off our chest" is necessary if we are to be emotionally and spiritually healthy.

Among the many things we should pray for are: salvation (Psalm 85:7); spiritual establishment (Psalm 119:5, 133); spiritual revival (Lamentations 5:21); divine vindication (I Kings 18:36); preservation and support (Psalm 69:17); prosperity (Nehemiah 1:11); for the sinful (Luke 23:34); and the list goes on.

The Rev. E. M. Bounds revealingly evaluates the prayer life of ministers, and people alike, in his classic book <u>Preacher and Prayer.</u> He says:

> What the church needs today is not more machinery or better, nor new organizations or more and novel methods, but men whom the Holy Ghost can use--men of prayer, men mighty in prayer. The Holy Ghost does not flow through methods, but through men. He does not come on machinery, but on men. He does not anoint plans, but men--men of prayer.[3]

Surely, to pray is to not only acknowledge our total dependency upon God for all that we are and have; but to say, "I love you, Precious Father!" We need human and divine love to sustain us. Yet, God yearns too for our adoration and worship! Truly, the only way we can do much for God is to ask much of Him in prayer. In reality, nothing lies beyond the reach of prayer except that which lies outside the will of God.

As we learn to pray in the Spirit (see Ephesians 6:18) our key desire must be to please God and see His perfect will accomplished in and through our lives. As Jesus prayed, "Thy will be done" to His Father, so we must sincerely desire His will to be done. Charles G. Finney said that "prayer is not to change God, but to change us!" But, as faith without works is dead, our prayer must not only be desirous of God's will (changes) for our lives, but reflect the seeking attitude: "Lord, show me what I might do, in a practical, human way, to implement your will. Evangelist D. L. Moody once remarked: "Prayer is a serious thing for we may be taken at our words." Too many times we are content to pray but not to act! Be assured that God will not be manipulated or exploited. If we think God is like some "jack in a box" that we call on when we are in need, we are sadly in error. If God for us is "God in a box," then J. B. Phillips' analysis is correct: our God is far too small! Furthermore, we are to be our Lord's hands and feet, not just His grandstand spectators and supporters. He calls us to be participators in His worldwide ministry of reconciliation.

Believe me, when we pray, God most always reveals His will in "close to home" personal ways that usually involve us in the job of ministry. Do we truly believe God when He says: "If ye shall ask anything in my name, I will do it" (John 14:14). We just cannot "cop out" and say we are too busy to pray. In actuality, we are too busy not to pray in our frenetic day of living. We need the fellowship and leadership of God every moment of life, and especially, we need the encouragement and power of the Holy Spirit for the tasks of life that God wants us to tackle. It is imperative that you decide now to set aside a regular time each day to pray and read God's Word. The morning is a good time, for the day is preceded by a private conference with the lover of your soul. Remember, a prayerless Christian turns out to be a powerless Christian! Pray without ceasing!

C.R.T. PROGRESS PRINCIPLE NO. 3--BE FILLED WITH THE HOLY SPIRIT!

Much has already been said about the Holy Spirit, but please indulge me for a few thoughts more. Jesus declared: "God is a spirit: and they that worship Him must worship Him in spirit and in truth" (John 4:24). So often, we think of the Spirit of God as an it, rather than as a Person. The

You Are What You Think

Spirit is God and our "link" to Him is through thought and prayer. Our Lord Jesus Christ dwells within our souls, through His Spirit, and sincerely beckons us to relax and let Him lead us in the paths of righteousness (see Psalm 23). Always remember, that we vitally confirm our faith in God, and our relationship with Him, if we are being led by the Spirit of God (Romans 8:16).

We can only know the mind of Christ if we are in constant touch with Him through His Spirit. His Spirit bears an "up-to-the-second" witness with our spirit that we are his children, and He confirms that our attitudes and behavior are in accordance with His desired will for our lives.

D. L. Moody once exclaimed that "The Holy Spirit is God at work!" Praise God, when His Spirit totally invades your soul; laziness, fear, and procrastination will be no more. The fire of the Lord in your soul will prompt you to be busy doing the will of your Father. Look at Acts, chapter two, and see what happened to the followers of Jesus when they were filled with God's Spirit. They were changed men and women who were "in tune" with God and responsive to His will. Nobody is curious enough to stop off and look at an old office building. Maybe a few would hesitate to see some smoke coming from its roof. But, let it really burn, then see how many pause in fascination to watch it be consumed! So it is, when the fire of God's Holy Spirit begins to burn in our hearts; a fire of holy love for God and man! "If we live in the Spirit, let us also walk in the Spirit" (Galatians 5:25).

Remember too, we are not only commanded by the Lord to "Be filled with the Spirit" (Ephesians 5:18b) but to grieve not the Spirit of God (Ephesians 4:30); that is, refuse to be sensitive to His ministry. A word of caution here, the sin that Christ said could never be forgiven in man is that of blaspheming against the Holy Spirit (see Mark 3:28, 29)! In my opinion, the committing of this sin means that we have lost our vital sensitivity to the Spirit of God. It is evidenced in that we no longer desire the close, intimate fellowship with our Lord. We could become like so many in Scripture (a notable example is Samson, Judges 16:20b) who almost lost their souls by spiritual carelessness and yielding to this world's lustful temptations. The Lord warns: "My Spirit shall not always strive with man" (Genesis 6:3a).

Shostrom and Montgomery observe another danger: "Having lost sensitivity to the gentle promptings of the Holy Spirit, the rigid person may set out to accomplish very worthy goals but in the process do much damage and destruction because of his steamroller approach to life."[4] How can God really bless what He (His Spirit) is not involved in? Obviously, He cannot! We begin the deadly process of leaving God out by neglecting His counsel. Remember, God's Spirit is a manifestation of His love to us and without question, His love in our hearts always will triumph over pride and eventual spiritual desensitization. "Walk in the Spirit, and ye shall not fulfill the lust of the flesh" (Galatians 5:16).

A dear brother in the Nazarene ministry, G. Franklin Allee, once wrote:

> The work of the Holy Spirit within the heart is both destructive and creative. He deals out death to the self-life, and at the same time creates new life within. He not only applies the purging of the cross; he fills with holiness. He more than destroys the works of the Devil; He enthrones Christ within the soul. While He burns up the chaff, He also gathers out and saves the wheat.[5]

Dr. E. Stanley Jones, who for many years experienced and testified of God's saving and sanctifying power, wrote so much to this point on our need of the Spirit as Christians. He proclaimed:

> The Holy Spirit is the answer. One doesn't have to strive against the flesh or trust oneself. All he has to do is to consent, and the Holy Spirit takes over the inner life. Transformation sets in, and the transformation is not in mere action; it is transformation at the place where it counts most--the depths of the personality. The spring is cleansed and the flow is thereby purified.[6]

Come, Holy Spirit, we need you!

C.R.T. PROGRESS PRINCIPLE NO. 4--WORSHIP REGULARLY WITH OTHER BELIEVERS!

The Word is very clear on this principle! The Lord instructs that believers should give continual care to others (in love) and to take care in "not forsaking the assembling of ourselves together, as the manner of some

You Are What You Think

is; but exhorting one another: and so much the more, as ye see the day (of Christ's return) approaching" (Hebrews 10:25). Without question, the call to worship, and to fellowship with the believers, is a central theme of Scripture. Jesus emphasized this when He declared: "Thou shalt worship the Lord thy God, and Him only shalt thou serve" (Matthew 4:10b). Jesus consistently was found in the synagogue on the Lord's day and was occasionally called upon to speak. He exclaimed to the Samaritan woman that "the hour cometh and now is, when the true worshippers shall worship the Father in Spirit and in Truth: for the Father seeketh such to worship Him" (John 4:23). Jesus confirms the value of worship and the characteristic qualities it must possess if God is to be pleased--Spirit and Truth!

David, a man declared as one after God's own heart, admonishes: "O come, let us worship and bow down: let us kneel before the Lord our Maker." (Why?) "For He is our God; and we are the people of His pasture, and the sheep of His land" (Psalm 95:6, 7a). Throughout its pages, the Word encourages us to engage in private worship, (Matthew 6:6; 14:23); family worship (Deuteronomy 16:11); and corporate worship (Hebrews 10:25). We are to hear instruction and wisely accept its meaning for our lives (Proverbs 8:33, 34); and come before God in worship with a positive, receptive attitude. David said, "Make a joyful noise unto the Lord, all ye lands. Serve the Lord with gladness; come before His presence with singing" (Psalm 100:1, 2).

In addition, our Lord promises that when we gather together to worship Him, He will be in our midst and bless us by answering our prayers (Matthew 18:19, 20). We need worship in order to keep ever before us the vital importance of God, His Truth, and His mission. Furthermore, it is our joyful duty to worship so that we might read His Word, declare His gospel, sing His praise, and encourage one another in the faith.

Our family has always enjoyed camping in the mountains of the beautiful Pacific Northwest, and a special feature of such outings has been the times around the evening campfire. The fire crackles, pops, and warms us faithfully (enduring our almost endless talk), but then, sleep beckons us. Before retiring, however, comes the responsibility of "banking the coals" of the fire, so that when the cold morning comes, the hot coals will have kept each other's heat preserved and ready for new service. The coals

Neil C. Roth

keep hot because they are vitally close together. Christians keep "hot" for God when they regularly fellowship together around the person of Jesus Christ. Take note: Relationships with God or persons are not built by proxy or wishful thinking. They are built only if we build them. Learn to share yourself with those of like faith if you expect to grow spiritually. Psychologically, you need to closely relate with others of like purpose and affection because of the mutual affirmation and encouragement that is afforded. A word of caution in in order, however: We must not be drawn into having fellowship with each other <u>about</u> God, but guard carefully that our fellowship together will be <u>with</u> God!

Surely, God could dispense with us and all our engagements, but we cannot afford to possibly dispense our meeting with Him. As Rev. Jabez Burns has said,

> Our knowledge is yet imperfect--our faith feeble--our hope clouded--our love languid--our graces weakly. We might 'forsake the assembling of ourselves together' if we had no mercies to acknowledge--no sins to confess--no blessings to crave--no enemies to overcome--no soul to sanctify--no hell to escape--no heaven to gain.[7]

Along the same line, D. L. Moody once said that "Satan doesn't care what we worship, as long as we don't worship God." John Wesley confirms again our need to worship by stating: "The Bible knows nothing of solitary religion." Our fellowship must display a warmth that is winsome and redemptive if Christ is to be exalted. There are two ways of being united together in fellowship: frozen together or melted together! Which do you prefer?

The Lord Jesus established the Church on the earth as His means of getting the news out to all that He loves us. He loves the Church and gave Himself for it (Ephesians 5:25) so that we, the Church, might be sanctified and cleansed by the truth of His Word (Ephesians 5:26, 27). May this prayer be our motto: "When I pass my church I will drop in for a visit, so that when I'm finally carried in, the Lord won't say, 'Who is it?'" The following notice was displayed outside a church: CH??CH--What is missing? Worship regularly with other believers!

You Are What You Think

C.R.T. PROGRESS PRINCIPLE NO. 5--SHARE YOUR FAITH FREQUENTLY!

As Christians, we are called by the Lord to carry out the principle of the Great Commission. His command is crystal clear:

> Go ye therefore, and teach (make disciples of) all nations, baptizing them in the name of the Father, and of the Son, and of the Holy Ghost: Teaching them to observe all things whatsoever I have commanded you: and Lo, I am with you alway, even unto the end of the world" (Matthew 28:19, 20).

Interestingly, Jesus does not let anyone "off the hook" regarding this commandment. Age, position, wealth, beauty, degrees; none of these qualities exempt us from our duty! We are all to be living epistles, known and read by all men (II Corinthians 3:2). Furthermore, we are always to be in a state of readiness to witness about our faith in Jesus to anyone who might ask us why we have an everlasting hope (I Peter 3:15).

You might be thinking, "I thought all Christians had to go out and "button-hole" others and force the Gospel on them." Well, even though this method is repeatedly tried, the results are often dubious, at best. You see, God's plan is psychologically sound and so deceptively practical. He wants us to make people "thirsty" for the "Water of Life!" Also, Jesus called the Christian "salt" (Matthew 5:13), and our lives are to be so loving and winsome that the non-Christian will become "thirsty" (curious, inquisitive) about what it is in our lives that is radically different and more wholesome than the people of the world possess. Only Christ, the Water of Life, can create and quench such a thirst (see John 4:14)!

Without exception, if you are adhering to the first four C.R.T. Progress Principles, you will be like the cup that is continuously overflowing with God's praise and testimony of His blessing and goodness. Remember, we witness in two distinct ways: By word and by deed! In other words: we must know God's Word, and be willing and qualified to share it; then, we can live the Word by our actions of love and concern to all within our sphere of influence. We are to be more than reservoirs of God's Word and love. We are to be SPILLWAYS sharing the Living Water! Resist being like some Christians who are like Arctic rivers--FROZEN at the mouth.

Neil C. Roth

A small boy, who had just been operated on by the famous Viennese surgeon, Dr. Adolph Lorenz, after just regaining consciousness said, "It will be a long time before my mother hears the last about you, doctor."[8] Out of gratitude this boy will constantly testify to the skill of one who saved his life, with God's help, of course. How much more, then, are we grateful to our Lord Jesus Christ who has given us eternal life, abundant joy, and the Holy Spirit!

The great missionary Gordon once declared that the crucial spiritual lesson that we must learn is that: "We do not stand in the world bearing witness to Christ, but stand in Christ and bear witness to the world."[9] The Bible also says, "He that winneth souls is wise" (Proverbs 11:30b). We are each called to be ambassadors for the King of Kings (II Corinthians 5:20), and as ambassadors, let us be faithful in our witness, lest in the end, we be "recalled," for not doing our job. The Western Union man is called upon to deliver only the message <u>as sent</u>. We are called upon to faithfully communicate Christ's message of love, hope, and salvation, also <u>as sent</u>! Be an enthusiastic witness and booster for your Lord!

Dr. Henrietta C. Mears once stated that love and "kindness has converted more sinners than zeal, eloquence, or learning."[10] Always remember John 3:16. Share your faith frequently!

C.R.T. PROGRESS PRINCIPLE NO. 6--BE JOYFUL AND WHOLESOME!

Few persons in life, excepting the redeemed of the Lord, ever approach the emotional state that the Christian knows as joyous. For true joy can only come from knowing the Lord Jesus Christ in His fulness. The Apostle Peter said it so adequately: "Whom (Jesus) having not seen, ye love; in whom, though now ye see Him not, yet believing, ye rejoice with joy unspeakable and full of glory" (I Peter 1:8).

Jesus stated that He came in order to provide us with a more abundant life (John 10:10); and, that our joy might be full because of His ministry of Word and Spirit to us (John 15:11). Jesus strongly urges us to ask, in His Name, those things we have need of, so that our joy might be full (John 16:24). Humanly, David captures the saint's delight by declaring: "Thou

You Are What You Think

wilt shew me the path of life: in thy presence is fulness of joy; at thy right hand there are pleasures for evermore" (Psalm 16:11).

Someone once suggested a uniquely appropriate acrostic for joy. The "J" of joy stands for the fact that joy in the believer's life is founded upon <u>Jesus</u>, the source of all joy. If we put Him first in our lives, joy will be present. But, when we allow other gods to interfere (things, ideas, people, aspirations, lust--remember the provision, possession, and position principles?), then joy vanishes.

The "<u>O</u>" in joy indicates that our joy is sustained only when we share our love and faith with <u>others</u>. We can really only keep our faith and our joy by giving it away. What a paradox!

The "<u>Y</u>" stands for <u>you</u>. You are to respect yourself and nurture your spiritual life by God's Holy Spirit and His Word. <u>Jesus</u> first; <u>Others</u> second; and then <u>You</u> form the equation for successful Christian living characterized by real joy. Truly, joy is multiplied as it is divided up with others. Also, how redemptively impressive we are for God when we are genuinely joyful, loving, and thankful. This mode of expression will also convey a quality of peace to the world. Not just peace with God, but the peace of God--"at the very center of my soul I am being held without panic or anxiety!"

Not only is joy the quality that attracts the unsaved to thirst for the Living Water, but also that quality of being wholesome. The Bible calls us to be separated from sin, and its practice, but not to draw attention to ourselves by weird grooming, dress, or behavior. We are instructed to "adorn the Gospel of Christ in all things" (Titus 2:10b); that is, we are not to draw attention to our physical characteristics but display a meek and quiet spirit that brings honor to Jesus Christ (I Peter 3:3, 4).

We are also to be friendly, kind, and courteous to all persons and "as we have therefore opportunity, let us do good unto all men" (Galatians 6:10). The Lord admonishes the Christian to "abstain from all appearance of evil" (I Thessalonians 5:22) so that we will not bring shame and discredit to Him and His Church. God only knows what eternal damage is done by those Christians who are careless and carnal in their living.

First Mate Bob, of <u>The Haven of Rest</u> Radio Broadcast, once said, "Some Christians faithfully go out and sow their wild oats six days a week and then come into church on Sunday and pray desperately for a crop failure!" Oh, how we need to be so very careful with the consistent quality

Neil C. Roth

of our testimony. That moment of lustful enjoyment can often mean a lifetime of defeat and guilt! As Christians, we are free to do everything but not everything builds up the body of Christ (see I Corinthians 9:1-5; 26, 27). Upton Sinclair once declared that the "oldest form of slavery is self-indulgence." Instead of being a question mark for the Lord, we must become EXCLAMATION POINTS!!! Be joyful and wholesome!

C.R.T. PROGRESS PRINCIPLE NO. 7--BE POSITIVE; LIVE ABOVE YOUR CIRCUMSTANCES!

You have possibly heard the old saying, "Beauty is in the eye of the beholder." How very true it is that our dominant perspective of life (people and situations) essentially becomes us--our selves, our personalities. If we adopt a negative (I'm not OK or you're not OK) attitude, we begin to evade responsibility for positive achievement by being critical. Some psychologists have insisted that our life circumstances, parents, environment, yes, our genes, etc., are the culprits that keep us from happiness and fulfillment. These influences surely impact our development but, in reality, it is we, ourselves, that are primarily to blame for the quality of our personal lives.

Yes, we are responsible for choosing how we will react to our life circumstances, not mother, dad, or the I.R.S. You see, when we try and shift the blame to someone else, we are really trying to hide our own inadequacies. It is a psychological fact that we tend to find the faults in others that we are experiencing in ourselves. After all, we might say "we are the experts!" This is called projection in the professional language of psychology. Unfortunately, this is an extremely damaging process. Why? simply because it gets the individual nowhere--except backwards. For, throwing dirt at another usually only soils your own hands. J. G. Whittier once wisely wrote: "Search thy own heart; what paineth thee in others in thyself may be."[11]

The payoff for assuming a negative attitude towards circumstances, or people is, predictably, you will tend to become a negative person. In addition, the critical person invites criticism--of himself! Someone once stated it this way: "If you point one finger at another, you point the other three fingers at yourself." The real question lingers: Are you ready to assume

You Are What You Think

responsibility for your life and quit blaming others or circumstances for the "fix you are in?" If you are, then Cicero's words can be a starting point. He said, "I criticize by creation; not by finding fault."[12] Indeed, how beautiful his attitude is! Truly, we can never improve ourselves, and our life situation, by critical, negative attitudes.

E. Stanley Jones once described how to practically get rid of critical, negative attitudes. He wrote:

1. Make up your mind that the way of criticism is a road with a dead end. Nobody is changed except the critic--He is changed into a critical person.
2. Surrender the way of criticism as a way of life. Give it up like a shabby coat--for a critical personality is a shabby personality.
3. Begin to look for good in people and circumstances. As you do, a good spirit will come over you.
4. Don't criticize a person until you have projected yourself into his situation and see things from his standpoint.
5. Work out a positive technique of relationships based on the positive. A couple, eighty-nine years of age, were asked to tell how they were still in love with each other. They replied: '(a) A man and his wife should be considerate of each other; (b) Practice the Golden Rule in everyday life; (c) Count ten before you begin bawling out your mate--and then give a kiss instead.'[13]

In all that has been said, the bottom line is that we can and do choose who we wish to be. In other words, we become what we think. Victor Frankl, author of the best selling <u>Man's Search for Meaning</u>, and founder of the existential school of psychotherapy known as Logotherapy, explains that life can be made meaningful by adopting three dominant attitudes: (1) "Through <u>what we give</u> to life (in terms of restorative and creative works); (2) by <u>what we take</u> from the world (in terms of our experiencing values); and (3) through the <u>stand we take</u> toward a fate we can no longer change (an incurable disease, an inoperable cancer, etc)."[14] Frankl's experience in the Nazi concentration camp forced him to search for the truly foundational values that render meaning to existence. He found that one could survive where it really counts--in one's mind and soul!

Neil C. Roth

If we can learn to be positive to life even when circumstance seems to conspire against us, something life-changing can occur. The key is to be found in our sincere faith and commitment to Jesus Christ as Lord. For, if our circumstances find us in Christ, then we will find Christ in all our circumstances!

For a moment, practice emptying your mind, affirming "I am releasing anxiety, fear, insecurity, and all negative thoughts and replacing them with peace, courage, calm assurance, Christ's love and positive affirmation for myself!" You see, it is really up to you! Joshua told the nation of Israel, "Choose you this day whom you will serve." Mr. Negative or Mr. Positive? Bondage in Egypt or freedom in the Promised Land? Satan or the Lord Jesus Christ? Joshua did choose. Listen to his answer to the people: "...but as for me and my house, we will serve the Lord" (Joshua 24:15).

Begin now by filling your mind with thoughts of the Lord Jesus, those happy and pleasant thoughts that are founded on God's rational Word. Start teaching yourself that you can change for the "positive" and do all (according to His desired will) things as you experience Christ's help. Paul was not joking when he said, "I can do all things through Christ which strengtheneth me" (Philippians 4:13). In fact, we can best combat negative thinking with positive thoughts, just as evil is best thwarted by good deeds. Paul confirms this by saying, "Be not overcome of evil, but overcome evil with good" (Romans 12:21).

Shakespeare said, "There is nothing either good or bad but thinking makes it so."[15] James and Jongeward, co-authors of <u>Born to Win</u>, have firmly committed themselves to the notion that we can choose to lose or choose to win in life. But, they affirm, we are born to win, to be positive, to choose and acquire the best in life, if we will. Will you?

Paul exclaimed that nothing in life could separate us from the love of God. No, nothing except our negative attitudes, but he did confirm that "In all these things we are more than conquerors through Him that loved us (Romans 8:37). As E. Stanley Jones said, "Accept the positive resources of God. Begin to live on God's yeses. Be God's yes-man in the sense of saying yes to God's yeses!"[16] The positive look is the upward look! Look for the positive and good and you will begin to see them everywhere. Be positive and live above your circumstances!

You Are What You Think

C.R.T. PROGRESS PRINCIPLE NO. 8--LEARN HOW TO HANDLE TEMPTATION!

James declared: "Let no man say when he is tempted, I am tempted of God: for God cannot be tempted with evil, neither tempteth He any man: but every man is tempted when he is drawn away of his own lust, and enticed" (James 1:13, 14).

Essentially, temptation is the brother of lust. We begin to see who we really are, ourselves, by the temptations we experience. Satan is seeking, through temptation, to humiliate, defeat, and devour the Christian, and the non-Christian, alike. Dr. J. Wilbur Chapman once stated that: "Temptation is the tempter looking through the keyhole into the room where you are living; sin is your drawing back the bolt and making it possible for him to enter."[17]

Interestingly, temptation seems to hit us during leisure hours, when we are idle. Solomon spoke of how "idle hands make mischief" and surely criminal statistics bear this notion out. During times of loneliness, frustration, and boredom, we seem to be looking for something exciting to fill the void. Have you ever noticed that Satan makes all sin appear exciting in the temptation phase? But during, and afterwards? How frustrating, what little pleasure, and then--remorse, guilt, severed relationships, emptiness.

Practically speaking, keeping away from sin and temptation is the best way to deal with it. We know that temptation will come, but as children of God, we can choose to flee from it, rather than "roost" on it! The savoring of temptation is, in reality, the "desired-for" spawning of lust! We do not have to experience prison, drugs, alcoholism, illicit sex, divorce, murder, electric shock, or hell, itself, in order to properly understand the consequences and pain that each of these experiences may bring. We can, do, and must continue to learn from the experiences of others. Is there a law that says that we have to fall into their pit and suffer their woe? Jesus said: "Watch ye therefore, and pray always, that ye may be accounted worthy to escape all these things that shall come to pass and to stand before the Son of man" (Luke 21:36).

Is it now apparent? If we are in Christ, constantly living in His Spirit, and praying without ceasing, temptation will not affect us. His constraining love will draw us to fidelity, away from the life of lust. Remember, Paul met temptations that would have broken most men, but came through because of God's grace and power. He affirmed:

> There hath no temptation taken you but such is common to man: but God is faithful, who will not suffer you to be tempted above that ye are able; but will with the temptation also make a way of escape, that ye may be able to bear it (I Corinthians 10:13).

Furthermore, Jesus was "in all points tempted like as we are, yet without sin" (Hebrews 4:15b). Praise God, because He overcame temptation, we can too! Keep in mind, it is His love that holds us in check! James declared: "My brethren, count it all joy when ye fall into divers temptations; knowing this, that the trying of your faith worketh patience" (James 1:2, 3).

In her song, "God is Our Only Strength," Laurie Roth vividly describes Satan's subtle, yet deadly appeal:

> He comes in the name of sugar and spice,
> We grasp at his beauty, but should we pay that price?
> A soul is a terrible thing for one to waste,
> For the moment's illusion will soon erase!
> God is our only strength against this force.
> Without Him, we'd be torn apart, or worse![18]

The more you practice saying no to Satan, the easier it will be to say yes to the Lord Jesus Christ! Learn how to handle temptation!

C.R.T. PROGRESS PRINCIPLE NO. 9--BE EQUALLY YOKED TOGETHER WITH BELIEVERS!

If our Lord ever gave a principle which, when violated, has such devastating and far-reaching physical, emotional, and spiritual consequences, it is this one: "Be ye not unequally yoked together with unbelievers" (II Corinthians 6:14a). The Lord is clearly saying that the Christian must not form any kind of permanent alliances with unbelievers that create a oneness or intimate unity. Strictly interpreted, marrying an unbeliever would be forbidden.

Also, the forming of a business partnership with a non-Christian could be inferred. Broadly speaking, does the Lord extend this command to encompass our social relationships, as well? The answer may be "yes" and

You Are What You Think

"no," but let me try and explain. God's standard goes on to state "for what fellowship hath righteousness with unrighteousness? and what communion hath light with darkness" (II Corinthians 6:14b)? Herein, the Lord is clear that He wants us to maintain our vital intimate relationships with those of like-faith in Him. This includes close fellowship with those Christians with whom we meet on a regular social basis.

Obviously, we are to be a leavening and saltine influence on those who are not Christians; so we must go to them and let them know we sincerely care and hold respect for their person. In addition, we should be open to being a friend, if the Lord opens this door. But, it does not mean we lower our personal Christian standards in order to get along. We are to be in the world, but not of the world. We are called to stand in Christ and witness of His love. Surely, when that love is accepted, deeper levels of fellowship will follow and hopefully develop!

Regarding marriage, the Christian is not to marry one who is not a born-again Christian. Why? Simply because, how can two people form a truly intimate marriage relationship without being in agreement on their respective philosophies of life? It is impossible and God knows it. Read Ephesians 5:22-33 and hear what Paul says about the marriage relationship. He states:

Wives, submit yourselves unto your own husbands, as unto the Lord.

Husbands, love your wives, even as Christ also loved the church, and gave himself for it.

Why?

> That He (Christ) might present it to himself a glorious church, not having spot, or wrinkle, or any such thing; but that it should be holy and without blemish. So, ought men to love their wives as their own bodies. He that loveth his wife loveth himself (Ephesians 5:22, 25, 27-28).

These words of the Apostle clearly declare several principles. <u>One</u>, that God can only honor the marriage that is founded on Him and His Word. He knows that the relationship can never fully succeed as He intends, and desires, without there first being a spiritual bond, or unity, between Himself and the two individuals.

Neil C. Roth

<u>Secondly</u>, how can a husband and wife know true agape love without knowing and loving the Author of true love? Oh yes, counterfeit brands of love seem to be so nice, like frosting on a cake, but without Christ's Spirit in the heart, no person, and that includes you and me, can truly love, like Jesus wants us to love each other. Study the attributes of God's love in First Corinthians, chapter 13. Could you possibly, in your own wisdom and strength, love as described therein? You would have to say no! Well then, put the shoe on the other foot: Could your non-Christian mate possibly be able to love you, as Christ loved the church and gave himself for it? You see, by marrying the unbeliever, you are drastically short-changing yourself with a mate that cannot, by virtue of his nature, possibly know what God's agape love is! The answer is, and always has been--DO NOT MARRY AN UNBELIEVER!

Be careful here, however. Many fine Christian women or men who were lonely, or perhaps a bit desperate for companionship, entered into marriage assuming that their intended was a Christian because he or she said they were. Watch out here! Satan believes in God and trembles but his rebellion against God and His Truth is absolutely complete. The key is to be found in the potential mate's spiritual appetites, attitudes, and behaviors.

I am advocating a courtship period that will provide sufficient time to evaluate the sustained presence of several qualities in the intended spouse. These qualities are worthy of careful evaluation, for, if you marry in haste, as the saying goes, you can repent in leisure. Some questions you might ask: "Does he speak often of the Lord and enjoy the ministry of a Bible-believing and Christ-honoring Christian fellowship?" "Does he regularly read the Word and pray?" "Does he personally witness to others about his love for the Savior?" "Is he considerate and respectful of his beloved as a person?" "Does he think more highly of himself than is warranted by the Holy Spirit?" "Is his chief aim in life to seek first the Kingdom of God? (Matthew 6:33)

But take note, success in marriage, or in any relationship, consists in not only finding the right mate, or associate, but in being the right mate or associate! Many more pertinent questions need to be asked and be answered before the final decision could be made. Of critical importance is the question: "what level of love exists between us (if, because, or in-spite-of), and do we really like each other?" Someone was once heard to

You Are What You Think

say: "Choose a mate by your ear, not by your eye." Caution: Love at first sight usually results in divorce at first slight!

But in all practicality, any business partnership must ask many of these same questions. "What are the goals and philosophy upon which we wish to do business?" "Is the business going to glorify God or mammon?" "Is it going to exploit or serve?" "Is it going to be based upon honest labor and production, or upon making its gains at the expense of others?"

Paul said to us: "Stand fast therefore in the liberty wherewith Christ hath made us free, and be not entangled again with the yoke of bondage" (Galatians 5:1). In other words, you have been born-again as a free person. Stay free! Jesus said, "Take my yoke (we will pull together) upon you, and learn of me" (Matthew 11:29a).

Leslie Parrott, minister, author, and President of Olivet Nazarene College, reveals an often forgotten principle in his practical book, entitled <u>Easy to Live With</u>. When marriage, or any relationship, is being contemplated: "The real test of maturity is our ability to make ourselves easy to live with."[19] In essence, he is saying that we must prepare to become loving and lovable.

In addition, Dr. Parrott describes four characteristics that Christ teaches in the Beatitudes that promote the habits of happiness and help us in predicting a happy marriage or relationship. These personal qualities are: "(1) Adjustability (Matthew 5:3, 5, & 7); (2) Sensitivity (Matthew 5:7); (3) Absorbs the jolts of life (Matthew 5:11, 12); and (4) A personal faith in Christ (Matthew 5:6, 8; John 15:11)."[20] The lesson is clear as mountain air: NEVER TO BE YOKED TO ONE WHO REFUSES THE YOKE OF OUR LORD JESUS CHRIST. It would be like two oxen fighting each other in their yokes wanting to go their own ways. How can two walk together except they be agreed? Be ye equally yoked together and save yourself untold heartache!

C.R.T. PROGRESS PRINCIPLE NO. 10--BE FAITHFUL AND TRUSTWORTHY WITH GOD AND MEN!

Are you really honest? Can you be trusted with your friend's wife or your employer's money? The writer to the Hebrews said: "But without faith it is

Neil C. Roth

impossible to please him: for he that cometh to God must believe that he is, and that he is a rewarder of them that diligently seek him" (Hebrews 11:6).

The Apostle is surely referring to our faith in the fact that God exists. But, in a profoundly deeper sense, more than belief in the fact of His existence is necessary in order to have a relationship. We must come to believe deeply in God's integrity as a person! This means we view Him as One who is ultimately faithful and trustworthy! Also, this expectancy, that we can be trusted, is a hoped-for experience within all humans. How refreshing it is to meet someone who believes us. The saying, "A man's word is his bond" is not frequently heard or believed much any longer. Instead of trusting and being trustworthy, we insure ourselves against every form of deceitfulness and untrustworthiness! What a price we pay, because we have forgotten that honesty and integrity really do pay! In not exploiting others, they in turn learn to become more trustworthy.

Faith lifts the other person and says, "I have every confidence in you and know I can trust you without fear!" Marvelously, our faithful expectations of others, more often than not, begin to be fulfilled beyond our wildest dreams. This is because, faith elevates the soul, and lifts the spirit when we show it to God, and to our fellow sojourners here.

I repeatedly hear people comment on the lack of honesty and ethics they see evidenced in the business world. Yet, more tragic, in my opinion, is the so-called Christian (or church) who does not meet his financial obligations and who seemingly makes no sincere effort to inform the business of his payment intentions. What must the world think? You know what they think! "If Christians are like that, who needs them, or their church?" Thankfully, when Christ rules our lives, the Priority Principles, as they are energized by God's Spirit, are operational, in every way, in our dealings with others. Respect for others and ourselves, stewardship of goods, reputation (both our Lord's and our's), and true <u>we</u> love, are not only believed, but displayed in practice and behavior.

In addition, the Rotary Club four-way test of business ethics is most applicable to all areas of personal ethics. It is premised on four questions: (1) Is it the truth?; (2) Is it fair to all concerned?; (3) Will it build goodwill and better friendships?; and (4) Will it be beneficial to all concerned? Someone once stated: "It is often surprising to find what height may be obtained merely by remaining on the level."[21] Be challenged to be

You Are What You Think

honest and trustworthy, for nothing so baffles another, especially if he is dishonest, as much as finding another who is treating him honestly and with integrity. Ralph Waldo Emerson once said, "The greatest homage we can pay for truth is to use it."

Jesus declared, "But, let your communication be, Yea, yea; Nay, nay; for whatsoever is more than these cometh of evil" (Matthew 5:37). What has He really said here? To be sure, He has commanded us not to swear oaths using God's name, etc., but more importantly, we must be people whose word can be trusted. The world will only be won to Christ as they begin to perceive Christians as loving, winsome, and trustworthy. Then, you see, faith is created, or restored, and lasting spiritual and human relationships will finally have a foundation that is sure. Be faithful and trustworthy with God and men!

CHAPTER REVEW AT A GLANCE

The Ten C.R.T. Progress Principles:

1. Read and study the Bible daily.
2. Pray without ceasing.
3. Be filled with the Holy Spirit.
4. Worship regularly with other believers.
5. Share your faith frequently.
6. Be joyful and wholesome.
7. Be positive--live above your circumstances.
8. Learn how to handle temptation.
9. Be equally yoked together with believers.
10. Be faithful and trustworthy with God and men.

As you review, try not to forget, <u>love</u> must be the Preeminent Principle in your life, if you are to succeed with the Progress Principles. Begin, right now, to practice these C.R.T. Progress Principles in your daily living. Remember, today will be yesterday tomorrow! Surely, the only adequate preparation for tomorrow is the right stewardship for today.

FOOTNOTES

1. Doan, Eleanor L. The Speaker's Sourcebook. Grand Rapids: Zondervan Publishing House, 1962, p. 34.
2. Ibid, p. 192.
3. Bounds, E. M. Preacher and Prayer. Grand Rapids: Zondervan Publishing House, p. 6.
4. Shostrum, Everett L. & Montgomery, Dan. Healing Love. Nashville: Abingdon, 1978, p. 49.
5. Allee, G. Franklin. Evangelistic Illustrations. Chicago: Moody Press, 1961, p. 217.
6. Jones, E. Stanley. How to be a Transformed Person. Nashville: Abingdon-- Cokesbury, 1951, p. 244.
7. Burns, Jabez. 500 Sketches and Skeletons of Sermons. Grand Rapids: Kregel Publications, 1959, p. 254.
8. Allee. op. cit., p. 390.
9. Doan. op. cit., p. 284.
10. Ibid, p. 137.
11. Ibid, p. 74.
12. Ibid, p. 74.
13. Jones. op. cit., p. 241.
14. Frankl, Victor E. Psychotherapy and Existentialism. New York: A Clarion Book, Simon & Schuster, 1967, p. 15.
15. Doan. op. cit., p. 262.
16. Jones. op. cit., p. 140.
17. Doan. op. cit., p. 261.
18. Roth, Laurie J. Song: "God is Our Only Strength." All rights reserved, Copyright, 1981.
19. Parrott, Leslie. Easy to Live With. Grand Rapids: Baker Book House, 1973, pp. 12-18.
20. Ibid, p. 130.
21. Doan. op. cit., p. 127.

CHAPTER EIGHT

ACHIEVING EMOTIONAL CONTROL
THROUGH C.R.T. SELF-THERAPY

"Test yourselves to see if you are in the faith;
examine yourselves" (II Corinthians 13:5a N.A.S.).

"The imprudent man reflects upon what he has said,
the wise man upon what he is going to say."

Hopefully, by this time, you have not become overwhelmed by the presentation of Christian Rational Thought Psychology and its numerous precepts, principles, and insights. I do commend you for considering the book's contents to this point and assure you that this final chapter, toward which we have been moving, will systematically illuminate the very practical and life-changing C.R.T. self-therapeutic approach.

C.R.T. Therapy is most effective, as a tool, in the hands of a Christian, professional, minister, counselor, or psychologist in the helping professions. But, without hesitation, I can recommend its use by anyone who wishes to grow and develop as a rational Christian person. By growth and development, I refer to all possible levels, including the intellectual, emotional, and spiritual.

There is ample evidence supporting the concept of self-management in counseling. Major self-therapeutic strategies include activities in self-observation, environmental planning, and behavioral planning (see Thoresen & Mahoney[1]). Many different therapists have developed behavioral change techniques that the client can use to check the accuracy

Neil C. Roth

and rationality of his perceptions, thoughts, and beliefs. In effect, the results are seen in new, rational integrative learning and behaviors that are centering about one's relationships and reactions to the total environment (people and things). These then, become a replacement for the old irrational, disintegrative, self-defeating ideas and behaviors (see Bandura[2]; Ellis[3]; Kaufer and Philips[4]; Krumboltz & Thoresen[5]).

In the future, it is apparent that, even though behavioral counseling will tend to emphasize intervention through the counselor-counselee relationship, increased focus will be upon assisting clients to learn how to better cope with their difficult life situations and develop more perceptive and effective prevention attitudes and behaviors.[6]

Self-therapy is engaged in, by millions of people each day, as they remain open to the lessons of life. This therapeutic growth takes place because of the existence of an environment of love, hope, and faith between people, and with God. Truly the atmosphere for positive change is characterized by the central principle of genuine (agapē) love that persons experience with each other and with their Lord. Martin and Deidre Bobgan, in their extensive and provocative study dealing with the compatibility of Christianity and Psychotherapy, list three therapeutic principles (in addition to being instructed in God's Word) that have been consistently effective since human relationships began. They cite "listening/talking; confessing/accepting; and thinking/understanding."[7]

Because of their simplicity, we often fail to relate these principles to the ministry of the Holy Spirit, and certainly to the therapeutic support of concerned Christian brothers and sisters. In the present context, when we talk with God, He always listens (II Chronicles 7:14); when we listen in quietude, we will know Him (Psalm 46:10). When we carefully analyze psychotherapy, it is people talking and listening to each other. Hence, our Lord Jesus Christ is accurately described as the "Counselor" by Isaiah (Isaiah 9:6). Praise God, He does listen and speak to us through prayer, the Word, and through His precious Holy Spirit.

The confessing/accepting aspect implies that there will be a spirit of freedom to share any thought or problem without criticism or reprisal. Jesus Christ calls upon us to be brutally honest with Him about our true selves. Only in His presence, can we truly find an atmosphere of acceptance that is characterized by unconditional positive regard, and

192

You Are What You Think

freedom from threat (see Matthew 11:28-30). Carl Rogers, the father of Client-Centered Psychotherapy, not only espouses the above tenets, but feels strongly that every person, when given unconditional, positive regard, and when provided a threat-free environment, has the inherent ability to diagnose his own problems. Then, as a result of insight, he can discover and move toward psychic healing and self-actualization.[8]

Frankly speaking, without Jesus Christ in the center of our being, our identities are sadly lacking the affirmation and confirmation we need as persons. The Apostle John reinforces this thought when he urges that we confess our sins so that we might be forgiven and cleansed. But much more happens to us, in that, catharsis, that momentous relief that comes when we tell someone of our sin and trauma, is experienced. In forgiveness, we are affirmed by Jesus Christ as autonomous persons who are indwelt by a friend that sticks closer to us than a brother and who says "because I live, you really count as a person!" The time of spiritual refreshing is widened in the generation of (or restoration in the case of the Christian) our personal relationship with God, and man, that is characterized as a "walk in the light" (I John 1:5-9). Furthermore, this catharsis is often accompanied by both intellectual and spiritual insight.

The activity of thinking/understanding is not only descriptive of our cognitive and emotional response to life and God (through gained insights) but certainly of spiritual insights that God grants to us through the medium of faith, hope, and love. Paul prayed for the Christians at Ephesus

> That the God of our Lord Jesus Christ, the Father of Glory, may give unto you the spirit of wisdom and revelation in the knowledge of him: the eyes of your understanding being enlightened; that ye may know what is the hope of his calling, and what the riches of the glory of his inheritance in the saints (Ephesians 1:17, 18).

The Bobgans add this commentary, "While these processes...may occur in psychotherapy, they are limited in such a setting because they are used for other purposes than for a person to come into a deeper and fuller walk with God."[9] Surely, the Lord has called out Christians to counsel others in the power of His Holy Spirit. It would be well to remember, however, that Jesus Christ is the most eminently qualified counselor!

A word of caution is warranted: C.R.T. self-therapy will probably be less than effective when used by those who are suffering with moderately to serious emotional distress. The following criteria may be helpful in assisting one in deciding upon the seriousness of the individual's adjustment problems.

First--Intensity. Are the reactions of the individual inappropriate, or out of proportion, to the situation? For example, does he always go into a rage when any gratification is hindered or denied?

Second--History and Duration. Typically, emotional distress and dysfunctional behavior patterns of long-standing (usually a year or longer) are considered to be more serious than those of shorter duration.

Third--Contact with Reality. Is fact constantly confused with reality? Many persons, like exaggerators, fantasizers, and pathological liars, do not or cannot distinguish between fact and fiction.

Fourth--Conflict Zone. Does the individual's total personality seem to be affected? Do the symptoms, like exaggeration or withdrawal, seem to pervade every area of the person's experience?

Fifth--Treatment Response. Has the person responded to therapeutic assistance in the past? Remember, some persons do not will to get better, so resist any therapeutic help!

Of critical importance, decisive referral to a competent Christian helping professional should be made for those persons who exhibit the signs of emotional distress mentioned in the preceding criteria. This is not to say that the C.R.T. Therapeutic steps might not be helpful to a mildly distressed individual with long-standing symptoms. On the contrary, after all other therapies may have failed, either partially or fully, C.R.T. Therapy, with its emphasis on the ministry of the Word and the Holy Spirit, may be just the encouragement for the distressed person to begin to desire personal change and growth. So much is dependent upon the individual's will and capability to discern reality at the time of encountering C.R.T. self-therapy. When in doubt about the seriousness of any individual's emotional condition, it is always good counsel to seek trained Christian professional psychological counsel.

Because most of us do not purposely desire to be unhappy, emotionally distressed, or unfulfilled in life, it becomes essential that we learn how to control our emotional responses by first learning how to control our

You Are What You Think

thinking. To successfully accomplish this goal, we need to remember that our Lord's precepts and principles must become part of our thinking and being--then feelings will be naturally appropriate and reflective of His intention and design for us.

Watchman Nee has stated most insightfully:

> We should remember that in walking after the spirit, all our actions must be governed by principles, since the spirit has its own laws and principles. To walk by the spirit is to walk according to its laws. With spiritual standards, everything becomes sharply defined. There is a precise standard of right and wrong. If it is "yes" it is "yes" whether the day is clear or cloudy; if it is "no" then it is "no" whether exciting or depressive. The Christian's walk should follow a distinct standard. But if his emotion is not handed over to death, he cannot abide a permanent standard. He will live by the whim of his vacillating feelings and not according to a definite principle. A principled life differs enormously from an emotional life. Anyone who acts from emotion cares neither for principle nor for reason but only for his feeling.[10]

Before proceeding through the eight C.R.T. Self-therapeutic steps, remember that your problem is probably not unique to the annals of human experience. For sure, the Lord knows about it in every detail and wants to assist you in its solution. It would be appropriate to pause right now and ask Him to illuminate your mind and heart to see His perfect will for your life in this matter.

This prayer, or one like it, might be helpful for you to use:

Dear Lord Jesus,

> I sincerely and committedly place myself in your therapeutic hands and ask that your blessed Holy Spirit shall reveal to me an accurate understanding of your precepts and principles, and the presented C.R.T. Insights, so that I might be guided by Christian rational thought into accurately and realistically assessing my cognitive, emotional, and spiritual condition, and be granted

Neil C. Roth

insight into the causes and solutions surrounding my besetting emotional and spiritual problems.

Thank you for hearing and acting upon my request for help.

In Jesus' Name, I Pray,
Amen.

Furthermore, keep in mind that many experiences in life leave scars that can never be completely erased. God promises forgiveness and redemption but physical and emotional scars are fixed. In a redemptive way, they are useful in reminding us of those elements of life to be avoided like the plague! But, thankfully, the Lord entrusted us with the power, through our human will and power of choice, to select for ourselves the attitude we might wish to assume toward any event or condition in life. Our unregenerate and carnal wills are generally prone to select attitudes and behaviors that are not in keeping with God's desired will. Truly, we are to place Jesus Christ in the driver's seat in this respect. We are what <u>we choose</u> (Jesus and us) to think about any experience in life!

Aldous Huxley put it in a slightly different but similar way: "Experience is not what happens to you; it is what you do with what happens to you." God has a redemptive solution for each of our problems if we will only trust Him to work it out in our lives (see Romans 8:28).

You might ask, "What about the situation that I can't change, like a terminal illness or business reverse?" or "Who can fully know God's desired will for every situation in life?" Remember, the Lord wants us to have His ways of thinking ("the mind of Christ") and His ways are keyed to utter truth and respect for persons. J. Grant Howard, Jr. has given us a very timely treatise on <u>Knowing God's Will and Doing It</u>. In discussing how we can discern the Lord's desired will (and, incidently His thoughts and attitudes), two factors that relate to God's Word and to His work, are presented as key discovery components in Figure 8.

Assuredly, the Word gives to us God's desired will for every life but it does not give us a comprehensive flight plan for every detail of life. This is where faith comes in: to fully trust God for those times and places in life we do not fully understand; and, to choose "His" redemptive attitudes

You Are What You Think

which ultimately bring all things into spiritual harmony within our lives (Romans 8:28). Paul's prayer for the Colossians echoes his concern that they might "be filled with the knowledge of His will in all wisdom and spiritual understanding" (Colossians 1:9b). What better prayer could we pray for ourselves?

It is discovered in the	It is discovered in the
WORD OF GOD	**WORK OF GOD**
Its precepts	in the world (external) and
Its principles	in the person (internal) through:
	circumstances,
	counsel,
	consequences,
	conscience,
	common sense,
	compulsion, and
	contentment.
This is the primary and sufficient revelation of the will of God for the unbeliever and the believer.	This is the secondary and supplementary revelation of the will of God.

--J. Grant Howard, Jr.[11]

Figure 8 THE DESIRED WILL OF GOD

In addition, before starting through the eight C.R.T. self-therapeutic steps, let stress and tension go. <u>Relax</u> and <u>be calm</u>! You will not be able to think rationally and clearly unless you keep your mind and body relaxed. Escape to a quiet place and clear your mind of all thoughts and think only of peace and tranquility. Perhaps you can imagine a beautiful mountain lake scene and put yourself into the picture.

Also, sometimes by exercising properly, we can relieve much hypertension that blocks lucid and fruitful contemplation of a truth. You can reliably count on the promise that there is rest for your soul in Jesus Christ (Matthew 11:28-30). He meets us when we signal our frustration

Neil C. Roth

with self and fruitless motion! The Lord calls us to listen to Him with total attention--"Be still and know that I am God" (Psalm 46:10a). David knew from experience that there was real "rest in the Lord" (Psalm 37:7).

Now, let us proceed to the C.R.T. self-therapy approach to straight thinking. The eight C.R.T. therapeutic steps for straight thinking are presented in Figure 9. An acronym using the word STRAIGHT is employed to assist the reader in remembering the essential steps of therapy. Please keep in mind that the same eight "straight" steps would be followed by the C.R.T. therapist in counseling with those individuals who would not be able, by virtue of some hindrance (eg.: serious emotional distress), to initiate and pursue their own self-therapy. C.R.T. self-therapy will be potentially effective if you are sincerely desirous of dealing honestly and courageously with your particular problem and accepting God's truth, as revealed by the Word of God, as your rule and guide for living. Self-analysis is never easy, however, but do not give up! The Lord will guide you with His counsel!

Order of
CRT self-
therapy steps:

1. <u>S</u>timulus--event or situation that you experience. Often is thought to be the problem.

4. <u>T</u>hought/s--are your thoughts rational or irrational as compared with Biblical precepts and principles, C.R.T. principles and insights, and with reliable experiential truth?

2. <u>R</u>esponse/s--feelings/emotions brought about by the stimulating event or situation. (eg.: fear, jealousy, guilt, envy, sympathy, love, depression, etc.

3. <u>A</u>ppraisal--rationality of thoughts in step 4. Compare your thoughts with C.R.T, precepts, principles, and insights, as well as experiential insights, etc. (Use the C.R.T. Problem Appraisal Inventory for recording your therapeutic findings- -see figure 11).

5. <u>I</u>nsight--discovery and understanding of inner nature of your problem.

6. <u>G</u>arbage day--saying No (and meaning it) to the irrational, self-destructive thoughts.

You Are What You Think

7.   Honesty--to face truth about God, self, and others. Acceptance of moral and spiritual responsibility.

8.   Trusting--Jesus Christ with your "total" life. Commitment to His Word. Saying "yes" to the rational, Christ-centered productive and loving thoughts, attitudes, and actions. Goal-setting for spiritual objectives. Now, you should:

        (1) Choose appropriate attitudinal and behavioral goals, and

        (2) Record these short and long-term goals on the C.R.T. Problem Appraisal Inventory and on the C.R.T. Personal Growth Covenant (see figures 11 and 15).

        (3) Enlist the moral and prayer support of a significant-other person. Have this person witness your intentions with his signature. Set a schedule of periodic feed-back conferences with him to report your progress.

The above therapeutic steps are based on the assumption that nearly all emotions (step 2) are caused by what we think (step 4) of, or about, the stimulus, and not caused by what happens to us (step 1), that is, as a result of the stimulus.

Figure 9 THE EIGHT C.R.T. SELF-THERAPEUTIC STEPS FOR STRAIGHT THINKING

We shall now work our way through the C.R.T. steps one by one. Keep in mind that the acronym using the word STRAIGHT does not suggest the exact order to follow in self-therapy, but does remind us of the essential factors of the therapeutic steps to consider. The order of these steps is determined by the prime assumption of this book, that being: (1) Nearly all emotional responses are caused, not by the events or experiences of our lives, but by (2) What we think about these events or experiences. Then, (3) it follows that since we can control our thinking and wills, we can learn to challenge irrational, Satanic thoughts, and by God's help, replace these thoughts with rational Christ-centered thoughts that are in line with His Word and Will. The end result of leaving our irrational, Satanic thoughts unchallenged and unchanged is that of emotional frustration and eternal fatality. When our beliefs/thoughts are energized by the love of Christ, emotional stability, fulfillment, and eternal life become the end results (see figure 10).

Neil C. Roth

YOU ARE WHAT YOU THINK
WHEN CONTROLLED
by

<u>Satanic Irrational Thoughts</u> | <u>Christian Rational Thoughts</u>

<u>B</u>eliefs (Carnal) | <u>B</u>eliefs
<u>E</u>ntertained and | <u>E</u>nergized by the
<u>L</u>eft (unchallenged) | <u>L</u>ove of Christ
<u>I</u>rrational bring about | <u>I</u>nspire
<u>E</u>motional | <u>E</u>motional
<u>F</u>loundering and | <u>F</u>ulfillment and
<u>S</u>adness | <u>S</u>tability

Figure 10 C.R.T. THOUGHT CATEGORIES

C.R.T. THERAPEUTIC STEP NO. 1: STIMULUS

Our first step toward discovering whether our thoughts are rational, or not, is to clearly understand a very simple but revolutionary concept: Namely, that what happens to us--we are cussed out, the tire goes flat, the boss fires us, a tornado hits, a loved one dies, the dog bites the neighbor, etc., etc.,--does not cause us (in most cases) to react emotionally. What does cause us to react emotionally is what, and how, we think about what has happened to us and around us during our daily lives. With this in mind, the stimuli of life are essentially powerless to effect our emotional life unless we allow them to! I am not referring to certain physical stimuli that would elicit automatic reflex responses like eye blinking, muscle twitches, etc. I do refer to those stimuli that impinge upon us that impact the intellectual and spiritual spheres of our consideration. The Priority Principles essentially deal with these provinces (centering on: the lust of the flesh, the lust of the eyes, and the pride of life).

You Are What You Think

A crucial flaw in most people's thinking occurs at this point: namely, that what happens to us is the culprit; the cause of our emotional distress (for review, refer to chapter three, for physical and psychosomatic causes of emotional distress)! Always remember that most stimuli have no power over us until we respond to them. Then we become personally effected and affected. Many times we are merely reacting to other people's reactions!

Jesus Christ has promised that we can, with His empowerment, withstand any temptation that is common to man" (I Corinthians 10:13). The word temptation used is close to being synonymous with the word stimulus because a person can be enticed by his own lust to yield to almost any stimulus (temptation). Frankly, we are like the temper of steel, being tested in the fires of life in order to see how true we are. It is only through being tested that our real worth is confirmed (see I Corinthians 3:10-15 for discussion on testing and works).

Now, if you are engaging in self-therapy, record the stimulus (what happened) situation at step one of the C.R.T. Problem Appraisal Inventory. (Notice, you will need to duplicate a copy (or copies) of the Inventory if you intend to engage in self-therapy).

C.R.T. THERAPEUTIC STEP NO. 2: RESPONSE

The next time something happens to you, identify the stimulus (eg.: a tire went flat, the phone rang in the middle of your shower, etc.) and then monitor your emotional response. Then ask yourself, "what feelings or emotions am I experiencing as a result of the stimulus situation?" "Am I angering, frustrating, depressing, bittering, sympathizing, joying, loving, to name a few?"

Again, if engaged in self-therapy, record your emotional and behavioral reactions to the situation at step two on the C.R.T. Problem Appraisal Inventory.

C.R.T. THERAPEUTIC STEP NO. 3 AND 4: APPRAISAL OF THOUGHTS

The appraisal process is more than just evaluation of our thinking. It is an action that is directed toward improved understanding and a desire

Neil C. Roth

to discover truth. To assist you in quantifying and clarifying the quality of your thoughts, the C.R.T. Problem Appraisal Inventory has been provided in figure 11. It is designed to follow the first six C.R.T. Therapeutic steps (see figure 9) through, in order, as the appraisal process is being experienced. As a further aid, the Ten Person Precepts, the Three Priority Principles, the Ten Progress Principles, and the Seven Cardinal Insights

Name_____   Date_____

Step 1   Stimulus: Step 2   Responses/s:
         (What Happened?)_____   (a)
                                                       Emotional: _____

         _____   _____
         _____   (b) Behavioral: _____
         _____   _____
         _____   _____

Step 3   List the possible   Step 4   Now, evaluate rationality of
         interpretations/thoughts that   each interpretation/thought
         may explain what happened.   in the light of the C.R.T.
         List your own first.   Precepts, Principles, Insights,
                                                       and proven experiential truth.
                                                       State why! Cite evidence. State
                                                       whether rational or irrational.

         (a) _____   (a) _____
         (b) _____   (b) _____
         (c) _____   (c) _____

Step 5   "How should I have
         responded?" (List rational
         responses according to God's
         precepts and principles. Cite
         Scripture verse and precept,
         principle, insight.)

           Christian Rational Response   Biblical-Insight Reference

         (a) Emotional: _____   (a)_____
         _____   _____

         (b) Behavioral: _____   (b)_____
         _____   _____

You Are What You Think

Step 6 Improvement Steps to   Target Completion
        Facilitate Personal Change
        and Growth. Target
        Completion

        Short-Term Goals: Date: Long-Term Goals: Date:
        (a)_____/_____   (a)_____/_____
        (b)_____/_____   (b)_____/_____

Figure 11 C.R.T. PROBLEM APPRAISAL INVENTORY (FOR USE IN SELF-THERAPY)

For Successful Christian Living are each provided for easy reference in this chapter (see figure 12).

In Appendix letter B, a listing of selected scriptures are provided that are arranged according to rational and irrational thought categories, and the by-products of such thinking. It would be most helpful to have a Bible handy for precept and principle study purposes. Also, do not be reluctant to underline key Bible verses or passages and write significant insights down in the margins. We learn and remember best when we reinforce our minds through kinesthetic activities, and by sharing our newly discovered insights with a significant-other person.

Now to the appraisal of our thinking. Hopefully, we have come to the realization, that our emotional responses are a nearly direct result of what we think about the stimulus (what happened to us, or others) situation. Our next step is to evaluate the validity, reliability, and rationality of the data that has been programmed into our minds and has now become our thoughts.

The following questions form the base of this inquiry: (1) What are the possible reasons/interpretations that might possibly explain why the stimulus situation occurred? For example, why did the tire go flat on route to work? Some possible reasons might be: overheating, excessive wear, defect, Murphy's Law at work, etc. (For those in self-therapy, record answers to this question at step 3 of the C.R.T. Problem Appraisal Inventory.)

(2) Were my interpretations rational or irrational in the light of the C.R.T. Precepts, Principles, Insights, and proven experiential truth? Our

Neil C. Roth

emotional response/s will give us a strong clue to the answer to this question. For example, if I became exceedingly angry at the tire for going flat, then my emotional reaction is not based upon rational thinking. Why? Because tires have no being or mind and they are the inanimate products of man's ingenuity. If we could reliably determine that the tire failed due to a factory worker's neglect, we might be on more solid ground to be upset. But, as a Christian, can we? After all, there may be a dozen good reasons, other than neglect of duty, that hindered the factory worker from producing the tire free from defect! But, what if he purposely flawed the tire during creation? Then, he probably is being overcome by a negative attitudinal problem and is not able at that particular time to function in the best interests of the buying public, his company, or himself. Besides, we are told to pray for those who persecute us or despitefully use us (Matthew 5:44)!

At this point, check out your interpretations/thoughts against the C.R.T. Precepts, Principles, Insights, and proven experiential truth (many of the 12 irrational ideas of Albert Ellis are helpful appraised insights--see chapter 6, pp. 199-201. Also refer to the C.R.T. Auxiliary Trait Checklist, figure 13, which makes use of Maslow's list

----

****

<u>The Central Principle--The Love Principle</u>

****

<u>The C.R.T. Person Precepts</u>
(Paraphrased Version)

1. Please love me solely for I am your creator and God and I sincerely love you.
2. No substitute god is necessary--I am your all in all and will meet all your needs.
3. Speak of and to me with love and respect.

You Are What You Think

4. Communicate and fellowship with me--I want to hear from you regularly.
5. Respect and love your mother and father.
6. Respect and love all other persons--life is sacred.
7. Be faithful in marital and all other human relationships.
8. Be trustworthy with the resources and possessions of others.
9. Be truthful in all thought and conversation.
10. Be content with what God has given you.

****

The C.R.T. Priority Principles

1. Flee lust--Respect your body--Trust God for needs (the "provision" principle).
2. Seek God first and foremost and He will provide material blessings according to His will (the "possession" principle).
3. We are saved to serve--not to be served (the "position" principle).

****

The Seven Cardinal C.R.T. Insights

1. If you <u>will</u> to change, you can!
2. You can <u>stop blaming</u>, and <u>assume</u> <u>responsibility</u>!
3. You can learn to <u>control your thinking and emotions</u>!
4. You can <u>find your life by losing it</u>!
5. You can learn to <u>face reality without fear</u>!
6. You can learn to <u>love and be loved</u>!
7. You can learn to <u>become a problem-solver</u>!

****

The C.R.T. Progress Principles

1. Read and study the Bible daily.
2. Pray without ceasing.
3. Be filled with the Holy Spirit.

Neil C. Roth

4. Worship regularly with other believers.
5. Share your faith frequently.
6. Be joyful and wholesome.
7. Be positive--live above your circumstances.
8. Learn how to handle temptation.
9. Be equally yoked together with believers.
10. Be faithful and trustworthy with God and men.

★★★★★★★

Figure 12 RECAP OF C.R.T. PERSON PRECEPTS, PRIORITY PRINCIPLES, INSIGHTS, AND PROGRESS PRINCIPLES

Self-rating Scale										To what degree do you possess the following traits?
1	2	3	4	5	6	7	8	9	10	1. Realistic perception of the world. (Rose-colored or clear glasses? Free from or bound to past, present, or future events.)
										2. Acceptance of self, others, and the world for what they are. (Unconditional positive regard and respect for all persons, and the world.)
										3. Spontaneity in behavior and inner experience. (Enthusiasm and zest in response to the real and spiritual worlds.)
										4. Focus of interest on problems rather than self. (Critical or redemptive spirit-- positive or negative mind-sets.)
										5. Capacity for detachment. (Can think on spiritual and philosophical matters.)

You Are What You Think

6. Independence in the sense of self-containment.
   (Unduly dependent upon others--independent and content to enjoy the company of oneself.)

7. Freshness of appreciation of people and things.
   (Moving toward others and things with love and respect--moving away in fear.)

8. Capacity for profound mystical experiences.
   (Hungering and thirsting after God and His righteousness.)

9. Identification with the human race.
   (Accepting or rejecting being human and finite.)

10. Deep emotional relations with small circle of friends.
    (Are not afraid to risk self--afraid to risk self.)

11. Democratic attitude and values.
    (Believe in moral boundaries that grant all persons equal rights and respect.)

12. Ability to discriminate between means and ends.
    (Does the end justify the means according to Scripture?)

13. Philosophical rather than hostile sense of humor.
    (Can we laugh at ourselves and with others?)

14. Creativeness.
    (Do we feel compelled to creatively contribute to God and man?)

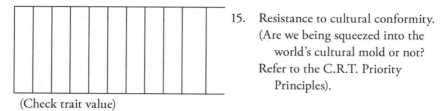

15. Resistance to cultural conformity. (Are we being squeezed into the world's cultural mold or not? Refer to the C.R.T. Priority Principles).

(Check trait value)

Figure 13 C.R.T. AUXILIARY CHECKLIST

On a scale of 1-10 (1 = lowest no up to 10 = highest yes), ask yourself, "How do I rate myself regarding the degree of trait possession in the above list?" A score of 125-150 probably indicates high rationality (high degree of self-actualization); 100-125 = moderate rationality (moderately high degree of self-actualization); and lower scores would suggest a low degree of rationality and little movement toward self-actualization.

C.R.T. AUXILIARY TRAIT CHECKLIST FOR THE EVALUATION OF RATIONAL THOUGHTS

(Adapted from Maslow's List of Traits Most Commonly Found in Self-Actualizing People)[12]

of traits found in self-actualizing people. This check list can assist you in evaluating the rationality of your thinking with regard to key philosophical and spiritual ideals. Though not exacting, the total score earned may suggest some evidence of the need for thinking to be challenged and modified. Are your thoughts/interpretations in line with proven facts? Are your thoughts rational or irrational? Are they carnal or spiritual? (You may wish to refer back to the C.R.T. Model of the Mind in chapter 6 and review the thinking, attitudinal and behavioral characteristics of the carnal and spiritual minds. Also, see the C.R.T. Model of Man in chapter 7 for additional review).

For self-therapists, record your answers to these questions at step 4 of the C.R.T. Problem Appraisal Inventory.

Keep in mind, when attempting to determine rationality, some of the pitfalls that hinder clear thinking such as hasty generalizations, prejudice,

You Are What You Think

semantical errors, negative mindset, temptation to psychological closure (forming a conclusion without complete data), and drawing invalid conclusions from our premises (see chapter 6, Cardinal Insight no. 3).

But, "what," you ask, "if I discover that the evidence from my investigation was not conclusive?" In other words, you found that the data was unclear, incomplete, inaccurate, unavailable! Then, have the personal courage to keep your interpretations tentative! No one really wants to be shown up as ignorant or stupid, so we all, at times, force a conclusion with insufficient data in order that we might say, "I know." But wait, in reality we are generally more humiliated and shamed when we are found out to be not all-knowing! Remember, only God is omniscient! Trust His Word for the right answers!

Also, learn to say to yourself and others, "I DON'T KNOW." This response will be refreshing to others and bring relief to you. Why? Because you can stop pretending to know everything, and avoid living under the burden of being "right" about everything. We must constantly remind ourselves that only God is perfect and the perfection He calls us to is a relative kind--we are to be perfect as He enables redeemed humans to be perfect, <u>in</u> <u>Him</u> (see Matthew 5:48). This is an "impossible perfection" made possible by God's redemptive grace as revealed through Jesus Christ!

Not only is it difficult not to say "I am right," but it is just as hard to say "I am wrong." Bear in mind that you will not have to say as many "I am wrongs" if you start right now by not saying so many "I am rights." Forethought spares afterthought!

I am convinced that most of the emotional distress we experience is experienced because we too hastily formulate our conclusions without proper foundation of fact. Why not be tentative, for if you find out later that you have been slighted, angering is still open as a response option. Hopefully, however, as a Christian, a more excellent way of responding will be chosen.

C.R.T. THERAPEUTIC STEP NO. 5: INSIGHT

At this step, an understanding of the bottom-line, previously hidden nature of your thinking and behavioral problem, becomes known. You

Neil C. Roth

might exclaim: "Eureka! I am now aware of the self-defeating, irrational thoughts that have been stimulating and supporting my distressing emotional habit (or responses)!" It is precisely here, when insight is arrived at, that most people fail to progress toward changing their faulty ideas and behaviors. For many, the problem rests with the fact that they seem to have no real self and are largely dependent upon others for almost total confirmation and support. According to the Word of God, you can only be truly independent if you are willing to let go of your carnal self and take hold of the self-hood that Jesus Christ can create in you!

Another hindrance to acting affirmatively on the insight we have is our general lack of frustration tolerance. We always seem to want everything NOW! We are a society of "instant" this and that, with very little patience with, or practice in, growth, tolerance, and development. We say constantly, "Don't deprive me," or tell ourselves "the bankcard is always available!" This quick gratification trait is further revealed in the hidden statements we make to ourselves such as, "I can't stand rejection," or "I can't stand frustration." In effect, we constantly keep reindoctrinating ourselves with immature, irrational, self-defeating ideas that keep us from profiting from the insight we already have!

Also, insight is a result of our thinking that says: what has happened to us has had antecedent aspects. In other words, an effect or affect has a prior cause! Then, we should consider what we do to reindoctrinate ourselves. We must examine the negative, personal (or other-directed), statements and behaviors that are failure-oriented. Again, we must be courageous to face the truth about what we discover about our ways of thinking. We just might be prejudiced, bigoted, or hostile, all for no defensible, rational reason. "Don't give me the facts, my mind's already made up" is a more common condition than anyone realizes, I fear.

Insight is coming to grips with the real problem of your life, whatever that may be. In most cases, however, it centers around our attitude toward God, self, and others! Many times, our real problem does not immediately surface because the presenting--observable problems are symptomatically obvious to others and oftentimes hidden from ourselves. For example, we are angering because we did not get our way in a certain situation. We are aware of our anger (as are others around us) and continue to perpetuate it

You Are What You Think

by telling ourselves that "it is terrible and tragic not to get what we want!" This is an obvious example of a presenting-observable problem.

But the real problem is not angering, or frustration but what these emotional expressions are symbolic of: a basic selfishness that says, "I am the only one that really counts in this life. No one else dare hinder me or I'll be unhappy and angry!"

Note that anger consists of two main parts: (1) "I didn't get what I wanted and I'm angry" and, (2) "Since I didn't get my way, I'm going to punish the person (or thing) that kept me from getting my way!" The first phase of anger, characterized by irritation, annoyance, and resentment, is less serious, in that we can usually defuse it without suffering drastic consequences. But, when our anger reaches stage two, we are usually acting out behaviors that are increasingly hostile and usually directed toward other persons. In some respects, those who can express their anger outwardly are hampered less with inward stress than those that hold their angry feelings in. When anger is not expressed outwardly, it typically turns into depression. This happens because depression is a societally acceptable emotional reaction, whereas, anger is not.

Our self-induced depression takes several forms: (1) <u>Guilt</u>-<u>caused depression</u>, due to real or imagined offenses. Regarding our real offenses, down deep we are angry at ourselves for getting caught, or in suffering alienation from man and God, and the loss of self-esteem; (2) <u>Feeling</u> "self-pity" because something in life was unfair or unjust. Again, we did not get what we wanted; and (3) "<u>Other pity</u>" <u>depression</u> that involves us in feeling sorry for the less fortunate. With the exception of grief depression (that is short term in duration), most every depression has anger at its base and is irrational in nature. Other depressive states include: manic-depressive (high--low mood swings); neurotic (loss of self-esteem); post-partum (after birth); success (no challenge left); involutional melancholia-hypochondriacal (affects the older person); and, psychotic (delusional symptoms due to guilt).

Guilt, a feeling of wrong-doing, is needed to hold anti-social impulses in check. It can, however, be harmful if we are feeding ourselves irrational thoughts like: "I am a bad person and can't do anything right," or, "I am so sinful to be enjoying this picnic today when I should be home working." Real offenses toward God or others should provoke guilt, but

Neil C. Roth

when founded upon imagined transgressions, it is extremely irrational and worthless, and should be decisively challenged.

Sometimes, the insight into the nature of the real problem does not surface immediately but is deferred until a later time. So, do not be alarmed if no "bells ring" or "sirens blow" to signal your problem-insight! You may have to take considerable time to sort out your thoughts and kindred emotions, and "try on" some new, and perhaps disturbing ideas. The Word of God is noted for uprooting old irrational ideas and behaviors. Listen to the Apostle Paul:

> For the word of God is quick, and powerful (living and active), and sharper than any twoedged sword, piercing even to the dividing asunder of soul and spirit, and of the joints and marrow, and is a discerner of (quick to discern) the thoughts and intents of the heart (Hebrews 4:12).

The marvelous truth here rests in the fact that the precious Holy Spirit will grant you His insight when you are ready to receive it! You see, God is intensely concerned that we have the mind of Christ. After all, Jesus Christ is the real therapist, not ourselves or another human being! (For self-therapists, record your insights in the space under step 5, "How should I have responded?" on the C.R.T. Problem Appraisal Inventory). Also, for further assistance in evaluating some types of emotional problems, refer to the C.R.T. Emotional Problem Guide (see figure 14).

C.R.T. THERAPEUTIC STEP NO. 6: GARBAGE DAY!

We have probably all heard of Fibber McGee and his chaotic closet which, when opened, spued out all manner of trash and junk onto the floor. Well, we humans are also guilty of not ridding ourselves of the sin and hindrances that so easily "gets us down" (see Hebrews 12:1) and keeps us from running the race of life as free-born persons. The Apostle Paul states that "Everyone who competes in the games (races) exercises self-control in all things"

You Are What You Think

Emotional Problem	Caused by	Recommended Solution	(Note: The Word of God has a perfect solution for each problem listed below. Consult your Bible!
Neurotic love "If" "Because"	An inaccurate conception of self and the beloved; Narcissistic, fails to see what is good for each.	May be incapable of love-- some love actively, some passively. Needs therapy in form of educative counseling on what real agapē love ("in-spite-of") is. Finding Christ is the bottom line answer (Ephesians 5:28-33; I Corinthians 13).	
Feelings of Inferiority	Self-image unacceptable; fails to live up to personal or other's expectations.	Needs to identify deficiencies and select more realistic goals. Must recognize that God values him as a most-respected person. Others can help by affirming his worth too! (Acts 10:34; John 3:16).	
Shyness	Lacking social skills.	A form of inferiority. Urge social contact in atmospheres (social and church groups) that are not snobbish or artificial (Acts 2; Hebrews 10:25).	

Neil C. Roth

Guilt	Real or imagined transgressions.	Analyze whether guilt is real and if it is, urge for confession of sin to men and God (I John 1:9). If imaginery, then urge to appraise, challenge, and change irrational thinking. May need professional help.
Fears	A normal learned response to an active threat; has an object.	Face the feared person or object. Talk about it with someone. Desensitize your fear by encountering it soon after the first negative experience (I John 4:17, 18; II Timothy 1:7).
Phobias	Fears without reasonable basis of fact.	Same as above. May need professional help in overcoming this fear (I John 1:6-9).
Anxiety	Social, vocational, romantic, personal unrest. Has no object.	Uncover cause--face it--remove it. May require professional help (Matthew 6:34; Philippians 4:6; I Peter 5:7).
Jealousy	Active or passive anger tied to actual or supposed loss of (always) prestige or love to a rival; social in origin. Caused by a sense of inadequacy.	Evaluate strengths and weaknesses. Develop more personal and social competencies to increase self-esteem (James 3:13-18; Matthew 5:43-46).

You Are What You Think

Depression		Anger--"I didn't get what I wanted and that is bad." (Differs from depressive--like symptoms of normal grief due to loss of loved one. Time heals).	Challenge thinking; replace selfish thoughts with God-centered ones. Do something for others. Get involved with others in positive situations. Change goals to more realistic ones that have a chance for succeeding (Psalm 43:5; Isaiah 4:10; Acts 27:22).
Anger-- (underlying reaction)	Hostility (directed toward people)	A key idea: "I didn't get what I wanted from people, plans, etc. I feel inferior and I don't like it."	Challenge irrational thought by asking: "Why should I always get my way?" Because, "Others live in this world and deserve to get their way too!" Give in sometimes (Proverbs 10:12; I Corinthians 13); usually others will too.

Figure 14 C.R.T. EMOTIONAL PROBLEM GUIDE

(I Corinthians 9:25a, N.A.V.).

In other words, we must come to the place where we are ready to say to God, ourselves, and others that "I want to change, I must change, I will change!" This can only occur when, after digesting our newly-revealed insight, we have the courage to say no (and mean it!) to the destructive, carnal, irrational, and Satanic attitudes and behaviors. This is a true GARBAGE DAY! No more do we pile the sinful irrational trash back into the closets of our minds but we rid ourselves of it FOREVER! (For review, see chapter 6, Cardinal Insights 1-4).

Then, it is time to move on to the next step of our therapy. (For self-therapists, you will be discarding (on the altar of the Lord) your mental, emotional, and moral "garbage"--all of those irrational thoughts and behaviors listed in step 4 of the C.R.T. Problem Appraisal Inventory).

215

Neil C. Roth

C.R.T. THERAPEUTIC STEP NO. 7: HONESTY TO FACE REALITY!

As a result of "dumping your irrational, carnal attitudinal and behavioral garbage," that is, "saying no to sin and irrationality," it is now the time to say that GREAT AMEN to God's ways. Saying yes to God's will is the only way to gain true fulfillment and satisfaction in this life, and in the life to come. Listen to the beloved Apostle, John: "Beloved, if our heart condemn us not, then have we confidence (boldness) toward God. And whatsoever we ask, we receive of Him, because we keep His commandments, and do the things that are pleasing in His sight" (I John 3:21-22).

The confidence to face the reality of our lives, and the Reality of the universe, will only come when we are ready to see things as they really are, in God's light; by His standards. Then, we can have true confidence because no sin will be in our nature to condemn us. God's confidence will help us accept: (1) who we are; (2) where we are; (3) what we are doing; and, (4) where we are going. This does not mean we are to be content with the status quo! Quite the contrary; we should continue to grow and develop in the nurture and nature of our Lord and Savior, Jesus Christ (see II Peter 3:18; II Thessalonians 1:3).

Benjamin Franklin once said, "What you would seem to be, be really." Really be real, and honestly face (1) who you are in God's sight; (2) where you are going in this life; (3) what you are doing, all within His awareness; and (4) where you will spend eternity in the next life.

In addition, there are four central ways that people can attempt to deal with their problems. Watch out by avoiding the first three ways of coping, for they all end up short-circuiting one's physical, mental, and spiritual health. People can (1) take <u>flight</u> by running away from their problem. Vagrancy, evasion, divorce, and many kinds of mobility are prime examples. The ego-defense of exaggerated fantasy or daydreaming could be associated with the fleeing of reality.

Then, there is the tactic of starting a (2) <u>fight</u>--lashing out (blaming others) in physical and psychological ways such as gossip, hostility, lying, stealing, murder, war, etc.

In addition, we sometimes try to (3) <u>forget</u> our problems through the mediums of alcohol, drugs, sex, excessive work or play, fantasizing, sleep,

You Are What You Think

etc. In the final analysis, these strategies seldom are very effective because they all tend to focus on the symptoms of the problem, but never on the real problem itself. In effect, these coping devices are a form of a lie, in that we are unwilling to view ourselves in a true light. So, when we lie and face it not, and swallow the lie, it poisons us, and we become bitter!

Hence, for real solutions, we must inevitably muster up the courage to (4) <u>face</u> our real problem/s with naked honesty! Rochenfoucauld once said, "True courage is shown by performing without witnesses what one might be capable of doing before the world."[13] Our courage is critically tested in the secret, quiet place of our minds and souls where only God can truly know us. David prayed for such an honest spirit: "Search me, O God, and know my heart: try me, and know my thoughts: and see if there be any wicked way in me, and lead me in the way everlasting" (Psalm 139:23, 24). (See chapter 6 and the 5th Cardinal Insight for further review).

C.R.T. THERAPEUTIC STEP NO. 8: TRUSTING JESUS CHRIST WITH YOUR TOTAL LIFE!

Hopefully, this final step of your self-therapy will be the first step of a long series of self-examinations in which you will joyfully learn to engage (see II Corinthians 13:5). Absolute surrender to Jesus Christ is the only prudent choice to be made. Resistance to Him can be projected only until the last breath of life, but what then? Ultimately, every knee shall bow and every mouth shall proclaim that Jesus is Lord!

Ample research evidence suggests that the first three words we humans learn to say are "ma ma," "da da," and "no"! Christ Jesus is calling us to quit saying "no" and start saying "yes" in our wills to our spiritual survival. Truly, we can only eternally survive if we believe the words of the Living Word. Rev. Jim Elliot, who gave his life in martyrdom for Christ in Ecuador, captures the futility of resisting God's call to discipleship. He said, "He is no fool that gives what he cannot keep in order to gain that which he cannot lose."

Our Lord Jesus Christ is calling us to "taste and see that He is good!" This tasting process involves the gradual development of a hungering and thirsting for righteousness (see Matthew 5:6; John 6:53-60). Jesus' words, when appropriated to our souls through insightful understanding and commitment, free up the channels of human and divine communication, and promote physical and spiritual healing. The glorious end result is new life that is evidenced by increased hungering and thirsting for new truth.

After experiencing this period of consideration of Jesus' words, we soon begin to savor and appreciate the Lamb of God, the Living Word. We truly begin to love Him, as He first loved us! Faith, we must remember, comes as a result of our reflective hearing and prayerful consideration of the rationality and veracity of the message that God has revealed through Jesus Christ in the Word (Romans 10:17).

Words create life and death! Marriages are consummated, businesses formed, divorces occur, wars are waged; all because of what men say to each other with words. The most important words spoken brought about the creation. Be once again amazed by reading Genesis, chapter 1 and 2, and witness when God spoke words, the world and its inhabitors became reality. God's words (Truth) created, and keep on creating as each of us decide to make them real and vital parts of our reality!

Much has been already said in previous discussions about the conditions of salvation that we must meet (see C.R.T. Cardinal Insight no. 4 in chapter 6) if we are to be "born again" Christians. Someone once said, "If you don't go to heaven before you die, you'll not get there afterward." We have no other choice open to us for salvation but to confess our sin with godly sorrow and accept the only remedy for sin--the death of Christ on the cross at Calvary. We cannot be saved by perfect obedience to the commandments because we cannot keep them perfectly. We cannot be saved by imperfect obedience because our Lord cannot accept imperfect obedience. So, it remains that our only hope and solution is Calvary. Jesus said, "And he that taketh not his cross, and followeth after me is not worthy of me. He that findeth his life shall lose it: and he that loseth his life for my sake shall find it" (Matthew 10:38-39).

Our Lord is calling us to rationally consider His Word and urges us to respond to the only fulfilling and eternal way of life that man can choose--the way of trusting Christ with our total life. After all has been said, we have to come back to the overriding truth reflected in the C.R.T. Central Principle, the love principle (see chapter 5): "Thou shalt love the Lord thy God with all thy heart,... soul,...mind. Thou shalt love thy neighbor as thyself" (Matthew 22:37, 39b).

You Are What You Think

Therapeutically, no vital changing can occur in any personality unless the changes we desire to see effected are in concert and obedience with the perfect will and laws of God for our lives. God has a blueprint for each human being that reflects His master plan (desired will) encompassing every minute detail. In essence, the Lord has recalled the human race back to the heavenly repair shop for extensive repairs because we have damaged our souls and bodies through gross neglect, abuse, and misuse. He has offered us a free "regenerative" personality face-lift and a "new loving spirit!"

The Lord has been clear to state that the reason we are in such a spiritual mess is that we have failed to heed the rules as stated in the maintenance and drivers' manuals, the books of the Holy Bible. Listen to God's promise for our restoration as given to the prophet Ezekial long ago:

> A new heart also will I give you, and a new spirit will I put within you; and I will take away the stony heart out of your flesh, and I will give you a heart of flesh. And I will put my spirit within you, and cause you to walk in my statutes, and ye shall keep my judgments, and do them (Ezekiel 36:26, 27).

How sad it is that the following fact seems to be one of the best kept secrets in the world. Simply, that we can learn to live victoriously in Jesus Christ in and through His Holy Spirit, and not be bothered by trying to keep His commandments in our own strength any longer. "How?" you ask. Because, they will be kept automatically by the Spirit of God loving in and through us (see Hebrews 4:9, 10).

On the other hand, self-love is self-conscious and seeks its own ends, whereas, God's love in our hearts is God-conscious and seeks only His will. God's love, revealed in the agapē-type love, rests on bedrock reality--God is love. Agapē always points to Jesus Christ, and true spirituality is asserted unconsciously, as a pure spring issues forth. E. Stanley Jones puts it like this:

> Eros has little room for gratitude. It gives itself because of what it gets. It has the atmosphere of the bargain counter--I give this, you give that. There can be little or no place for bubbling gratitude--it is rather a bargaining 'gimme.'

Neil C. Roth

> Agapē has little room for anything but gratitude. For God gave Himself a hundred per cent for nothing. He loved us, not because we were good, bad, or indifferent; He loved us--full stop. Anyone who comes in contact with that overwhelming agapē must respond in bubbling gratitude if he responds at all.[14]

After trusting the Lord with your total life, it will be important to put your newly acquired insight to work. This can be accomplished through the setting-up and acting-out of appropriate and realistic goals that will assist you as the mediums of change.

As a <u>first</u> step, review again those recorded aspects of your thinking, attitudes, and behaviors that contradict the C.R.T. precepts, principles, or experiential insights. (See steps 4 and 5 of the C.R.T. Problem Appraisal Inventory.

<u>Secondly</u>, analyze step five of the C.R.T. Problem Appraisal Inventory for possible ideas that will suggest positive actions to be taken in order to implement desired (mentioned in task 5) and needed changes. Conferring with your significant-other person about these ideas might be helpful at this time.

<u>Thirdly</u>, choose appropriate (in keeping with God's Word and proven experience) and realistic attitudinal and behavioral goals. They should be decidedly specific, such as, "I will read the Scriptures for fifteen minutes per day beginning today." Or, "Everytime, I begin to experience anger, I will monitor my thoughts and analyze whether or not my potential or real reactions are in keeping with God's ways." These are specific objectives that can be quantified and qualified by any person who desires to change. A short-term goal might be: "I will spend 30 minutes a day with my son in recreational activity for the next six weeks." A long-term goal could be: "Over the next year, I plan to take my family to church each and every Sunday for both morning and evening services." Or, "I plan to read the Bible through by the end of this calendar year."

The <u>fourth</u> task is to write down your short and long-term goals at step six of the C.R.T. Problem Appraisal Inventory. Evaluate them for Christian appropriateness, practicality, and realism. Our Lord is not the author, or affirmer, of confusion. Be organized and clear in your goal-setting, and you will have a far better chance to accomplish their fulfillment.

You Are What You Think

Finally, the <u>fifth</u> task is to prepare the C.R.T. Personal Growth Covenant upon which you will record your desired short and long-term goals for personal improvement (see figure 15). Then, enlist the moral and prayerful support of a significant-other person with whom you will share these goals. This individual should be a Christian whom you trust and feel confidence in. Your minister, friend,

_____

I, _____, with God's help have experienced the following attitudinal and behavioral insights that have made me aware of needed improvements in my life. These insights are:

(1) _____

(2) _____

(3) _____

I do now solemnly commit myself, with God's help, and that of my friends, to the completion of the following attitudinal and behavioral goals:

Short-Term Attitudinal Goals (Be specific)	Objective Completion Date	Date Objective Actually Completed
(1)_____	_____	_____
(2)_____	_____	_____
(3)_____	_____	_____
Behavioral Goals (Be Specific)		
(1)_____	_____	_____
(2)_____	_____	_____
(3)_____	_____	_____
Long-Term Attitudinal Goals (Be specific)		
(1)_____	_____	_____
(2)_____	_____	_____
(3)_____	_____	_____
Behavioral Goals (Be specific)		

Neil C. Roth

(1)_____   _____   _____

(2)_____   _____   _____

(3)_____   _____   _____

I acknowledge my sacred responsibility, to God, to myself, and to my witness, in diligently pursuing and, if at all possible, completing the goals of this covenant.

_____   _____

Signature of Covenant-Maker   Date of Covenant-Making

_____   _____

Signature of Witness   Date of Witnessing

Figure 15 C.R.T. PERSONAL GROWTH COVENANT

spouse, neighbor, or counselor might be just the right "significant-other person." Once selected, share with him/her your goals and ask for their moral and prayer support. Please do not feel reluctant to ask a Christian to share your goals, for this is his duty as a Christian. Paul said, "Bear ye one another's burdens, and so fulfill the law of Christ" (Galatians 6:2).

In addition, have them witness your decision to grow by signing the C.R.T. Personal Growth Covenant. Be sure to give them a copy and, of course, you keep a copy for frequent personal reference.

Ask them to pray with, and for you, and then request that they might meet with you several times during the period your goals are being pursued. Research has consistently shown that sharing our goals with a significant-other person assists greatly in helping the individual to successfully achieve their goals. The Bible repeatedly emphasizes the importance of confessing our decision to follow Christ before all men (see Matthew 10:32; Romans 10:9, 10).

Also, do not be discouraged by possible failure to always reach your stated goals. Remember, that nobody is born with good habits and attitudes! Only Christ can help you to build these. But do analyze the reason/s why you failed to fulfill your goals. If it appears to be because of irrationality of thinking, decisively challenge those ideas and immediately set new goals

You Are What You Think

and begin to pursue them with confidence. Again, share your set-back with your goal-witness and begin again to change and grow!

We are human beings with many limitations. Learn to accept yourself as you are and that can become a solid foundation to build upon. Stanaifer once said, "Do not get discouraged; it may be the last key in the bunch that opens the door." Goethe stated: "We must always aim at the bull's eye--although we know that we will not always hit it." In other words, if we do not try to achieve the absolute best, how can we hope to reach the relatively good? Keep in mind that miracles never happen until we take aim at something impossible! With Jesus Christ in your life, you need not be discouraged. He said, "Be of good cheer; I have overcome the world" (John 16:33b) and He promised that we would overcome too if we trusted Him completely. (For review, see C.R.T. Cardinal Insight no. 7 in chapter 6).

In summary, let us review the eight C.R.T. Therapeutic Steps for straight thinking. First, we experience something or someone (step 1, stimulus) and then experience a feeling/emotion (step 2, response). Commonly, humans blame the situation or other persons for their emotional distress. "He made me mad." "She made me do it!" "The schools have caused my distress." etc., when really, situations or events do not cause us to feel/emote good or bad, but what we think about them brings about our emotional response/s (step 2,

With these points in mind, step 3, appraisal, focuses on the hard work of self-evaluation. That is, the honest and objective discovery and evaluation of the "real" facts surrounding the causation of our irrational thinking and emotional distress. In this regard, we look critically at our thoughts (step 4) that describe for us the event/s or experience/s (step 1). At this juncture, we analyze whether our thoughts were rational or irrational, and, after weighing all the possible evidence (from God's Word, counsel, common sense, circumstances, consequences, compulsion, conscience, etc.) we hopefully gain insight (step 5) into our besetting problem/s and or need/s.

Garbage Day (step 6) is rather self-explanatory. It is at this point of therapy when we say, "I'm sick and tired of sin, failure, negativism, joylessness, and am going to trade it all in for something infinitely better!" It is saying no to the worst in our lives so that we can say yes to the best! Steps 7 (honesty to face truth about God, self, and others) and 8 (trusting Christ with our total life) are the obvious last steps that are tied to our

Neil C. Roth

acceptance of reality and responsibility for goal setting and commitment to Jesus Christ as Lord and Savior.

Frustratingly, we have only scratched the surface in our brief discussion regarding self-therapy. Do not hesitate to contact competent Christian professionals (ministers, with training in counseling, counselors, psychologists, or psychiatrists) if you sense being "in over your head" with confusion and/or emotional distress. If you are able to work through the C.R.T. self-therapeutic steps, perhaps questions regarding your abilities, personality characteristics, intelligence, vocational interests, or skill aptitudes will be raised in your mind. Generally, standardized tests in the above categories are available for administration at university and college counseling centers, through professionals engaged in private practice, and sometimes through church-sponsored counseling centers. These tests can confirm to you many important aspects of your intelligence, personality, interests, and aptitudes, and basically provide a moderately accurate image of the real you.

Furthermore, I would urge you to begin weighing every negative emotional response on the scales of God's holy standard, His Word. When anger comes, ask "why did I anger?" Go through the C.R.T. therapeutic steps and discover what the prompting motivation was. When guilt arises, fight the temptation to rationalize, and evaluate why you feel guilt in the light of God's precepts and principles.

Remember, you can control your thinking and keep it straight if you program your mind with God's precepts and principles. Let me urge you to get into God's Word and draw it lovingly to your heart. Truly, if a man will keep God's commandments, they will keep him. If he chooses to break God's laws, they will break him!

In closing this chapter, God's call to rational thinking and behavior is ever clear. Charles H. Spurgeon captures the essence of God's desired standard:

> The Holy Spirit acts as a Comforter through the Word, and sheds abroad those benign influences which still the tempests of the soul. Nothing is a stumbling block to the man who has the Word of God dwelling in him richly. He takes up his cross daily, and it becomes a delight. He is neither stumbled by prosperity, as

You Are What You Think

so many are, nor crushed by adversity, as others have been; for he lives beyond the changing circumstances of external life.[15]

Finally, the poet Grenville Kleiser has written a most memorable poem entitled "Thoughts" in which he urges us all to keep our thoughts strong, clear, right, and true.

What valuable counsel! After all, YOU ARE WHAT YOU THINK!

FOOTNOTES

1. Thoresen, C. E., and Mahoney, M. J. <u>Behavioral Self-Control</u>. New York: Holt, Rinehart & Winston, 1974.
2. Bandura, Albert. <u>Social Learning Theory</u>. Englewood Cliffs, N. J." Prentice-Hall, 1977.
3. Ellis, Albert. Rational-emotive therapy: Research data that supports the clinical and personality hypotheses of R.E.T. and other modes of cognitive-behavior therapy. <u>Counseling Psychologist</u>, 1977, pp. 2-42.
4. Kanfer, F. H., & Phillips, J. S. <u>Learning Foundations of Behavior Therapy</u>. New York: Wiley and Sons, 1970.
5. Krumboltz, J. D., & Thoresen, C. E. (Eds.). <u>Counseling Methods</u>. New York: Holt, Rinehart & Winston, 1969.
6. <u>Ibid</u>.
7. Bobgan, Martin & Deidre. <u>The Psychological Way</u> / <u>the Spiritual Way</u>. Minneapolis: Bethany Fellowship, Inc., 1979, p. 168.
8. Rogers, Carl R. <u>On Becoming a Person</u>. Boston: Houghton Mifflin Co., 1961, pp. 44, 47-49, 62, 283-284.
9. Bobgan and Bobgan. <u>op</u>. <u>cit</u>., p. 172.
10. Nee, Watchman. <u>The Spiritual Man</u>. Volume Two, New York: Christian Fellowship Publishers, Inc., 1968, p. 194.
11. Howard, J. Grant, Jr. <u>Knowing God's Will and Doing It</u>. Grand Rapids: Zondervan Publishing House, 1976, p. 125.
12. Ewen, Robert B. <u>An Introduction to Theories of Personality</u>. New York: Academic Press, 1980, pp. 354-358.
13. Allee, G. Franklin. <u>Evangelistic Illustrations</u>. Chicago: Moody Press, 1961, p. 133.
14. Jones, E. Stanley. <u>Christian Maturity</u>. Nashville: Abingdon Press, 1952, p. 147.
15. Allee, <u>op</u>. <u>cit</u>., p. 40.

CHAPTER NINE

EPILOGUE

"Until a man has found God, he begins
at no beginning; he works to no end."
--H. G. Wells

We have seen that Christian Rational Thought Psychology is really an attempt to return the study of human behavior and counseling to their prime Creator, Jesus Christ. If we truly believe the Word of God, then representative statements like "for in him (God) we live, and move, and have our being" (Acts 17:28a) and "I am the way, the truth, and the life" (John 14:6a) should tell us that any study of man must begin with the Source of all life and creation.

For this central reason, C.R.T. Psychology has been premised on the notion that God's Word is completely valid, reliable, and true. Hence, no improvement was needed to enhance the philosophical base of C.R.T. Psychology. This is not to say that viable truths regarding human behavior discovered by dedicated researchers and clinicians are not welcomed when compatible with the Word of God. All truth, wherever found, comes from its ultimate source, Jesus Christ, the Truth.

So, C.R.T. Psychology is formulated upon the rather simplistic but profound idea that man, being made in the image of God, was created to walk with God in loving obedience and fellowship. Man's free will, and Satan's lure, brought man into a state of alienation with God. So, God, sent His Son, Jesus Christ to complete the divine plan of redemption for man's possible return to fellowship. Jesus called man back to the keeping of the Ten Commandments by way of His agapē love as He revealed it on the Cross of Calvary.

Since the commandments could never be fully kept by man, Christ sent His Holy Spirit to empower His children with a fervent, holy love. This agapē <u>we</u> love was the "constraining" power that would enable man to keep the law. Supremely loving God, and our neighbor as ourselves, was suddenly made realizable for the first time in history.

C.R.T. Psychology holds that man's moral and spiritual alienation (from God) has caused him grievious physical, emotional, and spiritual distress which is characterized by selfishness, fear, alienation from his fellows, physical and emotional breakdown, and great sadness with life in general.

In addition, a primary idea upon which C.R.T. Psychology rests is that God calls all men to rationally consider His invitation to repentance, salvation, and sanctification. Also, that Satanic, irrational thoughts must be challenged and replaced with Christian, rational thoughts that represent the mind of Jesus Christ. (See Romans 12:1, 2; Philippians 2:5; Isaiah 1:18, etc.).

C.R.T. Psychology is also premised upon the notion that if man will obey the perfect laws of God, as fulfilled in and through Christ, then, it will be possible to experience a life that is characterized by "love, joy, peace, longsuffering, gentleness, goodness, faith, meekness, temperance" (Galatians 5:22), (where no law is needed in response). This new, abundant life will be actualized in the lives of all who have trusted and committed themselves to Jesus Christ, and who are filled and led by His Holy Spirit.

In addition, C.R.T. Psychology proposes that human beings can learn to victoriously control their cognitive, emotional, and spiritual lives by heeding the following precepts, principles, and insights:

1. The C.R.T. Central Principle--The Love Principle. "Thou shalt love the Lord thy God with all thy heart, ...soul, ...strength, ...mind; and thy neighbor as thyself" (Luke 10:27).
2. The C.R.T. Person Precepts as revealed in the Ten Commandments (see Exodus 20:3-17).
    (1) Please love me solely for I am your creator and God and I sincerely love you.

You Are What You Think

(2) No substitute god is necessary--I am your all in all and will meet all your needs.

(3) Speak of and to me with love and respect.

(4) Communicate and fellowship with me--I want to hear from you regularly.

(5) Respect and love your mother and father.

(6) Respect and love all other persons--life is sacred.

(7) Be faithful in marital and all other human relationships.

(8) Be trustworthy with the resources and possessions of others.

(9) Be truthful in all thought and conversation.

(10) Be content with what God has given you.

3. The C.R.T. Priority Principles of I John 2:15-17;

(1) <u>The Provision Principle</u>--"The lust of the flesh" (2:16). Lust or love is the issue here. Flee lust, learn to respect the body as God's holy temple, and trust God for the inate basic physical, psychological, and spiritual needs related to sustenance and fulfillment.

(2) <u>The Possession Principle</u>--"Lust of Eyes" (2:16). Seek God first and foremost, and He will provide material blessings according to His will. The concept of being a good steward is central to this principle.

(3) <u>The Position Principle</u>--"Pride of Life" (2:16). We are called to become servants. We are saved to serve, not to be served. Trust in God--not self!

In reality, the Priority Principles are fully represented in Jesus' Words: "Seek ye first the Kingdom of God, and his righteousness; and all these things shall be added unto you" (Matthew 6:33).

4. The C.R.T. Progress Principles of the Christian life;

(1) Read and study the Bible daily.

(2) Pray without ceasing.

(3) Be filled with the Holy Spirit.

(4) Worship regularly with other believers.

(5) Share your faith frequently.

(6) Be joyful and wholesome.

(7) Be positive--live above your circumstances.

(8) Learn how to handle temptation.

(9) Be equally yoked together with believers.

(10) Be faithful and trustworthy with God and men.

5. The C.R.T. Seven Cardinal Insights for Living are reflective of the major issues that man must face in order to fully develop and mature as a Christian. They are:

    (1) If you <u>will</u> to change, you can!

    (2) You can <u>stop</u> <u>blaming</u> and <u>assume responsibility</u>!

    (3) You can learn to <u>control your thinking and emotions</u>!

    (4) You can <u>find your life by losing it</u>!

    (5) You can learn to <u>face reality without fear</u>!

    (6) You can learn to <u>love and be loved</u>!

    (7) You can learn to <u>become a problem-solver</u>!

If man is to achieve and maintain physical, cognitive, emotional, and spiritual well-being, he must totally commit himself, by faith, to God, through Jesus Christ, His Son, and to His Holy precepts and principles as just stated.

After being confronted with the foregoing precepts and principles, the searching and seeking person probably would ask: "How can I find out whether or not I am thinking rationally and reacting emotionally to life as Christ would have me to?" The Bible admonishes each Christian to constantly be in a state of monitoring his thoughts, attitudes, and behaviors. This is accomplished when we are living and walking in God's Spirit, looking to Him for counsel through prayer, and checking in regularly with His Word for directions on how to live a holy life.

The eight C.R.T. Therapeutic Steps for Straight Thinking provide a self-analysis frame-work within which we can examine our current thinking and behavior. As a result, we can discover if our thinking and behavior is in accord with the previously-stated precepts, principles, and insights of God's Word.

You Are What You Think

After all is said, the life-changing truth still shines: You can become a child of God, or greatly improve your present Christian experience, by learning that you can control your thoughts and emotions through the able assistance of our Lord Jesus Christ, and of course, C.R.T. principles and precepts.

Remember, situations or events do not need to affect you negatively. Christ calls us to view life developmentally, optimistically, and with realism. These three perspectives, synchronized by God's Holy Spirit, will always allow you to keep life in proper emotional and spiritual balance. Skill, in thought and emotional control, will not come overnight but will probably develop in small increments. Learn to courageously challenge your thoughts and behaviors daily and sincerely <u>desire to improve</u>! The Lord promises that He will grant you the "desires of your heart." Believe Him and grow!

Above all, keep your heart and mind committed to loving: loving God--loving others--loving yourself, as you ought. This is the most important psychological insight and rational thought that man can attain. E. Stanley Jones puts it this way:

> Love is an emancipating passion. It breaks the tyranny of self-preoccupation and frees the powers by getting them outside of themselves. But while it emancipates from self, it also gives a self back to itself. But now it is a self you can live with--it is a lovable self because it is a loving self.[*]

What will it be? Despair or joy? Lust or love? Frustration or fulfillment? Failure or success? Eros or Agape? Irrationality or rationality? Satan or Christ? Death or Life? ONLY YOU CAN CHOOSE! <u>YOU ARE WHAT YOU THINK</u>!

---

[*] Jones, E. Stanley. <u>Growing Spiritually</u>. Nashville: Abingdon-Cokesbury Press, 1953, p. 132.

APPENDIX A

C.R.T. STATEMENT OF FAITH

Tenets:

That the Bible is the inspired Word of God and contains His redemptive revelation to man.

That God is, and seeks to establish a genuine spiritual relationship with every human being (John 1:1-18).

That every human being has been made in the spiritual image of God (Gen. 1:26) the Father, Son, and Holy Spirit.

That every human being, after willfully rebelling (attitude and spirit of sin) against God's moral law, is guilty of violation of this law (sinning) and subject to the inevitable consequences of sin, namely, physical and spiritual death (Romans 3:23; 6:23; 1:20-32).

That God, in order to redeem man's moral nature and restore present and future fellowship with man, sent his only Son, Jesus Christ, to reveal His love for man and the conditions of salvation from sin, namely, belief in and commitment to Jesus as the Son of God and to His Word as ultimate truth for living (John 3:3-21). The confirmation of our born-again experience is love, obedience, and possession of the Holy Spirit.

That God, in redeeming man through personal faith in Jesus Christ, calls redeemed man to a life of personal holiness and righteousness to be realized as the Spirit of God indwells man's life (a life characterized by faith, holiness, and obedience), all

Neil C. Roth

the days of his earthly life (Luke 1:74, 75; Romans 5:1-21; Deuteronomy 10:12).

That God, through His love, as revealed in Jesus Christ, constrains us to be faithful to His Word and His will, and to avoid sin at every cost. When we do sin, and confess it, God is faithful and just to forgive our sin and to restore us to full fellowship with Him (I John 1 and 3).

That redeemed man's primary task is to glorify God (the Father, Son, and Holy Spirit), and to be ambassadors of Christ's message of redemption and reconciliation to all men who are lost and condemned (John 3:18).

That God's salvation of man will enable him to be victorious over the world and its lust and to experience the peace of God through the indwelling Spirit of God. Furthermore, all who are in Christ, through the New Birth, shall inherit eternal life and be accorded a place in a heavenly home prepared for the redeemed by the Lord (Romans 8: Revelation 21-22).

That the Ten Commandments stand and are fulfilled by Christ, and the love of God as revealed in Christ (Mark 12:31, 31; Matthew 5:17; Romans 10:4; Deuteronomy 4:40).

APPENDIX B

CHRISTIAN RATIONAL THOUGHT APPLIED TO SELECTED SCRIPTURES

	Scripture	Rational Thought (God's Law)	Result of Obedience	Irrational Thought (Sin)	Result of Sin
Association vs. Separation	Psalm 1:1 Blessed is the man that walketh not in the counsel of the ungodly, nor standeth in the way of sinners, nor sitteth in the seat of the scornful.	Walk with God	Blessed	Walk with ungodly	Not blessed
	I Cor. 15:33 Be not deceived: evil communications (companionships) corrupt good manners (morals).	Be not deceived	Maintain good morals	Be deceived by evil companionships	Corruption
Blessings vs. Afflictions	Matthew 11:28 Come unto me, all ye that labor and are heavy laden, and I will give you rest.	Come to God	Find rest	Those who do not come to God	Remain heavy-laden

Theme	Scripture				
	John 10:28 I give unto them eternal life; and they shall never perish, neither shall any man pluck them out of my hand.	Accept God's gift (eternal life)	Never perish; safety in God's hands	Do not accept God's gift	Perish from nonacceptance
Blindness vs. Vision	1 John 2:11 But he that hateth his brother is in darkness, and walketh in darkness, and knoweth not whither he goeth, because that darkness hath blinded his eyes.	Love our brother	Live in the light	Hateth his brother	Walk in darkness; does not know where he goes; blinded
Defilement vs. Cleansing	1 John 1:7 But if we walk in the light, as he is in the light, we have fellowship one with another, and the blood of Jesus Christ his Son cleanseth us from all sin.	Walk in light	Fellowship one with another	Walk in darkness	Defiled with sin
Liberality vs. Covetousness	Romans 8:2 For the law of the Spirit of life in Christ Jesus hath made me free from the law of sin and death.	Following law of Spirit of life	Free from law of sin and death	Following law of sin	Bondage to sin and death

Theme	Scripture				
Life vs. Death	**John 5:24** Verily, verily, I say unto you, He that heareth my word, and believeth on him that sent me, hath everlasting life, and shall not come into condemnation, but is passed from death into life.	Believe on Jesus Christ	Everlasting life; shall not come into condemnation	Not believing in Christ	Condemnation; death
Love vs. Hatred	**John 13:35** By this shall all men know that ye are my disciples, if ye have love one to another.	Love one another	Men shall know we are Christ's disciples	If we have not love one for another	Are not Christ's disciples
	John 3:16 For God so loved the world, that he gave his only begotten Son, that whosoever believeth on Him should not perish but have everlasting life.	Believe on Jesus Christ	Have everlasting life	Do not believe on Jesus Christ	Shall perish

Carnal vs. Spiritual	Romans 8:6 For to be carnally minded is death; but to be spiritually minded is life and peace.	Be spiritually minded	Have life and peace	Be carnally minded	Death and fear
Obedience vs. Disobedience	Matthew 7:21 Not everyone who saith unto me, Lord, Lord, shall enter into the kingdom of heaven; but he that doeth the will of my Father which is in heaven.	Do the will of the Father	Shall enter kingdom of heaven	Does not do the will of the Father	Shall not enter the kingdom
Sowing vs. Reaping	Galatians 6:8 For he that soweth to his flesh shall of the flesh reap corruption; but he that soweth to the Spirit shall of the Spirit reap life everlasting.	Soweth to the Spirit	Reap life everlasting	Sow in flesh	Reap corruption
Steadfastness vs. Instability	James 1:8 A doubleminded man is unstable in all his ways.	Singleminded	Stable	Doubleminded	Unstable in all ways

Worldliness vs. Unworldliness	Matthew 16:26				
	For what is a man profited, if he shall gain the whole world, and lose his own soul? or what shall a man give in exchange for his soul?	Seek first His kingdom	All these things will be added unto you	Gain the whole world	Lose his soul

---By Linda Graves, 1980